To
Diana,
Pass on the Joy,
of Family Legacies,

Lauren Littauer Briggs

Psalms 18-1-7

# MAKING
# THE
# BLUE PLATE
# SPECIAL

## FLORENCE LITTAUER
## MARITA LITTAUER
## LAUREN LITTAUER BRIGGS

LIFE JOURNEY®
*Bringing Home the Message for Life*

COOK COMMUNICATIONS MINISTRIES
Colorado Springs, Colorado • Paris, Ontario
KINGSWAY COMMUNICATIONS LTD
Eastbourne, England

Life Journey® is an imprint of
Cook Communications Ministries, Colorado Springs, CO 80918
Cook Communications, Paris, Ontario
Kingsway Communications, Eastbourne, England

MAKING THE BLUE PLATE SPECIAL
© Copyright 2006 by Florence Littauer, Marita Littauer, and Lauren Littauer Briggs

First printing, 2006
Printed in the United States of America

1 2 3 4 5 6 7 8 9 10 Printing/Year 11 10 09 08 07 06

Cover Design: Koechel Peterson & Associates, Inc., Minneapolis, Minnesota

All Scripture quotations, unless otherwise noted, are taken from *The Living Bible*, © 1971, Tyndale House Publishers, Wheaton, IL 60189. Used by permission. Scripture quotations marked: "NCV™" are taken from the New Century Version®. Copyright © 1987, 1988, 1991 by Thomas Nelson, Inc. Used by permission. All rights reserved; "NKJV™" are taken from the New King James Version®. Copyright © 1982 by Thomas Nelson, Inc. Used by permission. All rights reserved; NLT are taken from the Holy Bible, New Living Translation, copyright © 1996. Used by permission of Tyndale House Publishers, Inc., Wheaton, IL 60189. All rights reserved; AB are taken from the Amplified® Bible, Copyright © 1954, 1958, 1962, 1964, 1965, 1987 by The Lockman Foundation. Used by permission. (www.Lockman.org.); and MSG are taken from *The Message*. Copyright 1993, 1994, 1995, 1996, 2000, 2001, 2002. Used by permission of NavPress Publishing Group. Italics in Scripture have been added by the authors for emphasis.

Library of Congress Cataloging-in-Publication Data

Littauer, Florence, 1928-
Making the blue plate special : the joy of family legacies / by Florence Littauer, Marita Littauer, Lauren Littauer.
p. cm.
ISBN 0-7814-4298-2
1. Family--Biblical teaching. 2. Family--Religious aspects--Christianity. I. Littauer, Marita. II. Briggs, Lauren. III. Title.
BS680.F3L58 2006
248.4--dc22
2005027301

# CONTENTS

To view pictures of many of the people, places, and objects
mentioned in this book, please go to
www.makingtheblueplatespecial.com.

# BLUE PLATE SPECIAL OR SPECIAL BLUE PLATE?

## *FLORENCE*

Starting in 1892 the Harvey chain of restaurants and diners served daily "Blue Plate Specials"—a full meal on a divided blue plate, both quick and inexpensive. By the 1920s, the term "Blue Plate Special" was accepted in American society to mean a cheap meal offered with different items each day and containing meat, potatoes, and vegetables. There were "no substitutions." In the beginning the plates were solid blue, and later they varied to a blue willow pattern. Amazingly enough, my husband's grandparents had twelve blue willow plates they used for family cookouts, and somehow we inherited them. I wasn't impressed at the time, but now I'm glad I have these twelve willow designed, compartmentalized plates all in perfect condition without even a chip or crack.

This book is not about these old dinner plates but about any plates, goblets, or other heritage items you might have. Our stories will challenge you to look around and hunt up some collectibles you can use in home decor or as inheritable keepsakes for your family and friends.

When my daughters and I got together to discuss the topics for this book, we got more and more excited as we realized how many collectibles we had among us. We laughed when we realized both girls possessed antique bedroom sets with vanity dressing tables and tall dressers. Lauren's came down from her great-grandparents on my husband, Fred's, side, and Marita's are from her husband's family.

As we thought of more stories, I confessed that I had almost wiped out our entire heritage in one day. When my grandmother died, leaving an attic full of antiques, I was somehow assigned to clean it out. Having grown up with old furniture and mismatched dishes, I wanted no memories of my poverty-filled childhood. Nor did I want any sad or broken relics that had been relegated to the attic. It was a hot summer day when my young brother Ron and I climbed up the narrow stairs to Grandma's attic. As our heads rose up above the floor level and our eyes became accustomed to the dim light, we gasped in unison at what had accumulated in fifty years. Endless piles of unlabeled boxes, old dresses and uniforms hanging on nails around the walls, Uncle Donald's black iron printing press from his days in trade school, and a portrait of Queen Victoria peering through the slats of an old crib. There was no way we could sort this out in the one day we had to do it, so we backed up the borrowed dump truck to a spot under the attic window and began to push Grandma's treasures out the window into the truck below. My mother, watching our youthful zeal and lack of sentiment, stood sobbing as we threw her heritage away.

In the years since then, I have deeply regretted my thoughtless disposal of our family history. My mother and grandmother are both dead, but I'm writing this as a belated apology to them and a challenge to you not to send your heritage to the dump.

Thankfully, my mother had retrieved a few heirlooms before I got there to empty the attic, and I cherish the cradle she was placed in, the rocking chair her father made, and the large portrait of her as a baby.

I'm glad I saved her wedding picture, since I threw away the dress. Can you understand why I now have my wedding gown on a dress form in my living room?

Think about your life as you read through this book. What symbols of your childhood are still around somewhere, perhaps in a box in an attic, neglected and unappreciated? Everyone has a legacy to leave, but often no one knows about it. Perhaps it's time for you to pull out some of your family history.

Frame it on the wall,

Drape it on the hall,

Show it to them all.

Find your blue plate and make it special!

# MAKING THE BLUE PLATE SPECIAL
## *Florence*

*L*iving in those three rooms behind my father's small variety store—a precursor to 7–11—was an embarrassment to me as a teenager. My friends had real houses with dining rooms and pretty dishes; we ate from chipped plates around a table in the store. At a young age, I longed for the better things of life and took every opportunity to advance myself.

## PORK WITH PANTIES

One day, I read an ad in the paper for a free cooking demonstration put on by the gas company. They would show us how to prepare an entire meal and give us the recipes.

I convinced my mother to go with me to the Paramount Theater, where a teacher wearing a waitress-type uniform showed us how to create a dinner featuring a crown roast of pork garnished with pink pears. She told us that our local butcher would be happy to tie a loin of pork into a circle for us. To make pink pears we had only to put a drop of red food coloring into an open can of pear halves. By the time the roast was done, the pears would be pink.

The thought of such a lavish dinner presentation was so exciting that I talked all the way home about the steps of preparation. Mother, lacking my enthusiasm, let me know she was just along for the ride.

My first problem arose with the butcher, who, never having made a crown roast, questioned me. "What are you trying to do, go fancy on us?" I insisted he could tie a loin into a circle. After grumbling a bit more, he accepted the possibility and began to rope the pork together. I held my finger on the knots so he could tie the twine tightly, and by the time he finished the crown, so much string was wrapped around it that it looked as if it were in bandages. The butcher, although pleased with his artwork, admonished me, "Don't keep coming in here with more crazy ideas." When I told him I needed "panties" to decorate the top of each rib, he laughed, apparently picturing my undies atop the roast. From then on he informed his customers, "The Chapman girl is putting on airs."

I called the gas company to find out where I could buy "panties," and they said they'd give me the leftovers if I'd come get them. I did. When I arrived back home, I followed the recipe card, stuffed the center of the crown, and put it in the oven to roast.

Now I needed a "presentation plate," because the teacher had said that placing this creation on something ordinary would ruin the whole effect. My mother wouldn't let us use anything really good, as we were saving the few things we had for some better day. I begged her to unlock the china cabinet and let me remove a large royal blue plate I had always admired.

The pork roasted perfectly, the pears dyed effortlessly in the can, and the little pink frilled panties stood elegantly on top of each rib. Displayed on the big blue plate, the crown roast of pork was the most beautiful presentation I had ever seen. My father carried it around the store to show the customers what his smart little girl had created. They all gasped in amazement as he exclaimed, "This really is a Blue Plate Special." Some asked, "What are those funny paper ruffles for?" and I, in my newfound culinary wisdom, explained that all crown roasts wear little panties for trim. That's what makes them special!

As I look back on a childhood of meatloaf and Spam, that meal still stands out in my mind as the one time we rose above the ordinary.

In contrast, Fred was brought up with meals served by a maid. So when I married him, he expected me to be a gourmet cook and replace the maid. I worked hard at new recipes and even preheated the plates as he instructed. Then one day I remembered the blue plate. The next time I visited my mother, I asked if I could have the special dish. "That old blue plate?" she asked. "Oh, I gave that away to Cousin Elizabeth. It matched her dishes." Gave it away? Gave my plate away? I couldn't believe my mother would do that to me. "You'll have to get it back from her. Ask her for it back," I pleaded. My mother never wanted to cause trouble for anyone, so although she agreed to ask, she wouldn't push. Gratefully, Cousin Elizabeth didn't care that much, and I got the blue plate back.

In my years of marriage, I've made few crown roasts of pork, but I have the plate for it whenever I do. When I told this story to some friends recently, I took the old blue plate out of the cabinet. As I looked down at it, I felt a tug at my heart and suddenly could hardly talk. Why? I felt the pride of that little girl with the drab childhood who produced one culinary triumph: the crown roast decorated with rosy pear halves and adorned with the pink panties, sitting on the bright blue plate. I could see it all again.

I've eaten better meals since then, and I own more impressive plates. But I'll always hold on to that special blue plate, for it represents how hard I tried to rise above my ordinary circumstances.

Do you have a memorable blue plate, a cherished goblet, or a favorite spoon? Display it. Talk about it. Pass the story on. Don't let the sweet memories die.

## INTANGIBLE TREASURES

As a child I had very few treasures—a Shirley Temple doll, a few Nancy Drew mystery books, and the blue plate. Due to the Depression, there was no money for extras, and because we lived in such cramped quarters, there was no space to save anything. But what we lacked in tangible collectibles, we made up for with an underlying faith in God and two types of talent: words and music.

My father, Walter Chapman, was born in England. Shortly after his family came to America, his mother died in childbirth. The baby she was delivering died as well. My father had to leave school to care for his young brother while their father, a harness salesman, traveled New England. Although Dad worked in a grocery store from age sixteen on, his lack of education did not stop him from learning. He helped his brother with his schoolwork, and he read whatever books he could obtain. He inherited his father's "gift of gab" and sense of humor.

As my brothers and I grew up, Dad amused us with funny tales of his childhood and taught us rhymes and pithy sayings with big words. One we can say in unison to this day is "People who live in transparent domiciles should refrain from hurling geological specimens promiscuously." Before we went to first grade, we had to memorize a response to give the teacher in case we couldn't answer a question: "Not knowing to any degree of accuracy, I dare not assert for fear of erring therein."

We memorized Bible verses, and all of us recited them in church. We were in all the pageants and excelled at everything to do with words, acting, and humor. In spite of our family's lack of money, we had an exciting childhood with a constant audience of customers willing to listen to our newest recitations.

Because of our inherited talent and Dad's consistent encouragement, we all became speakers of one sort or another. I taught English and speech at the high school and college levels, Jim became a chaplain, colonel in the US Air Force and is still a minister in Ohio. Ron, a radio DJ since he was sixteen, recently retired with much fanfare as the top radio personality in Dallas history.

How grateful we are for a father who cared enough to pass on his love of the English language to three eager children who took his instruction to heart and have established a family legacy of learning.

## A LASTING LEGACY

Have we passed this passion along to others? Both of my daughters are articulate speakers and writers. Lauren has three sons to pass her talent to and Marita trains potential speakers and authors through our CLASSeminars.

Jim's six children all have master's degrees, two are ordained ministers, and two have PhDs. Ron's daughter has been a radio personality since college.

Think about your family for a minute. Has there been a thread of talent throughout the generations, some special skill that has been passed down? Has this ability been noticed and encouraged?

While our dad shared his love of words, our mother passed on her musical ability. Born in Canada, she was raised in Massachusetts in a family that was centered around church music. The seven children all took music lessons and formed their own ensemble. Sadie was a church organist and well-known piano teacher; my mother, Katie,

taught violin and cello; and Annie wrote the words to their composi-
tions. Ruth and Jean played the violin, and Bill and Donald
accompanied them on their cornets. In honor of the MacDougall
musicians, I display in my living room my mother's first violin and her
cello. The old hymnal Aunt Sadie used as she directed the church choir
graces my piano.

How has this musical ability passed down to those of us still living
today? Aunt Jean's son, Edward, has a master's degree in church music
and is being honored this fall for his forty years as minister of music at
First Church of Christ of Farmington, Connecticut. In college, my
brother Jim played the leading role in many operettas. He now com-
bines his preaching with singing and reading the symphonic poetry he
has written. Ron played the trumpet in the Haverhill High School
band and has an exceptional singing and speaking voice.

Although I was not a soloist, I used my musical talent to direct
musical comedies in the high school where I taught and later in professional community theater productions. My daughter Lauren and
her husband, Randy, are both singers in their church's choir and the
local community chorus. Classical music plays in their home, and
their three sons are all professional musicians.

Are talents passed down from one generation to another? Do certain families have similar professions and occupations? What about
your ancestors and your children? Is there any connection between
them or transfer of abilities and interests taking place?

This book is not a biography of my life but a presentation of creative ideas, many of which have been experienced in our family. My
daughters, Lauren and Marita, and I have been preparing for this book
for several years. We eagerly encourage you to consciously pass on your
talents, possessions, and passions to your family members and to teach

others to collect significant artifacts and to share their ideas. With families scattered around the world these days, it is more important than ever to unite our families in faith, in words, and by establishing a living legacy that will last through many future generations.

Make each one of your blue plates special!

# 1

# LIVING UP TO THE LEGENDS
## $\mathcal{M}$ARITA

When my mother, sister, and I first began discussing the idea of writing a book on leaving a legacy, we each threw out ideas of what we thought it should contain. Like all of our books, this one is intended to be a "Christian" book, but I questioned the spiritual element of it. Is this book to be more than a collection of touching stories? Why should Christians care about leaving a lasting legacy? Does it matter what people say about us after we are gone?

My life has been blessed by having very little experience with death. However, when my father and a good friend's husband died within a year of each other, my focus shifted. When you sit in the pew at a funeral and listen to the eulogies friends and family members offer, you cannot help but wonder, *what will they say about me?* I remember my friend's comments about her husband at his funeral. She talked about what he did for everyone and how he made people feel. She closed her commendations by saying, "That is the legacy Mike has left us."

Yes, Mike left a legacy. My father left a legacy, as will each of us. The question is what kind of legacy are we leaving?

I heard a story about a distant family member who died. As the deceased was not a churchgoing man, a minister who did not know him was brought in to officiate the service. As the minister interviewed the family to gather enough information to do his job, he asked for some good things that could be said about the deceased. After a long pause, one son said, "In his later years, when he got mad, he didn't stay mad as long as he used to."

Will your legacy be like that of my distant relative, or will it be more like the high praise my father and Mike received? Will it be worth recording like the saints throughout history whose names have been written in Hebrews 11, the chapter of the Bible referred to as the "Hall of Faith"? Will you live up to the legends?

## WHAT THE BIBLE SAYS ABOUT LEGACY

I began my search for the biblical foundation of this entire "legacy" concept with Hebrews 11. There we see Bible characters whose qualities made them legendary. I did a study of several members of the Hall of Faith: Noah, Abraham, Isaac, Jacob, Joseph, Moses, and Rahab, and I found that, like us, none of them was perfect. In fact, most of them committed what we might consider "big" sins. Yet God viewed them, out of all of the men and women in the Bible, as "obtain[ing] a good testimony" (Heb. 11:39 NKJV).

Despite our sins, our imperfections, and our failures, don't we all hope history will record us as having obtained a good testimony? Joie Fields shared with me her concern in this exact area. She wrote,

*As I read about the concept of this book, I wept, because the knowledge that we leave more than treasures and possessions for those we love has been in my heart for so long. The heritage passed to me was one of dysfunction from generations past. In my attempts to give my children a new heritage, I poured out love, protectiveness, and nurturing. The imbalance in my attempts came through a lack of discipline and correction of wrong ways and thought patterns. Because of this imbalance, my children did not learn many necessary lessons to prepare them for adulthood. They resented what they saw as my obsession with Christianity and doing things the way the Bible said to do them, so they chose a different path.*

*Often, in recent years, I have wondered if they would someday read my writings and truly know my heart. I have wondered if they will remember the depth of my love when they were not especially lovely. I have wondered if they would recall the times I cradled them and did my best for them. I have questioned God concerning the legacy I will have left those I love most—my children and my grandchildren. Will all I've done to make up for the imbalance in my life before Christ count at all in the memories of my children? Will the grandchildren think about the things I have tried to teach them concerning the kingdom of God while dancing with them and playing in the sandbox? Will any part of my life count for anything once I am no longer here?*

Joie, and all of you reading this, Abraham, Isaac, and Jacob all did things wrong with their children. Yet, as the Living Bible says, they "won God's approval" because of their faith. Despite anything we may have done wrong, we can still live up to these legends. Your life will count after you are no longer here.

In reviewing the lives of certain members of the Hall of Faith, I found that each had three distinct, common traits. Each had a rendezvous with God, each had a righteousness before God, and each had a relationship with God. These three qualities are the characteristics that founded their legacy.

As you look at your own life and the legacy you will leave, I encourage you to start by studying these three qualities. Be sure they are present in your own life. Have you had a rendezvous with God? Have you met him? Does your life have righteousness before God? Do you have the character traits of these saints? Do you have a relationship with God? Do you have ongoing interaction with him? If you do, the Bible tells us you will have won God's approval, and, through faith, you will have obtained a good testimony.

## PASSING ON YOUR FAITH

Share the stories of what God has done in your life and in your family. It may be that you'll share what God has brought you out of rather than a strong family history of faith.

Write down the story of your own journey with God.

Mark meaningful verses in your Bible, share a few words, in the margins, about why they are significant, and include a few notes from sermons or from your own studies. Pass this down as an heirloom of your heart for God.

I encourage you to spend some time reading God's Word, reviewing the legacy characteristics of each Hall of Faith member, and reflecting on your own life.

## THE BIGGER PICTURE OF LEGACY

So, now that we see the scriptural foundation for living a legendary life, why should we care? What will it do for us? In looking at my own life and through my biblical study on the topic, I find that the bigger concept does three things for us. It gives us a

> sense of history,
> sense of purpose, and
> sense of legacy.

### A Sense of History

Question: What is the biblical model for remembering where we come from?

Answer: The many genealogies listed in the Bible.

When I read 1 Chronicles 1–9 or Matthew 1:1–17, I don't really read, I skim. All of those "who begat whoms" are tedious reading. Yet, we know nothing is in God's Word by mistake. So why did the writers of the Bible include all that information that seems boring and irrelevant to most of us today? Because knowing a person's background provides a sense of history.

Regarding the opening of Matthew's gospel, the study notes in *Barclay's Daily Study Bible* offer this insight:

*It might seem to a modern reader that Matthew chose an extraordinary way in which to begin his gospel; and it might seem daunting to present right at the beginning a long list of names to wade through. But to a Jew this was the most natural, and the most interesting, and indeed the most essential way to begin the story of any man's life.*

*The Jews were exceedingly interested in genealogies. Matthew calls this the book of the generation of Jesus Christ. That to the Jews was a common phrase; and it means the record of a man's lineage, with a few explanatory sentences, where such comment was necessary....*

The reason for this interest in pedigrees was that the Jews set the greatest possible store on purity of lineage. In the biblical context, one's genealogy—one's history—teaches us lessons, "stories handed down to us from former generations" (Ps. 78:2–3). It is for this reason 1 Chronicles 29:29 says, "Detailed biographies of King David have been written in the history of Samuel the prophet, the history written by Nathan the prophet, and in the history written by the prophet Gad."

In the Bible, these detailed accounts helped a person know where they were from—it told a lot about them. Unlike the Jews of Bible times, we are not going to lose our right to be part of God's people because Christ's death on the cross insures our membership, but understanding our own history helps us know from whence we have come.

As I look back at my own family history, I see how it has influenced who I am today. For as many generations back as I know, many of my family members were active in the church and involved in Christian work. I have an uncle and a cousin who are both ordained ministers. My mother's cousin is a church organist and my mother's aunt Sadie, who would have been my great-aunt, was also a church organist. Church attendance and Christian work are a part of my heritage.

As I look around my house, many things decorating my home are a tangible reminder of my history. My brother, Fred, has the cradle that was used by many generations of my mother's side of the family. His daughter, named after me—Lianna Marita—was rocked in this cradle, as were my sister, my brother, and I. My mother and her mother were too. My great-grandfather made the cradle for his daughter Katie, my grandmother. These family treasures serve as a daily reminder of our history. That is why throughout this book we encourage you to search your own family history and find items that give you a sense of family—not to keep them in storage, but to be visual reminders every day.

*O my people, listen to my teaching. Open your ears to what I am saying. For I will show you lessons from our history, stories handed down to us from former generations. I will reveal these truths to you so that you can describe these glorious deeds of Jehovah to your children and tell them about the mighty miracles he did. For he gave his laws to Israel and commanded our fathers to teach them to their children, so that they in turn could teach their children too. Thus his laws pass down from generation to generation. In this way each generation has been able to obey his laws and to set its hope anew on God and not forget his glorious miracles. (Ps. 78:1–7)*

## A Sense of Purpose

As you think about your own legacy, you'll discover that it will be closely tied to your purpose. Each of us has a specific purpose.

The Bible tells us God's purpose in Ephesians 1:7–12 (NCV):

*In Christ we are set free by the blood of his death, and so we have forgiveness of sins. How rich is God's grace, which he has given to us so fully and freely. God, with full wisdom and understanding, let us know his secret purpose. This was what God wanted, and he planned to do it through Christ. His goal was to carry out his plan, when the right time came, that all things in heaven and on earth would be joined together in Christ as the head. In Christ we were chosen to be God's people, because from the very beginning God had decided this in keeping with his plan. And he is the One who makes everything agree with what he decides and wants. We are the first people who hoped in Christ, and we were chosen so that we would bring praise to God's glory.*

From this passage, we can see that God's clearly stated purpose is to offer salvation to the world.

Scripture also gives us Christ's purpose, found in Romans 14:9 (NLT): "The reason Christ died and rose from

## THE MOST IMPORTANT THING

The spiritual well-being of our children is our most important task as parents. Choose a few of the following suggestions to continue building a godly heritage for them:

Begin a regular family devotion and prayer time.

Read age-appropriate books with spiritual lessons or godly values. Discuss the biblical truths they illustrate.

As a family, choose a Bible verse of the week. Read it together at dinner and discuss how it might have been helpful or applicable that day or how God fulfilled that promise.

Take time to talk about the lessons you and your children learn at church.

Include your children in your activities when you put your own faith in action. Bring them along when you prepare and bring a meal to someone in need or paint the church building.

Encourage your children to serve others by mowing a neighbor's lawn, befriending a lonely classmate, or some other age-appropriate activity.

the dead to live again was so he would be Lord over both the dead and the living." Here we see Christ's purpose is to be Lord.

Next we'll look at Paul's purpose of pleasing God as found in 1 Corinthians 9:26 (NLT): "So I run straight to the goal with purpose in every step."

If God has a purpose, Christ has a purpose, and Paul has a purpose, shouldn't we? We do! We have both a greater purpose—a big picture purpose—and a more specific purpose. Our greater purpose is delineated for us in 1 Thessalonians 2:4 (NLT): "For we speak as messengers who have been approved by God to be entrusted with the Good News. *Our purpose is to please God, not people.* He is the one who examines the motives of our hearts." This is an easy purpose to grasp, not so simple to accomplish, but clear to comprehend.

Understanding our specific purpose is the harder task, since it's different for each person and may change depending on our stage of life and God's plan for us. In Acts 20:24 (NCV) Paul writes, "I don't care about my own life. The most important thing is that I complete my mission, the work that the Lord Jesus gave me—to tell people the Good News about God's grace." Though Paul faced many difficulties, including prison and persecution, he knew his mission, and that clear vision and focus enabled him to continue when others might have given up.

I find the same thing to be true for me. Knowing my purpose in life—what God has called me to do—drives me and keeps me moving forward. When I feel imprisoned by an overwhelming workload, I press on. When I am persecuted by someone who doesn't agree with something I wrote or the way I said something—or when I simply may have been snappish on a day I was tired—in my humanity, I want to quit. Once I drag my head out from under the pillow where I have been sobbing to God, however, I realize that if I quit, Satan wins. I remind myself that because God has called me to do this, he will equip me—and he does.

In my life, I have three distinct purposes, and all of these influence the legacy I am leaving in this world.

First, I have a purpose for my business, CLASServices, Inc., which has developed into a clear statement: CLASS is a complete service agency providing resources, training, and promotion for both the established and aspiring Christian speaker, author, and publisher. Shortened, we offer communication skills and skilled communicators. This purpose statement helps me remember what God has called me to do. An entrepreneur at heart, I'm constantly dreaming up new business ideas. But before I embark on a possible tangent, I ask myself if the new idea fits within this purpose.

One of my favorite ideas I have long wanted to pursue is making recordings for tourists in New Mexico. My husband says I am the unofficial champion of New Mexico. The state has some great things to offer, and I think it is undiscovered and underappreciated. When my guests come to town, I have several full-day tours outlined for them—complete with articles about the various places they'll see. Wouldn't it be great if when you picked up your rental car at the Albuquerque airport, you could pop in a CD with interesting narration and interviews with experts who would describe the rock formations or the Indian ruins as you travel past them? I can just hear it: "You should now be at mile marker seventy-two. On your left is …" While this idea enthuses me, does it fit within God's purpose for my business? Sadly, no. If I were to devote my time to this endeavor, it would be a distraction from God's calling for me. I stay focused on his purpose, not my plans.

For my personal speaking and writing ministry, I believe God has

**Y**ou're a nice girl, but you're not college material." So said my high school guidance counselor in my senior year. I knew I had done well in school, and on certain subjects I had excelled. I really wanted to go to college, but those clear words of discouragement said, "Forget it."

What was I to do with my life?

My father, a quiet, deeply religious man, suggested I pray and ask the Lord what purpose he had for my life. But I was impatient. I needed to know right then.

I decided to join the Air Force. I could travel the world and learn valuable skills. After making the necessary contacts with the Air Force, I waited to hear from the recruiter to finalize plans for the physical I would need before I could join. The recruiter called and told me he had one more question he had forgotten to ask me: "Do you have any lung disorders?" I was surprised at his question—it seemed irrelevant to me —but I had to be honest. "I've had asthma much of my life, but it's under control and not really a problem anymore." He then said, "I'm sorry, but we cannot accept your application because of your asthma."

I silently questioned, "Because of a little asthma? Is that a reason to keep me out?" I was devastated. Here I was a senior in high school with no plans for the future. Others were accepted to college, but what about me? I felt like a big failure.

One day my dad came downstairs to my room and said, "You can't sit and cry

called me to help people put together the pieces of their lives within the framework of God's Word. Because I have a deep conviction that everything I speak and write on must be grounded in God's Word, I offered to write this chapter. Before we developed this "legacy" topic, I wanted to be sure it was within the framework of God's Word. Clearly, it is.

For my personal life, God told me that my purpose is to love my husband extravagantly as is stated in The Message in Ephesians 5:2: "Observe how Christ loved us. His love was not cautious but extravagant. He didn't love in order to get something from us but to give everything of himself to us. Love like that." For many months I had for the rest of your life. Have you considered that God wants you to do something other than the Air Force?"

I sat back and realized I hadn't even thought about what God wanted for me. My Dad suggested that I go to our community college for one year while I considered God's plan.

"I don't think I'm smart enough."

"Your mom and I believe you're that smart, and we know that with God's help you can accomplish anything."

I was scared, but with my parents' encouragement, I went to college and loved it. That first year I made the dean's list every quarter! I decided to transfer to Concordia University, and when I graduated, I had two majors: Director of Christian Education and Elementary Education. After college, I served in various churches for about ten years as a youth minister before I was married.

I never forgot the words of wisdom and perspective my dad shared with me. I was able to encourage many kids in the youth ministries in which I served, because I know what it is like to struggle. But I also know what it's like to have someone believe in me. Most importantly I know all things are possible when I follow God's purpose, not my own plans.

*—Michelle Diercks*

"Love Extravagantly: Not to Get, But to Give" written in eyeliner pencil on my bathroom mirror as a daily reminder to treat my husband in a way that is contradictory to human nature. When I do his laundry, cook for him, or do any other task I might not totally enjoy, I remind myself that I am loving him extravagantly, not getting but giving.

While I have to be reminded of God's purpose for my personal life, in my parents' marriage, it was my father who needed a gentle reminder. My mother remembers, "In Fred's early Christian life, he realized he had a critical nature and was more apt to tell me what I had done wrong than to offer me praise for what I had done right.

As God made this clear to him, he taped a note on his dashboard that said, 'Praise Flo.'"

## STRENGTHENING CHILDREN'S FAITH

Encourage them to participate in family prayer time.

Allow them to "catch" you in Bible study or prayer. Stop for a moment to show and explain what you are doing or studying.

When children share their concerns, stop to pray with them about their worries. When they share their joys, praise God with them in prayer.

When possible, share biblical teachings on the issues they face each day in your regular conversation. Consider memorizing applicable verses together.

Whatever your purpose is in life, once you know it, I encourage you to translate it into a single statement, a purpose statement; something you can tape on your dashboard, write on your mirror, or put on a sticky note you can tack onto your computer to help you make decisions and guide your life like a compass.

Do you know God's purpose for your life, your "mission"? If not, spend time in prayer, asking God to show you what he wants you to focus on. Then write it out to keep in front of you as a tangible reminder.

### A Sense of Legacy

History is what came before us; legacy is what comes after us. When you know your history—you know where you have come from—and you know your purpose, you are uniquely positioned to pass what you've learned on to others. You live your life with a sense of legacy—thinking about the differences you can make in the world and what people will say about you.

Isaiah 8:16 tells us to "Write down all these things I am going to do, says the Lord, and seal it up for the future. Entrust it to some godly man to pass on down to godly men of future generations." Each of us can take the lessons we have learned and pass them on to others.

Likewise, Colossians 3:16 admonishes us with these words: "Remember what Christ taught and let his words enrich your lives and make you wise; teach them to each other and sing them out in psalms and hymns and spiritual songs, singing to the Lord with thankful hearts."

What have you learned that you can pass on to others? This book is full of ideas we hope will inspire you and cause you to look at your own life—and home—differently. After reading the stories presented here, Diane Baier Spriggs told us how they changed her perspective. "All of us are a part of the great 'sea of humanity,' but I don't want to be a wave that comes and goes and is then forgotten. I want generations of my family that follow after me to know that I lived and that I loved. I want them to know Grandma Spriggs had a real and personal relationship with God and that she wanted them to have one too."

Much of what I have learned in life I learned from my mother. I often joke that my seminary education was homeschooled before homeschooling was fashionable. I combine what I've learned from her with my own experiences, observations, and research and pass it on to others—who in turn pass it on to others. Second Timothy 2:2 says, "For you must teach others those things you and many others have heard me speak about. Teach these great truths to trustworthy men who will, in turn, pass them on to others." That is the true essence of leaving a lasting legacy.

# 2

# KEEPSAKES AND FAMILY TREASURES
## *FLORENCE*

$S$ince I grew up living in those three rooms behind my father's
store, there was nothing of material value for us to save. As a case
in point, we had no living room furniture—the store was our living
room and our dining room.

### THE BANANA SPLIT DISH

We had a booth where customers would sit and eat what was then
called a "college-ice," today, a sundae. For an extra dime, they could
have a banana split. My mother would take out the flowered dish,
slice a banana down the middle, and top it with three scoops of different colored ice cream. Then, she would pour Hershey's chocolate
syrup over one scoop, crushed pineapple on another, and strawberry
on the third. There were no whipped-cream bombs in those days to
fluff up these creations, but Mama would pull out one red maraschino
cherry from a jar and drop it onto the middle scoop for decoration.

We children wanted a fancy ice cream but were always told it
was too expensive for us. However, once a year on our birthday
afternoon, we could sit in the booth and Mama would make us our
own "college-ice." Somehow I managed to save one of those long,

narrow dishes—the size of a split banana. Though its glazed finish is cracked like a road map and the bumpy flowers are dulled down, the dish represents the whole era of the Depression and the War, when an ice cream sundae once a year was a major event.

## YELLOW THUMBTACKS

During that same period, we had a small kitchen behind the store. There was a glass-pane door between the kitchen and store that Mama tacked a towel over on Saturday nights when we took our once-a-week baths in the black-slate kitchen sink. As a teenager, I was horrified to sit naked in a sink containing only six inches of water, with nothing between me and the male customers but a towel, worn down to the nub and thumbtacked to the door.

We sold cards of thumbtacks in the store, so we used them to tack up everything, including the worn-out towel. I saved a card of the yellow thumbtacks, which now sits on a shelf in my home office. What was frightening then, as I sat nude and fearful that my brothers might open the door into the store and expose me to the customers, is today both humorous and nostalgic.

Recently, my two brothers and I counted the bathrooms in our homes and vacation homes and realized we have eighteen bathrooms among us. Is that overkill considering the poverty-filled childhood and the black-slate sink?

## SUNDAY DISHES

In that same kitchen was a cream-colored, drop-leaf table with four matching chairs. My mother sat on a stool since she had to get up frequently to wait on customers. The table had been a wedding purchase of my parents in 1925—before the Great Depression hit. We ate at that table unless the store got busy, in which case we moved our plates to the booth in the store and took turns waiting on the customers.

We normally ate on old plates that did not match, but on Sundays we used the special china Mama had received as a wedding present. "Only on Sundays," Mama stated. "We have to save the set for better days." When I asked one day, "Will we have better days?" the question hit her so hard that she plunked the pile of Sunday dishes onto the table and ran crying to the little bedroom. I didn't know what I'd said to upset her, so I went in to ask.

"I wanted so much better for you than this awful place." That was the first time my mother ever expressed her feelings about our life in the three rooms behind the store.

I knew I didn't like our little crowded place, but I'd never realized it bothered Mama. She hadn't grown up in poverty. Her father was a foreman in a carriage factory, so she and her six brothers and sisters had been well cared for, and all had music lessons. She and her sister, Sadie, had adjoining studios where they taught piano and violin.

When she married my father, he was a chain-store manager. They rented a little white house, and life had looked good. But then the Depression hit, and the entire company my father worked for closed down. For a time, my father—in his late fifties with three children to support—had to take a timekeeper job for a WPA (Works Progress Administration) street paving gang. My mother, twenty years younger, taught violin to help financially, and we ate whatever the government gave away for the week. I remember the month of canned red beets and corned beef hash with canned purple plums for dessert.

With borrowed money, my father bought the Riverside Variety Store, and we five moved into the rooms behind the store. Ron was one year old, James was five, and I was nine. I was ashamed of where we lived, but I hadn't stopped to think how Mama felt about it until that day she cried over my question.

"I'm so sorry; I'm so sorry," she sobbed. "Forgive me for not giving you more." Having said her piece, she stood up abruptly, shook her shoulders, and pulled herself into her usual stoic demeanor. We went back to the kitchen and set the table with the simple white dishes with the yellow borders. We never referred to that brief, honest moment again, but at least I knew one reason why my mother was so serious and sad and why she sighed so deeply, so often.

Years later, when my mother closed the store after my father's death, I kept the one remaining dish from the yellow-edged set. To this day the sight of that plate, the banana-split dish, and the card of yellow thumbtacks brings a tear to my eye and a lump in my throat.

My son and his wife, Kristy, have an attractive cabinet in their living room. I was thrilled when I saw it contained my son's silver baby mug, his little engraved spoon and fork, and his grandfather's dog tag from World War I. As I looked with interest at this collection and his Bunnykins cup and bowl set, he pointed out that the other side of this glassed-in cabinet held treasures from Kristy's childhood. She explained that her grandmother had a collection of Lladro figurines in her home, and as a child Kristy liked to touch each piece carefully and had wished she could play with them. As she grew up, she came to admire these pieces for their beauty. She was thrilled when her grandma gave her and her twin sister each the figurine of her choice. Kristy showed me the prized possession and said, "I could have bought myself a Lladro piece, but this means so much more because it came from my grandma's personal collection."

When we give a personal possession, it becomes a family collectible.

As I've shared my stories of my childhood and have shown friends the blue plate and other dishes, people have responded with stories about items they've saved but never thought of displaying. Some have realized that they've not passed down the stories that give meaning to the special pieces. What a joy it is to link your memories to a tangible item and then to pass it on. Without the stories, what you have treasured is only an old dish to someone else. The following examples—some mine, some Lauren's, some Marita's, and some from friends—are further proof of family treasures that have made a lasting impact. As you read, think of something you remember. Find it, display it, and tell the story.

## THE HANDS THAT MADE THE CRADLE BY LAUREN

As mentioned earlier, my great-grandpa MacDougall was a carriage maker by trade. He was living in Nova Scotia when my grandmother, Katie Florence, was born two months premature. She was kept alive by being placed in a dresser drawer that was set on the open oven door, providing a constant source of warmth, a homemade incubator.

Because she was so small, her father made her a beautiful wooden cradle. It was a hand-rubbed, spindle-and-dowel cradle with wooden slats to support the mattress. Not only was it a marvelous piece of workmanship, but it was a piece of the MacDougall legacy.

My mother, Florence, was rocked in that cradle, as were her two brothers. When I was born, the cradle was passed down to my parents. Every one of my siblings found comfort and rest in that family heirloom. As my children were born, they each had their turn in the family cradle. Since I was the only one of the three siblings to have children at the time, the cradle was usually at my house.

When my brother, Fred, announced that Kristy was pregnant, I knew the cradle wouldn't be mine much longer. It was Mother's Day in 2002 when Fred and Kristy came to our home and I called for everyone's attention so I could share the history behind the presentation I was about to make. As I recounted the generations that had been rocked, loved, and cared for in this cradle, emotion overcame me. I was suddenly speechless—a rare moment for a Littauer!

Later, I went shopping with Kristy to pick out a new mattress and some bedding for the cradle, and not long after that, Lianna Marita arrived and took her place among the generations of babies who were rocked in that cradle.

I just received a note from Kristy that read, "Currently the cradle is occupied by one of Lianna's baby dolls, but soon our new little one will sleep in it!" My first nephew, Frederick Jack Littauer, is on his way.

## ELEPHANT MUGS BY MICHELLE DIERCKS

Troy and I were good friends before we started dating, but his grandmother passed away before we had our official first date, so I was never privileged to meet her. Shortly before this, Troy had moved into his own home, so as his family sorted through his grandmother's house, he inherited quite a few things—a tall grandfather clock, a dining room table, a hutch, and a buffet. He received the grandfather clock because he had always helped Grandma take care of it, making sure it was set and working properly.

I remember the first time I saw his home after he received all these treasures. The dining room set was beautiful, and his mother had had the chairs reupholstered as a birthday present for him. I was quite impressed that a bachelor had a beautiful dining room set. As I stood admiring the room, out of the corner of my eye I caught some unusual colors. I looked up, and perched on top of this hutch was an arrangement of elephant mugs. They did not fit with Troy's decor at all, so I asked him about them. He told me his grand-mother, a Republican, had bought these mugs for every year a Republican had been president. Since his grandmother had arranged them like that, he wanted to do the same.

After we were married, the elephant mugs remained on top of the hutch. Dinner guests often asked questions about the mugs, and we were pleased to send many of them happily away with an elephant mug that was special to them because of the year it represented. It seemed that no matter how many mugs we sent home with guests, there were always mugs left.

We moved after we had been married for a year. As we were put-ting things in their places, Troy put the mugs up on the hutch again. I never said anything, and over time we had more guests who were delighted to receive one of the mugs.

We recently moved again, and when it came time to put things in their places, I noticed that the elephant mugs were not around. I asked Troy if he wanted to put them on top of the hutch. He looked at me and said, "No, I'm ready to let that go."

I realized there are treasures that please the eye, and there are the most precious ones—those "treasures of the heart"—that are the hard-est to let go. I'm so glad I never told Troy what I really thought of those ugly elephants staring down at me for all those years. When I left the removal up to him, the elephant departure was painless.

## ELEPHANT TEAPOTS

When I (Florence) was a young child, my father won two teapots as prizes for a contest. They were cheap china pots shaped like elephants. The tail was the handle to lift the oversized pot and the trunk was the spout. Riding on the back of the animal and forming the lid was a little boy wearing a turban, who sat on an ornate carpet. These made-in-Japan creations would be considered junk today, but since my father gave me one to keep as a gift, I still have it.

## MEMORABLE TIMES

Think about your closest family members and their favorite activities. Take some time to enjoy those activities with them. Then, when possible, find a memento to remind you of those times together. For example, keep the cup and saucer you used when having tea with your grandmother.

Anyone with a modicum of taste would wonder why I have this gaudy gold-trimmed elephant on my coffee table, but it's the only tangible gift my dad ever gave me. My only token of my father's love is wrapped up in that elephant. The little boy broke off once, but I glued him back on top. The other pot is in my brother Ron's home amid his more valuable keepsakes. When I asked him why he kept it, he replied, "It's the only thing I have from Dad." So here we both sit late in life with two old elephant pots sitting among Wedgwood, Lladro, and crystal—symbols of a Depression-era childhood, where two cheap pots were about the best we ever hoped to get.

## DAD'S FIRST PAINTING BY JANET TAYLOR BIRKEY

My love of creating things and being "artsy" came from a gene I received from my dad. While neither of us had much training, we both read books on topics that fascinated us and watched television programs that showed the "masters in action." Neither of us ever reached professional artist status, but we both had enough talent to interest family and friends and to generate plenty of compliments for our efforts. As I look at the work we've done, I understand it's nothing necessarily special, except that it represents our courage to try, and fail—and try again.

As an adult, I moved away, married, and established my own home. After my children came along, I took art and hobby classes whenever the budget and babies allowed. I gathered enough craft supplies to fill a closet and constantly came up with new projects to ease that creative tension in my soul and to fill our home with yet another, shall we say, "memorable creation." Tubes of oil paint in every color and amount cluttered that tiny closet. They were new, used, crinkled, and rolled—and ready for someone to make magic with their contents.

I lived halfway across the country from my parents, and it was important to me to make their visits special and unforgettable times. Being a young housewife and mother left little flexible income, but I was clever enough to use what I had to turn one particular visit into something Mom and Dad would not forget. Since we lived near Dallas, I drove them over to Ross Perot's home—free, but exciting, since Dad was a Perot fan.

When Dad got out of the car at Ross Perot's, he insisted on taking a picture. Apparently, Dad got too close to the fence and set off a sensor. A voice came over the intercom: "Step away from the fence." I guess Dad hadn't gotten what he wanted in the picture, so he stayed just a bit longer to adjust the camera, and again, the voice came over the intercom: "Step away from the fence." We all had fun the rest of the trip telling him to watch out, that they probably had his face on camera now, and the FBI was going to follow him forever.

We toured Old City Park in downtown Dallas; it was more costly, but it filled an afternoon and was fun for my antique-loving parents. On days we didn't go anywhere, my daughter, Jennifer, their first grandchild, entertained us. There was something else that made the trip memorable—something that I wouldn't understand the value of for several years.

During the visit, Dad watched PBS painting shows. The painters on those shows made it look so easy! Dad wanted to paint, so we pulled out the numerous tubes of oil paints I had saved and bought a canvas. Then the magic began. That hot August afternoon, Dad painted his first of many oil paintings. It was a simple painting, done in cool blues and greens. The snow-capped mountains in the scene's background gave a soft base for the jagged rocks and pine trees that framed the crystal blue lake. His amateur application of the base paint gave a texture so diverse that it looked like he had painted the scene on a slab of stone.

We all admired his work, but he was not satisfied, so he wiped the scene away and scrubbed the canvas down with cleanser. Probably no teacher would ever suggest this procedure, but it gave the next attempt a unique pebbled look. Dad backed up, stared at the blank canvas with its ruts and ripples, and said, "Well, here goes."

By that point we were tired of watching, but he painted on without an audience. When he called us in to view his masterpiece, we saw a vastly improved production. There was an ethereal, misty touch to it and the cleanser coating gave added texture. As Dad backed up to look at it, he gasped, "It looks like heaven where we'll gather around the 'glassy sea.'"

Dad left his painting at our home, and it moved with us several times.

Dad died thirteen years later. As I looked at the paintings that followed his original, I could picture the look on his face as he painted each brush stroke. My mind could see him excitedly trying to tell my mother what would go into each painting. One day, as I talked to my mother about Dad's zeal for his late-in-life hobby, she suddenly asked, "Where's his first painting?" Oops! I realized I hadn't hung it in our new house. Where was it? The last time I remembered hanging it was four years before.

As I quickly counted back to where we were at that time, I concluded I must have left it in the basement of the girls' school where we had been house parents. I thought I'd packed everything when we moved, but the painting apparently was left behind. I almost felt that I was reliving losing my father.

I did the only thing I knew to do—although it was a long shot. I e-mailed the campus's office and explained what had happened. In a few short days, "Twistertornado" replied that she thought she had found my painting. My husband and I drove the six-hour round trip that weekend, and yes, the painting was there!

**MEMORABLE DECOR**

Are there objects from your past that have special meaning to you? How can you repurpose those items in your everyday life? For example, fill an old teapot with flowers, and use it as a centerpiece. Or, put your childhood marble collection in a special bowl or tin, and display it.

I now have the painting proudly hanging in my bedroom, and I will never lose it again. Each time I look at it, I see him waiting for us to come and stand with him around the "glassy sea," and I am reminded that I, like Dad, can leave a masterpiece legacy through the brush strokes I paint on the canvas of everyday life.

## WEDDING GOWN

As all young ladies do when they become engaged, I (Florence) started making plans for my great day. I wanted the wedding to be done as a coronation. Naturally, I would be the queen, and my pupils

**41**

(I was a schoolteacher at the time) would be my ladies-in-waiting. One of my students, who was an artist, started designing my royal gown, and the high school got more excited than if Queen Elizabeth were flying over.

One weekend I went to New York to inform my future mother-in-law of my wedding plans. She was the type of person who, besides being beautiful and adorned with large diamonds, had a firm grip on family activities and a final say on all decisions—large or small.

As we all sat at the table, Mother Littauer announced that after dinner we women would proceed to her lavish bedroom and help "little Florence" pick out her wedding gown. "Little" in this case did not mean that I was short and undernourished, but rather that I was insignificant in her eyes. Her use of "little" was similar to Leona Helmsly's calling her employees the "little people," a demeaning reference that helped the jury of "little people" send her to the big house!

When Fred's mother stated we were all going to choose my gown, I was shocked. As the sisters all talked joyfully about the glamour of gowns, I pondered over where these mystery gowns had come from. Were they secondhand? What if they chose a gown I didn't like? Then it came to me. Fred's family had a store in Miami called Bargain Bazaar. Mother was the buyer for all kinds of "distressed merchandise" they would purchase very cheap and then mark up several hundred percent. The whole family got excited when Mother bought a bale of ribbon at twenty-five yards for one cent and then sold it for five cents a yard—which still seemed to be a great bargain for their clientele and a thrill for them.

At one point when the conversation lagged, I dared to ask, "Where did you get these gowns?"

Fred's mother answered, "Oh, it was so much fun! I went to a sale

S hirley Temple was the most famous child movie star when I was growing up. She was everything I wanted to be and wasn't. She had blonde curls, dimples, and a beautiful face. Besides, she was in movies and could tap dance. When the Shirley Temple dolls came out, I wanted one so badly, but my parents didn't have enough money to buy me one. Somehow a rich lady in church heard of my plight and gave me the doll of my dreams. Through the years I've collected Shirley Temple souvenirs: paper dolls, coloring books, cups, glasses, and bowls. I've bought her biographies and videos of her movies. Recently, I found two pictures of her on eBay and had them framed.

Now that I have an adorable three-year-old granddaughter, I bought a white wooden display case for her special room at my house and have passed the collection on to Lianna Marita Littauer. As she nestles into her ruffled canopy bed, she now has the company of a new friend.

where a wedding gown factory had burned to the ground, but one storage shed was left standing, and I bought you a few gowns from the shed to try on. They aren't really burned, but they may have some water damage...." As she continued amusing the sisters with tales of the burning factory, I slumped in my chair, depressed. I had a pupil designing my queenly attire, and I didn't want a distressed dress with water spots and a singed train! No one cared what I thought, however, as up to the master bedroom we went.

Gratefully, the three dresses she had selected were not spotted or burned. I modeled each one with a forced smile. They all voted for the one I liked best and pointed out how lucky I was to have a mother-in-law who loved me enough to purchase three wedding gowns for me and not charge me anything at all!

I cancelled the artist's work on my potential gown and wore the "distressed merchandise" from the fire sale. After the wedding, Mother asked me to return the gown so she could sell it. I pretended to forget the request and eventually she got on with more important things.

When we moved to Palm Springs a few years ago, I unpacked the wedding gown, got a dress form that was being discarded from a store window display, put my gown on it, and stood a headless "me" in a corner of my living room. The fabric has not improved over the years, and of course, it wasn't too fresh to begin with; the lace has disintegrated in spots—but the train is still full enough to look dramatic against the carpet. The model form has more bosom than I ever had, and the gown looks better on the dummy than it did on me. She stands quietly there in the corner, a testimony to the homily that if you buy quality clothes they will last you at least fifty years!

## THE TEDDY BEAR BOX BY WENDY STEWART-HAMILTON

Several years ago, while shopping the pre-Christmas sales, I stumbled upon some charming cardboard photo boxes decorated with teddy bears. I jokingly told my husband as I unloaded five of them from the car and clutched them possessively in my arms, that I had "bonded" with them and just couldn't leave them at the store.

He only had one question: "What are you going to do with them?"

I smiled and told him I would think of something.

For the next few hours I thought about my teddy bear boxes. What would I do with them? What good was a teddy bear box? What could it hold? Why would a teddy bear box be more special than any other box?

As I thought about this, my daughter brought me a picture—a handmade, crudely drawn heart with smiley faces on it. It was then the idea for a Teddy Bear Box was born.

As I created the first Teddy Bear Box for myself, I placed Kayleigh's drawing in the bottom and smiled. Then I gathered the cards from my husband; memos and notes from friends; letters from my husband's grandmother to me; and other special pictures, postcards, and mementos I had been given over the last year—items that reminded me of how I was loved by others—and placed them in the box.

I then sat down and wrote this poem to put on the inside of the lid to my Teddy Bear Box:

DEAR LITTLE TEDDY BEAR BOX,
YOU ARE A PLACE WITH WINDOWS THAT NEVER LOCKS.
LOTS OF LOVE WITH YOU I SHARE,
TO REMIND ME OF THE ONES WHO CARE,
TUCKED WITHIN YOUR FOUR-BOXED WALLS,
AND READY FOR ME IF I SHOULD CALL.
NOT ALL DAYS ARE BRIGHT; SOME ARE GRAY,
AND FOR SUCH DAYS I TUCK AWAY
LETTERS, CARDS, AND THINGS FROM THOSE
WHOSE CARE ABOUNDS AND LOVE DOES SHOW.
IF I SHOULD SEEK, PLEASE LET ME FIND
THOSE WHO LOVE ME AND ARE KIND.

For the remaining boxes I wrote variations of the poem and created memory boxes for each of my children. For my younger children's boxes, I add special cards and notes from grandparents and friends, so they'll have them in one place when they're old enough to understand and appreciate all that was given to them. I also write notes, poems, and letters, chronicling a certain day or time in their lives and how I felt about their special moments. I have encouraged my oldest child, my stepdaughter, Kaile, to put her special memories in her box. Recently, I gave her another photo box that included our gifts for her high school graduation. I told her she could use this new box for storing stuff while she was at college, and she reminded me that she still had and used her Teddy Bear Box. I'll have to ask her if she puts copies of the e-mails I send her monthly called "Letters to Kaile on Her Way to College." These include Bible verses, tidbits of roommate wisdom, advice for making decisions, and wisdom for following God's purpose for her life. I also let Kaile know I'm thinking about her and praying for her.

Inside my Teddy Bear Box, I've added notes I've received from those whose lives I have touched through my ministry along with encouraging words from editors and friends concerning my writing or songwriting.

Just knowing these special words are in my Teddy Bear Box is enough to make me smile and keep me moving on when difficult circumstances or people cause me to question what God has called me to do within my ministry.

Since my initial purchase, I've bought five more Teddy Bear Boxes and have given them away for various occasions. I keep an extra box on the shelf in my closet at all times, ready to be given to someone— a friend, a family member, or just someone I met—who I feel might like or need a "warm fuzzy" memory box in her life.

## MOM'S TABLE BY MARITA

My mother and father's brothers and sisters were a part of my life, but it was my grandmother's sister with whom I was always the closest. It was Aunt Jean and Uncle Ethan's house where we spent beloved vacations as children. They had a small, two-bedroom home—the house itself was not the attraction, though we loved the full basement under the house and the large yard with a big vegetable garden.

Prior to marriage, Aunt Jean had been a schoolteacher. She loved children and wanted a house full. She had only one son, however,

who was nearly an adult by the time I remember spending time at their home.

When my sister and I visited, we felt very special; Aunt Jean doted on each of us as if we were the daughter she didn't have. I know now that several of my cousins felt the same way when they visited Aunt Jean, but as a child I had no idea I was sharing her affection with my cousins who visited at other times.

Aunt Jean and Uncle Ethan lived several hours from my parents— far enough away for their house to be considered a big trip, but close enough to make the trek several times each year. In addition to sharing her affection, Aunt Jean let us help her in the kitchen, canning the abundance of beans, peas, and blueberries grown in Uncle Ethan's garden. Uncle Ethan loved playing board games, and we frequently spent the evening playing scintillating games with him like Chutes and Ladders, feeling as if there were nothing he'd rather do.

When I was nine years old, my family moved across the country, and my life took on a new flavor—one without Aunt Jean and Uncle Ethan. Yes, we exchanged Christmas cards and birthday gifts, but it wasn't the same. Sometime during this separation Uncle Ethan died, and sometime later I got married. As my life settled into a new normal, Chuck encouraged me to visit Aunt Jean. I called her and invited myself for a true New England Thanksgiving dinner. The five days we spent there remain a treasured memory.

Although there were many great things about the trip, one of my favorites was the evening we spent in the basement—though it was much smaller then the picture imprinted into my childhood recollections. As Chuck and I moved through the basement asking questions about the various interesting objects found there, he was fascinated with some old books tucked into the rafters. He went home with a box full of old editions and Bibles that had been in the family for years—many more than one hundred years old. No one else had expressed interest in them, and even though Chuck was not blood family, Aunt Jean was happy to pass them on to someone who would care for them.

The treasure I took home was an old and uninteresting-looking table. It was a small, drop-leaf dinner table that had been painted and repainted to match a variety of decorating trends. Underneath all the layers, it was evident that it had a base of white paint with a brown "antiquing" finish. Aunt Jean, when asked about the table's history, told us that it had been in my grandmother's home—where my mother grew up behind the store. This table was the one my mother ate on every day. I knew my mother would treasure it. Since Aunt Jean viewed it as "this old thing," she was happy to let me take it home. Chuck disassembled it. We went to the local U-Haul dealer and bought a box to hold the table. We took the table home on the plane as "luggage." I brought it to a furniture refinisher and had it cleaned up and finished in a stain that would work with my mother's home. When I picked it up, it looked like a totally different table—it was beautiful!

That year for Christmas, the table was my gift to my mother. I remember how excited I was to give it to her, as I had never mentioned that I had found it in Aunt Jean's basement. By the time Christmas Day came, I had safely hidden the table in another room with a cloth covering it. When it was time to give her my gift, I had my mom close her eyes while Chuck carried it out—still covered—and set it in front of her. She opened her eyes, reached out, and felt around the edges before taking the cloth off. As she touched the curves of the corner design, she knew what it was even without looking at it. Her eyes grew big as she asked, "Is this the table from the store?" Even though nearly fifty years had passed since she had seen the table, she instantly knew what it was just by touching it!

We had fun recounting the story of finding the table, crating it up, bringing it home on the plane, refinishing it, and then waiting for Christmas to present the gift to her.

Now the table has found a home in her house, next to her desk where it reminds her of the stories that were told around it and inspires her to write her own stories for others.

## SHARING THE MEMORIES

Search through the precious mementos you have collected through the years.

Consider:

- writing the story of how you obtained the item and why it is meaningful to you.
- placing it in a safe, visible place where it can prompt memories and conversations.
- passing the item on to a family member who will cherish its meaning.

## THE SALVAGED TREASURE BY RAELENE SEARLE

Months before Chip and I were to be married in 1982, my great-great-aunt Edith died. As the one who needed household items, I was offered the opportunity to go through her home with my aunt and take things I could use or wanted that my grandmother, aunt, and mother didn't want or didn't have room for. Acquiring these family heirlooms and antiques fostered my appreciation of my family heritage.

Two of the many items I received are extremely precious to me: Aunt Edith's Cedar Lane hope chest and a crazy quilt she had made. On three of the quilt's blocks are stitched the following: the city where she lived when she completed the quilt (Orange Cove, California), the date she completed the quilt (February 10, 1921), and the words "Remember the Sabbeth Day." (Yes, the word *Sabbath* is spelled with an *e* on the quilt.) Another quilt, with hand-stitched red and white blocks, was put aside by my aunt to be given to my mother later.

Several years later, while visiting my mother and stepfather, I noticed Aunt Edith's quilt lying in the back of their truck. I asked her what it was doing there, and my mother told me they used it for protecting things they carried in the truck bed. I was shocked. It turns out my mother had no idea that the quilt—handed to her by Aunt Edith—was actually a handmade family heirloom. I retrieved the quilt and lovingly restored what I could of the tattered edges.

When my sister, Carla, became engaged to a man who helped his mother in an antique restoration and sales business, her interest in family heritage began to grow. When Tod's mother died, Carla quickly salvaged the family's quilts and heirlooms. Her home began to look like a lovely antique store.

Last year, Tod and Carla traveled to our home for my daughter's wedding. It dawned on me that Carla had never received any treasures from our side of the family. I decided to surprise her with the quilt I had salvaged from my mother's truck.

When there was a lull in the family activities, I brought the quilt out to where Carla and our mother were and told my sister I had a family gift for her. I recited the story behind the quilt—with input from Mom—of who had made it and how it had been rescued. What joy she had in finally having her first heirloom from her side of the family. What joy I received in giving her such a precious gift.

We each now have one of great-great-aunt Edith's quilts proudly displayed in our homes and a wonderful link to our past. I look forward to passing this quilt and other treasures on to my daughter so she can continue this legacy of love started with great-great-aunt Edith.

## QUILTS

In reading about Aunt Edith's quilts, I (Florence) was reminded of mine. My grandma MacDougall, like many women of her time, made her own dresses and those of her five daughters. With the scraps left over, she made patchwork quilts. When I visited her in the summer as a child, she would take me to the store, let me pick out fabric, and make me two dresses to start school. She always saved the leftover pieces to make a quilt, and I was excited each summer to find pieces of my dresses from the previous year in her newest quilt.

When she was in her eighties and was cleaning out some old things from her closet, she let me have a quilt created from a combination of my dress patches and hers. I still have that patchwork quilt, which I used to cover my babies, and even though it is faded and torn in places, it still gives me joy to see the patches of my childhood dresses.

## ALABASTER, ALABAMA

One day after I had spoken in Alabaster, Alabama, a gracious lady, Beverly Burks, invited me to her home. I had mentioned the writing of this book in my lecture, and she wanted to show how she decorated with old family keepsakes. As we toured her home, she pointed out the origins of special pieces, took pictures, and gave the photos to me.

An easel with a montage of family pictures stands just inside the front door. Beverly says guests stop right there to observe the collection. It sparks interesting conversations on family background.

Next is a curio cabinet full of plates, goblets, and other family collectibles and pictures. It includes an envelope from her grandmother postmarked March 10, 1920. On the wall is a framed map of the town where Beverly grew up. She highlighted Beverly Creek named for her by her father, a local conservation officer. Beverly says her children loved showing their friends "Mama's river" on the map. Draped below the map is an original Roy Rogers bedspread that her husband had as a boy.

Also in the foyer sits the old family organ. Beverly wrote on the back of the pictures she gave me, "My husband and I feel very fortunate to have the organ in our home. My mother-in-law and her two sisters were given the organ in 1934. I have a picture of the three of them, taken at that time, on the organ showing to whom the organ belonged. They had a lot of fun playing the organ for family and friends as we still do today."

My favorite place is the guest room decorated with keepsakes of her daughter. Hanging on a coat hanger is a fluffy blue dress worn by Jody in 1970.

Visiting the Burkses is not only food and fellowship, but also more fun than a trip to a museum.

## OVERDONE! by GOLDEN KEYES PARSONS

"Where are your cookbooks?"

"In a box in the garage."

As I opened the door to the garage, a whoosh of hot, humid, summer Texas air blasted me in the face. I stepped into the garage-oven and began digging through moving boxes. Bravely sticking my hand down into a box marked "Kitchen," imagining that anything from a scorpion to a snake might be prepared to latch on to my fingers, I pulled out a fistful of books. From between Betty Crocker and Martha Stewart fell the charred, dirty, smoke-smeared cookbook I compiled for our middle daughter as a wedding present.

I carried my finds into the cool, air-conditioned new home and spread them out on the kitchen table.

Indicating the singed cookbook, I called to my daughter, "Sweetie, I didn't know this made it through the fire."

My daughter smiled. "Yes, but I don't know if I can still use it. It's so smoke damaged."

The fire that ravaged their former home had blessedly occurred when they were absent. We received a phone call a few months before as we were leaving our Sunday morning worship service. Our daughter was sitting in the driveway, pregnant with their third baby, watching their home of only two years burn. Sobbing, she managed to blurt out, "Mom, our house is burning, but we're all okay."

Nearly all their belongings were either burned or smoke damaged. Boxes of goods that could be salvaged remained stacked in their garage.

I wiped the soot from the cover as best I could and opened to where I had written a sentimental inscription. It was still readable. I leafed through the treasured recipes one by one. None were completely destroyed, even though the edges of the pages were brown and crackled under my touch. The recipes I had included were favorites of our family that had been handed down through the years. I had envisioned the cookbook being passed from her children to their children.

I momentarily considered redoing the book, but as I continued to turn the pages, I realized that the intrinsic value of the legacy I intended to convey to my daughter was unaltered. To be sure, it had gone through the fire and was damaged, but the intent of the testament was intact. And, besides that, the ordeal it had survived gave it character.

We use that cookbook every holiday now, as the favorite, treasured recipes are prepared. And every time we open the scorched book, we praise God for the protection he offered our family and the legacy of love and good times.

## FREE TREASURE!

As you've read the stories in this chapter, I trust you've come to believe that family treasures don't have to cost much or even be worth much monetarily. What's important is the emotional value each thing holds. What's even more important is for you to tell the stories of the family keepsakes so future generations can treasure those objects—and the memories they hold as well.

# 3

# ENHANCING YOUR HOME
## *FLORENCE*

W hen I was a child, there was no such thing as "home decor." We had lived through the Great Depression, a time in which our mothers were grateful if they could put one decent meal on the table each day for their hungry children. We'd gone from the Depression into World War II, an era when a gourmet meal was a can of Spam covered with brown sugar and mustard, baked for thirty minutes, and sliced at the table as a Sunday roast. Our clothes were more "charity case" than "designer label," and there were no Joneses to keep up with.

By the time we got married in 1953, Fred and I were basically ashamed of the leftover furniture our parents had passed down to us. I wanted no reminders of a poverty-filled past. I wanted sleek modern pieces—even though we couldn't afford them. Our first bedroom set was a pair of dressers with purple marble tops, donated by Fred's grandparents. I painted over the chipped maple finish with a matte gray and added soft silver handles to make the furniture look new.

New was what we all wanted.

When my grandmother died, I helped my mother clean out the house. Looking back, I cringe in regret. The attic was what we would now call a treasure trove of antiques. My brother Ron backed up a truck under the attic window and we threw out what we considered to be junk. I remember tossing gold frames with pictures of our ancestors still in them.

My mother cried as we threw away her heritage. "Why would anyone want this old stuff?" we asked. Our aim for the day was to empty the attic and take the relics to the dump. Sentiment and tears were not deciding factors.

Gratefully, I did have a slight concern for my mother's desire to keep some things, and I let her salvage a few treasures. Today, I regret throwing away the MacDougall legacy. Those few things we saved ended up with me, and I have great attachment to them: the rocker my grandfather carved and polished; the footstool he made for my petite grandmother whose feet never reached the floor; the large picture of the first three children—Annie, Sadie, and Katie (my mother, who was six months old at the time). Now all precious, these items occupy prominent places in my home.

Throughout my lifetime, America has gone through numerous phases: living with the old and then rejecting the old, modern sleek and pseudo-antique. Now in a new century, we search for our roots and consider any relic of our childhood a treasure.

How can we translate our new love for the old to our home decor? What can we use to give personal significance to our surroundings and teach our children their family history at the same time?

Here are some suggestions. Enjoy!

## PICTURES

I remember as a child being in awe of the large picture of an austere and imposing woman hanging in my grandmother's living room.

When I asked about her, I learned she wasn't a relative but England's Queen Victoria. Seeing her ruling over the parlor, a room used only if the pastor or some equally impressive person came to visit, gave me the desire to grow up to be a queen. Her presence in that secluded room inspired me to check out library books on Victoria and find out what kind of person she really was. A picture of a historical person you admire hanging somewhere in your home can be a catalyst for conversation and a teaching tool for your children and grandchildren.

Unfortunately, the queen was transported off to the dump, ending my brush with royalty.

As I was growing up, home decor wasn't a consideration. We had only one picture of a noted person: the scene of Jesus at Gethsemane. He is kneeling by a rock and looking up to heaven, and I just knew he was saying, "Not my will, but thy will be done." When I was baptized, I chose the hymn "In the Garden" and pictured him with me. "And he walks with me, and he talks with me, and he tells me I am his own; and the joy we share as we tarry there, none other has ever known" (C. Austin Miles, 1912). When we closed the store, the portrait of Jesus was somehow left on the wall, but the picture remained in my mind. To this day, when I call out to Jesus, I see him kneeling in the garden.

My current living room is graced with a niche over the fireplace. It is arched at the top, about twenty inches wide, two feet deep, and two and half feet tall. It was crying for something unique to sit in it. Many years ago, I heard about an old, Catholic church that was being modernized. They were selling old pews, columns, and other decorative pieces. I wanted everything I saw but settled upon a carved piece the size of an end table. Miniature church spires rose up around the top, and as the crown over the priest's head, it was a one-of-a-kind piece. When I bought it for eight dollars, they threw in a newel post and a two-foot-high wooden cross, faced in gold leaf. I have used the carved piece in different ways in other houses—once as an end table—but when I saw the niche in this house I could hardly wait to try it there. Not only does it fit as if it had been made for the spot, but there is room on the mantel next to the niche for the gold cross and the newel post topped with an angel figurine. It's not the Sistine Chapel, but with a little imagination, you can get the feeling.

What pictures, objects, or figurines do you have around the house or in a box in the garage? Perhaps a new matting or frame would freshen up an old portrait. Perhaps an odd object you love could brighten up a special spot.

Remember, it's not the cost that gives these things value, but the emotional connection they give us to the past.

Larisee Lynn Stevens sent us some suggestions for making home decor more personal:

*In this mass-market world, we are led to believe we should dress alike, decorate our homes alike, and blend in with everyone else. Yet God wants us to set ourselves apart. If we read Hebrews 11, we see the people listed there in no way "blended in." We are not to make spectacles of ourselves, but neither are we to follow blindly what the rest of the world is doing. Before settling for being average, we need to consider that average is where the best of the worst and the worst of the best meet in the middle. We don't want to be either of them!*

*Decorating uniquely need not be costly. Certainly, it can be considerably less expensive than following a fashion trend. When I was first married, I couldn't afford to buy paintings (even the cheap ones found at the discount stores). If I was to have anything on my walls, it was going to be 80 percent what I had on hand (almost nothing), 15 percent imagination, and 5 percent creativity. I went to a "junk" store and found*

**A**s I toured a stately home in England, I was astounded to find the owner had covered an entire wall with a decoupage collage of pictures and snapshots of his friends, family, and travels. Princess Diana created a border around Prince Charles's bathroom at Windsor Castle with cartoons of him from the press.

Decorating is intended to express who you are, not the latest decorating trend. Think back to homes you've been in. I'll bet the ones that stand out in your mind are those that had a unique feature, something that told you who the owners were. While beautiful oil paintings hung in my mother's living room, the grandchildren remember the items in her whimsically decorated kitchen—especially the goofy cat clock her sister gave her as a joke. The cat's big eyes moved side to side with each second. The little ones were sure he was looking only at them.

What among your possessions represent you or your family in a personal way? If you don't have a feel for arranging, invite an artistic friend over to help. Ask her to be careful to stay true to the look you want to create and not take over the entire project.

*an old carpet beater and a wooden pestle used with a meat grinder attachment for a kitchen mixer. I also discovered two wooden open boxes used as drawer dividers—forerunners of the plastic ones we use today. I paid about two dollars for all these treasures. I already had odd plates from my mother's, grandmother's, and great-grandmother's sets of dishes.*

*My dining room became a salute to women of days past. I arranged the plates, wooden boxes, pestle, and carpet beater on the wall. I wound artificial ivy through the carpet beater, hung the wooden boxes sideways and laid the pestle in one and a cup and saucer from my childhood tea set in the other, then fastened the plates in a pleasing arrangement. I enjoyed that wall decor so much I kept it for thirty-five years. Only after I moved into an "open arrangement" home with very few walls did I give it up.*

## VACATIONS FOR THE HOME

When traveling, look for items with which to decorate your home, rather than the usual mementos for tourists. Here are some ideas:

Purchase inexpensive art reflecting or depicting the area you're visiting.

When taking photographs, consider taking a few scenic pictures that might fit well with your décor: an old barn for a country themed room or a city skyline for a modern home office.

Before the trip, research the types of arts and crafts the area is known for. Look for things that fit your style and represent the region. For example, quilted items in Amish country or woven baskets in the Southwest.

If you travel regularly, find a specific type of souvenir to collect. Be sure it's something widely available. This can be as simple as a keychain or as challenging as a specific type of pottery.

*My husband and I love traveling, and we have done a good deal of it. We also love old things. My foyer is wallpapered in road maps we've collected over the years, and dotted with favorite snapshots we've taken from around the country—a field of California poppies, a Texas windmill at sunset, and so forth. For a coat rack, I screwed old, outside water faucets to an old board and then hung it up. It certainly gets the conversation going quickly!*

## WALLS

What can you do with an open stairway wall? Hang pictures as high as you can reach or even all the way to the ceiling. Over the years I had collected pictures from various family members and those once-a-year school or family portraits. When family members died, I asked relatives for any pictures they were going to throw away. In addition to these pictures, Fred and I collected menus.

Since we were in the food service business at the time, we traveled twice to Europe with a restaurateur group. At each stop on our gourmet gala, we asked for one of their colorful, impressive, and often embossed menus. Usually they were happy to give us one, but some sold us their menus at a modest price. When we returned home, we had each menu framed with an appropriate trim for the country it came from: gold ornate for England, stark black for Sweden, Greek-key for Greece, super ornate for Italy.

The first time we did this, we filled an entire dining room wall that guests loved to admire. When we moved into this house, we decided to fill the stairwell from the bottom to the top. How did we do this? We pushed the furniture out of the living room and laid down masking tape the outline and size of the wall space. We then laid out the framed pictures on the floor in appropriate groupings. First came the family, next the menus, then framed certificates of graduations, marriage, and special honors.

Then a home decorator came in and reorganized our collection more artistically. To hang them all the way to the ceiling was a fascinating project. The decorator built scaffolding even with the top stair and wide enough to hold a high stepladder. He started at the top and worked his way down to the level of each stair, completely filling the wall. When guests walk in the front door they gasp in awe and ask, "How did you ever get those pictures way up to the ceiling?" For the price of the scaffolding and one day's labor, we have a wall that is one-of-a-kind. No one else in the world has our family portraits, our European menus, and our unique awards and certificates.

You might ask about the price of framing. By the time we put this wall together, most of the pictures were already framed. The menus we originally had framed professionally. We put the diplomas and certificates in frames purchased at Wal-Mart. The overall effect is truly awesome and for very little cost.

Do you want a one-of-a-kind wall? Especially a two-story one? You can do something similar yourself if you have a carpenter friend who will build the structure you need to reach the top, and if you (or your friend) are daring and not afraid of heights. The most fun is to watch people who have only one simple scene hung over their couch gasp at this wall in disbelief, wondering where we got a ladder that high, how we balanced it on the stairs, and how we dared to get up there in the first place.

When Emilie Barnes, my dear friend (and the author of many bestselling books, including *More Hours in My Day*) first saw the wall, she spent two hours studying and reading every item. She loved the wall and gave us an A+ in wall decor.

Larisee Lynn Stevens has given us an original idea. Perhaps it will stir your creativity:

*As a child, I was always intrigued by the fact that my mother was born in a covered wagon and in a different century than I. Now that I've lived into a new millennium, I understand it's no big deal. You go to bed one night in one century, the alarm rings the next morning, and you're in another. There is no magic moment in time; life just moves forward.*

*The stories my mother told of riding horses to school, of stampeding cattle, and of putting real candles on Christmas trees fascinated me. It seemed such a wide time span for one family—going from horses to cars and from lanterns to electricity! I never considered that my own siblings and I, from the oldest to the youngest, were spread over twenty-five years from one World War to another. The family portrait that hung in my parents' bedroom of my grandparents with all their children, my great-grandmother and great-great grandmother in their turn-of-the-century clothes, helped put faces into Mother's stories.*

*Soon after I was married, I found an old ironing board in a shed behind my mother's house. She explained that before she got an electric iron, she placed the wooden board over the backs of two chairs and ironed with flat irons heated on the wood stove. I decided to hang this board over my sofa as a background for the family pictures I had collected. Up went portraits of my mother's family, my father's family, my parents, and my husband's parents, each in an oval frame. After a trip to Disneyland, where we had our family picture made in Victorian dress, I added the new portrait to the collection on the ironing board.*

*Even though my décor was not "antique," I added a few antique touches to the room (an end-table skirt, some old books on a table, an oil lamp, and a modern copy of a spindle back rocker). The ironing board and its family pictures remained my focal point.*

*Each time I moved, the ironing board came with me. The unique display has graced homes in almost a dozen states and one in Europe. With each move, it always made a house seem like home, and it was always a conversation starter when people came to visit. When my son requested it for his home, I couldn't say no. I let him take it. I not only want my granddaughter to have a sense of family continuity, but of the life and work those women did for their families as well. When we look at those pictures, I will tell her of traveling Highway 66, of moon landings, and of life without television and computers.*

*As I share our family history with this precious child and show her the pictures of each character I mention, I will provide roots for her life and a legacy for her to pass on to future generations.*

## SHELVES AND LEDGES

In many of today's new housing projects, the models boast high walls, small alcoves, and designer shelves. If you are not too creative, visit these new models for ideas. Emilie Barnes is able to take a bunch of dead weeds, tie them with a pink satin ribbon, stick a silk rose on the satin bow, and create a unique and striking decoration. She once adorned a wall with an antique plow and other old farm tools. For a creative entry, a doll perched happily on each of the narrow steps leading to her granddaughter's loft bedroom. Anything you hand to Emilie will inspire her to create something beautiful—the proverbial silk purse out of a sow's ear.

A ledge sits high over one end of my living room. It's narrow, but I thought it might hold a simple bookcase. In fact, it holds two, side by side. By nailing the cases to the wall and filling them with the myriad extra books and college texts we had stored in the garage, we created a library in the sky. I considered getting a library ladder to make the books accessible, but I never got around to it. Since the display is over the front door, people don't see it when they first enter. But there's a moment when they suddenly look up and whisper, "Wow!" Once they take a good look, they all ask, "How do you get up there to read those books?" The family answers simply, "We don't read *those* books." Above the front door, where the ledge turns the corner, we placed a special chair next to the bookcase. It came to me from Aunt Sadie. When I was a child, Aunt Sadie had a private kindergarten in her home. Our vacations were often at different times, and I would help Aunt Sadie teach the children. (From my earliest days, I loved teaching.) When Aunt Sadie closed her little school, I kept one of the chairs. That chair sits on the ledge, holding a cabbage patch doll that was given to me the year I wrote *Out of the Cabbage Patch*. The doll is, of course, holding a copy of the book.

The use of unique touches from our own lives, such as Aunt Sadie's chair, makes our decorating different and personal. At one point, Patsy Clairmont had a similar ledge over her living room. She had an antique sewing machine, complete with a heavy, black iron foot treadle. As she stood and pictured the machine up on the ledge, perhaps with some fabric hanging out the front, she asked Les how he could get it way up there. While he was figuring out how to accomplish this task, Patsy exclaimed, "You have to realize that if you get it up there and I don't like it, you'll have to take it down." Les answered, "If I get it up there, you *will* like it." Les did get the sewing machine on the ledge and Patsy liked it.

## FAMILY TREE

When my children were small, I began sharing our family background. Without pictures, it was difficult for them to grasp which grandmother was which. I gathered old photos, framed them in gold ovals, and had a tree painted on the wall by their bedrooms. My baby picture was on the left with my forebears above me; Fred's family was on the right.

The problem was I had so few pictures of the Littauers because Fred's mother didn't understand my request and felt it was too much work to dig them out. When she first saw the tree with empty branches on Fred's side she asked, "Why is this tree so lopsided? Where are the Littauers?" When I explained that I'd asked her for pictures several months before, she remembered. Within days she arrived with a bag of portraits, I framed them to match those on my side, and we evened up the family tree.

I have suggested this motivational style to visitors who have enjoyed the family tree, but are certain that one side of their family wouldn't give them anything. One fellow author wrote me this story:

"I did what you said after my mother-in-law told me she had no family pictures. I felt funny filling only half the tree. But when my mother-in-law saw it, she about had a fit and asked, 'Why is it only your side?' Within a week she had dug through old boxes and come up with a commendable family. Now she brings people in to see 'her tree.'"

## DISCOVERING WHAT YOU ALREADY HAVE

Look through the objects you have in storage and find a few from various moments in your life or from your family history. Are there any that can be creatively displayed?

Your mother's old glass pitcher might be used as a vase.

The model ships your father liked to build could stand on the fireplace mantel.

Your grandfather's typewriter from his reporter days might be placed on your desk.

The photos, receipts, plane tickets, and souvenirs from a memorable trip could be arranged in a shadow box and displayed.

We have found, as we've done a new tree each time we moved, that our grandchildren look at the pictures of these people they've never met. They wonder who these ancestors were, what they did, and whether they look like any of them.

You can start rounding up your relatives' pictures and motivate your in-laws to action. There is no right kind of tree—we've had everything from bare branches with a picket fence to flowered trees to the current one with a mauve-colored trunk that matches our décor.

Be creative and you'll make a bare wall beautiful and have a conversation piece none of your friends can equal.

## COAT OF ARMS

Another personal wall can be created with the coats of arms from each side of the family. These can be found in kiosks at large shopping malls or from genealogy companies located in phone books or the Internet. I bought my Chapman coat of arms in a store in England. It is a simple shield with an arm sticking out the top. The fist is holding an arrow and a laurel leaf coronet indicating victory. The word *Chapman* means "a salesman; one who peddles goods door-to-door." My father had worked in a store from age sixteen when he delivered groceries on foot, managed SK Ames Butter and Egg Store, and owned our Riverside Variety store until his death; he was truly a "Chapman." He was born in Rochdale, Lancashire, England. He proudly shared his love of his native country with us three children, encouraging us to visit the homeland, a feat we all accomplished at different times. It was a special joy for me to visit the town hall in Rochdale—an impressive castle-like building—and find the records of my father's birth in 1878. In reading the available pamphlet, I learned that Rochdale was originally the sheep-shearing, wool-gathering center of Lancashire. Their symbol is a wooly lamb hanging in a sling waiting to be clipped. It's fun for our family to know where we came from and to pass the history on to our children and grandchildren.

Fred and I found the street where Dad had lived his first years. The street was still there with its old, old houses, but at the end of the street, the homes had all been razed and simple apartment houses built in their places. When we asked an elderly man how old the old houses were, he answered, "Older than anyone would care to remember." That ended our quest for dates.

On the last trip Fred and I made to Europe, we drove from Edinburgh to the west coast of Scotland in search of the original MacDougall castle. We crossed the country to Oban, a seaside village with many souvenir shops. As we stood near a monument to men killed in battle, we looked up, and there on an immense sheer bluff stood the remnant of the MacDougall castle. High above the town and facing the sea, the fortress effect was chilling. It was easy to see how almost impossible it would be for an enemy to scale the cliffs.

Yet the property had turned over a few times, most notably to their archenemy Robert the Bruce.

We found a Scottish lady who created special coats of arms. She showed us samples of what she could do with the MacDougalls'. "Which would you prefer," she asked, "the peasant coat of arms or the royal one?" What a question for me to answer! She explained that the royal insignia was added to as the lord won battles. It was adorned with gold threads and padded embroidery. On the top of the MacDougall shield was the armored fist holding a cross, which I assume meant they believed in God. The most exciting part was when this lady pointed out our family motto: "Victory or Death."

When I brought my new purchase home and put it next to the Chapman one, I could see the difference between the royal coat of arms, highly decorated and festooned, and the peasant one, stripped down to its basic shape and simplicity. If I were to determine my status in life by my coats of arms, I would be half Chapman peasant, stripped to my baser nature, and half MacDougall royal blood, fighting for victory and refusing to accept death as a possible reality.

The study of family crests and coats of arms is fascinating, and information is readily available, especially for England, Scotland, and Ireland. In searching for the Littauer side in Germany, we were stopped when we learned that Littauer means someone from Lithuania whose forebears came to Germany. No matter what family they were from, they were all labeled Littauers from the country Litauen.

With the Internet access there is today, finding your background is easy for some nationalities and has grown even more possible for many more.

Leave a legacy for your children so they will know where they came from and who they are.

## THE CEDAR CHEST BY RANDY BRIGGS, SR.

When my mother married in 1945, it was customary for a bride to fill a cedar chest with linens, blankets, and keepsakes she intended to take to her new home. Mom's was built by Lane and sat at the end of her bed as long as she lived. Every once in awhile, she would open it to get something out—allowing me a glimpse—but I never knew all that it contained.

When my mother died, Lauren and I inherited the chest. It contained family "treasures" I had never seen. I was thrilled to discover most items were carefully labeled and they included the black lace shawl my great-great-grandmother wore when she immigrated to America from Ireland in the 1840s, handmade quilts from my grandmother, my father's naval uniform from World War II, childhood toys my mother had played with, a piece of my parents' wedding cake, and old family jewelry. All rested safely within the confines of the chest.

Lauren and I have added to the contents of the cedar chest over the years. Only the most precious items such as

## WHEN YOUR FAMILY IS OFF THE WALL

Find some empty wall space for family pictures. Arrange them in a way that will help you remember the various relationships. Here are a few tips:

When visiting with relatives, ask to look through their family photos. Offer to make and pay for copies of your favorites.

Don't just look for formal portraits. Choose a few from each relative that are candid and reflect their personality.

When arranging the pictures on the wall, consider mixing in a few small items that represent the people in the pictures: a tiny cross-stitch for your great-grandma who loved sewing or a framed fishing lure for your uncle who took you fishing.

Buy some acid-free paper and pens to write down the names and relationships of the people in the pictures. Place your notes in the frame behind the photo.

baby shoes, baby blankets, and baby clothes from our sons have been placed inside. None of the boys really knows the contents, but one day they, too, will discover the family treasure chest!

## WELL-TRAVELED SPOONS

My (Florence's) aunt Jean was always my favorite person in our family, and I became an English teacher like her because of her encouragement.

When I became a traveling speaker, I bought souvenir silver spoons from each city I visited and sent them on to her as surprise presents. She loved receiving them. Once when she commented that she had no way to display them, my husband bought her a spoon rack, hung it, and filled it with her collection. A few years later when her rack was full, we got her another one. When she died in her nineties, her son, my cousin Edward, inherited the two racks filled with her spoon collection. I wondered what he'd do with them. I didn't have to wonder for long, as he sent the collection to me. I now have the silver spoons I bought for Aunt Jean on the wall in my kitchen. They have gone full circle and have returned to me.

What's circling around in your family? Will it end up with you?

## BICYCLE ART BY MARITA

Like most couples, my husband and I have different decorating tastes. If I'd allow it, he'd move all the furniture out of the great room—after all, we hardly ever use it—and fill it with motorcycles. He has a single, car-loving friend who knocked out a wall in his living room and drove a car he was restoring into the room so he could work in inclement weather. (You can see why, despite his status as a medical doctor and his charming personality, he is single!) Chuck thinks this was a great idea. I do not.

However, somehow in getting settled into our new home—which has a much bigger garage than our old house and a great room with a very high ceiling—Chuck moved two bicycles into the great room for storage. One is the bike his mother rode when he was a child, and the other was his first bike. Since he is now an avid cyclist, having these historical pieces feels important to him. Not to me. I am not excited about having these two bikes stuck in the corner south of the fireplace. When I have entertained, I have wheeled them into his office and closed the door. While I never return them to the corner, they seem to find their way back to the great room by themselves.

Recently, we spent a holiday weekend in Durango, Colorado. There, we ate in a restaurant whose décor included lots of old "stuff." The main dining area had a narrow balcony that went around three of the four walls. On one of the railings, the focal point was a child's old bike that peeked through the banister with an old child-sized man-nequin posed as if he were riding the bike. It looked cute. My master bedroom is a loft that overlooks the great room and has a railing. *Hmmm,* I thought. I could do something like that with Chuck's child-hood bike.

When we got home, I began creating this little scene that would incorporate Chuck's little red bike with my "castle" décor.

I already had misplaced décor in the bedroom: old school desks from my childhood. When I was little, my father had gone to an auc-tion at an elementary school that was being upgraded. There he purchased two old desks—probably from the early 1900s. They were the style with the seat attached to the desk behind it. Each unit has one desk and an attached seat. These were lined up in the classroom with one extra seat at the back of the row. My dad bought two desks and the one extra seat—giving our set a total of three seats. These old desks, with dark wood and rusty metal legs, were in our basement. My siblings and I played "school" with them when we were little. Since there were only two desks, I am sure my sister was the teacher, while my brother and I were the students.

When my family moved to California when I was nine, many items were stored in the basements of family friends—including the desks.

Once I got married and settled into my own home, the topic of these desks came up. I asked my parents, "Whatever happened to those old school desks?" They knew exactly where they were—in the basement of so-and-so's house. A few years later, Chuck and I took a vacation that allowed us to visit my childhood neighborhood. We tracked down the family, and they still had the desks! Chuck disassembled them in the driveway and packed them in U-Haul cartons. We took the cumbersome crates home on the plane as luggage.

Because our home at that time was too small for the child-sized desks, they stayed boxed up in the garage. When we moved from California to New Mexico, the oddly shaped containers came with us—never being opened or assembled.

When we moved into our current home—which has a cavernous great room and an open loft master bedroom—Chuck declared that we were no longer storing the desks. We were either going to open the boxes, assemble the desks, and display them or we were going to give them to my brother.

Well, those desks are a part of my history. Plus, we had gone to a lot of work to acquire them. I couldn't give them away! I acquiesced,

and we placed the assembled desks along the railing of the balcony-like master bedroom.

Therefore, with the mental image of the restaurant's decorative use of an old bicycle, I began adding a whimsical touch to my bedroom's décor. I remembered my boxes of old books; some books I'd acquired on a visit to Aunt Jean's while others were some of Chuck's finds from used bookstores. I dug through the still-unpacked-since-our-move-a-year-ago boxes and found several old school textbooks and children's books. I bought a realistic looking apple at a craft store. Then I arranged the books on the first desk and topped them with an "apple for the teacher." I lugged Chuck's childhood red Schwinn with fat tires and dull paint up the stairs and placed it in the grouping—topping it off with an almost-life sized stuffed schnauzer (our dog of choice) on the first desk's seat. Now I'm on the lookout for a child-sized mannequin to ride the bike and complete the collection.

With Chuck's childhood bike artfully incorporated into a display, I still had his mother's old bike stuck in the corner to contend with before I'd have the south end of the fireplace returned to "showroom condition."

A few months earlier I'd seen a display in a store that gave me a idea. They had placed barren trees in a rectangular acrylic planter an hid the Styrofoam that secured the trees with Spanish moss. To cre a "spring" look, the store had tied little lime-green bows—to give feeling of new leaves—to selected branches. I thought that would work in the open space next to my fireplace. So, while i still winter—before the trees began to get leaves—I went out in woods and cut down three small trees whose branches for shape I thought would work. I secured them in umbrella st the kind you would use for your patio table umbrella—tied li

ribbons to a few branches, and strung them with "twinkle" lights. The little trees alone added a nice touch and stayed like that for several months—until I got into my bicycle-decorating mode.

Chuck's mother's old bike—a dark green Raleigh—has a large willow basket I had purchased for him several years before so he could ride with his dog in the basket. I retrieved the basket from storage and attached it to the front of the bike. I then placed a tablecloth in the basket with a corner draping over the front. I bought a long, fake baguette of French bread at the craft store and begged a brown bag the shape of French bread from the grocery store. I added a few other appropriate items such as a silk bouquet of daisies, an empty wine bottle, and a couple of glasses to the collection, then arranged them in the basket and placed the bike in my tree grouping. I have searched the Internet and found a fake salami that I plan to order to complete my "picnic basket" theme.

In storage, I also had the croquet set I played with as a child when we visited Aunt Jean. It is clearly old and worn but has all its pieces. I got it out and assembled the stand—placing the balls and mallets in the appropriate spots. I rolled the cart into my "French picnic" scene.

Bicycles are still stored in my living space, but now they bring history with them and are great conversation starters. Now I describe my décor as "castle with whimsical touches."

## SPAIN: A SPIN WITH A STRANGER

In 1965, when my (Florence's) husband was the District Governor of Rotary in Connecticut, we attended an international convention in Madrid, Spain. One afternoon, while the men were at meetings, we wives were set free to experience the intrigues of the city. Not knowing where to go or what to do, I was standing by the front door looking

bewildered when a dashing Spanish gentleman approached me. "Are you looking for someone?" he asked. "Oh no," I replied. "My husband is at a meeting and I don't have anything to do." Impressed with my naiveté, he invited me to sit down for a brief history lesson of the country.

He told me how General Franco had led a revolution against the royalty and had taken control of the country in 1936. To get spending money for himself, Franco had been stripping down the uninhabited palaces of the royalty who had fled and selling off the furnishings. "I happen to be Franco's personal artifacts dealer, and my job is to clean out one palace at a time, display the pieces in a warehouse, and bring tourists in to see them." By then I was wide-eyed and fascinated both by his stories and his charm. After captivating me with the possibility of buying furniture that kings had sat on, he asked, "Would you like to see some?" I assumed he had them to look at there in the hotel so I said, "Oh that would be fun." He smiled, then led me quickly out the front door and into a black limousine parked conveniently at the curb. My new friend spoke in Spanish to his driver, and I began to wonder what he was telling him. More than that, I suddenly wondered, *Where is he taking me?* What would Fred think when his meeting ended and he found me missing? Worse, what if he asked the desk clerk if he had seen me and was told, "Yes, she went off with a stranger in a black limousine."

By the time I realized my predicament and that no one had a clue where I was going, it was too late to object. Could I yell? Who would hear me? Should I ask where I was going or take the easy road, relax in the plush seat, act sophisticated, and pretend I ran off with strange men every day? The latter seemed my only alternative. As we got outside the city, the tall buildings turned into warehouses, and soon we drove up to one. This did not look like any furniture store I had ever seen, especially not like one selling furnishings from a palace. As the chauffeur opened my door and helped me out, I looked for Lorenzo. (I had learned his name by then. However, it wasn't until later that I looked in a "book of names" and saw that Lorenzo means "a charming, suave Spanish gentleman, up to no good.") He was attempting to get into the warehouse by tapping on a small square window in a door. It was a "Joe sent me" type of approach.

The door opened, and Lorenzo guided me into a huge barn full of furniture. "This is all from one palace and Franco still has many to go," he said. I looked around at the disorganized array of chairs, tables, and couches but stopped when I saw a huge carved cabinet. The carvings on the doors were cut all the way through and backed by red velvet. I had never seen anything so royal! A small gnome-like person appeared from behind a screen and told me the price of this ornate piece. It was called a *biblioteca* and was taken from a palace library. He even told me the palace name, which I of course can no longer remember. While I was thinking over the price and my instant desire to own this piece, the little man pointed across the room to a table. Lorenzo explained that the table and four chairs went with the bookcase. Then the price did not seem much at all. As I examined the table, I was overwhelmed. Instead of legs, the table had heavily carved panels at each end with a carved connector between the ends. A thick piece of solid walnut formed the top. The chairs had tooled leather seats with studs and high, carved backs. One was a throne chair, bigger than the rest and obviously where the former king had sat to issue edicts to his subjects. I had to have this. "Could I come back tomorrow with my husband?" I asked the short man. He said I could not come because the place was closed on Sunday. Lorenzo spouted a few hot words in Spanish and the man changed his mind. "For you, we will be open."

Our ride back was more relaxed than our ride over, as I had seen Lorenzo really was an influential government employee and had nothing more devious on his mind than selling American women palace furniture. As I happily walked into the hotel, a guard grabbed me. He held my picture in his hand and asked, "Are you Señora Littauer?" When I nodded, he whisked me off to the front desk where a frenzied Fred was asking, "Have you looked in every room?"

When I showed up smiling and unharmed, Fred responded with a mix of relief and anger. "Where have you been?" I pointed to tall handsome Lorenzo and said sweetly, "That nice man took me shopping." Gratefully, Lorenzo stepped up and explained where we had been and that I had found some castle selections that I wanted to buy. "We will open up for you alone tomorrow." By then, Fred had regained his composure and promised to see him the next day at one.

Fred later explained to me that he had come out of the meeting and looked for me in the lobby. When he could not locate me, he had gone to the room and seen that I wasn't there either. The desk clerk told him all the ladies had gone shopping, but when they returned laden with bundles and I was not among them, Fred panicked. Where could I be? How could he find me in Madrid? Were there any police who could hunt for me? No one had any answers, but the security guard asked for a picture so he could spot me when I entered—as he assured Fred I would. And sure enough, I had arrived in a limousine with an unknown Spanish conquistador!

The next day, Lorenzo took us to the warehouse where we closed the deal and paid a huge price to have this castle furniture shipped to Connecticut. The huge bookcase was strikingly imposing on one wall, and the table, a true work of art, stood out as a piece of royal antiquity against our purple carpeting. The throne chair was so impressive that

Fred could hardly wait to sit in it and give out edicts to the children. Friends came in wide-eyed, and I truly felt like a queen. We had not noticed in Madrid that the carvings were bizarre animals biting each other in the foot while monkeys watched from the treetops.

When we moved to Arrowhead Springs, California, we left a twelve-room home for "Bungalow One," a dilapidated five-room motel. Each room followed the next one like train cars going around a curve. To go from one end of the house to the other, you either went through each room in sequence or went outdoors and crossed the patio. It was four bedrooms with one sitting room that could house little but the Spanish antiques. There was no kitchen, so I cooked on a hot plate on a porch. This was hardly a place to house royalty, so we "played peasant" for several years.

We ultimately built a house focused on the Spanish furniture: a little bridge spanned a moat to a ten-foot-high front door that opened right to the bookcase. The library table and chairs became the dining room set. We finally had a position of elegance for the Spanish antiques.

We've moved several times since then, and each time we only buy a house that will hold this special furniture. When I asked my children what each one wanted to inherit, they all wanted the royal furniture. If I only had an expensive dining room set, no one probably would care, but with this display of antiquity, each one hopes to receive it.

Whatever your family treasures, it is not just the furniture, the bicycle, or the commemorative spoons that matter; it is the legacy behind them that counts. Tell your children the colorful background of any special item in your home. It's the story that brings value to the antiquity.

# 4

# Food and Fellowship
## Marita

*A*t my table, I set a place for surprise. I serve opinion and some- times fact. I simmer good conversation," states an advertisement for Electrolux appliances. It continues, promising "In the well-lived home more than eating goes on around the table. It's a place for celebrations. A place for savoring. A place where friendships are forged."

Echoing the times around the table of my childhood, this ad caught my attention. While food was a focal point, it was not an end unto itself, but rather a means to an end—the end being celebrations savored and friendships forged. The food and festivities carry genera- tions of history with them; from previous generations through to those in the future.

## FOOD

How grateful I am that in our home we all learned to cook, and how to cook many of the family favorites.

### New England Favorite

My mother's family is from New England—Massachusetts specifi- cally. I have fond memories of going to Grammy Chapman's apartment for a Sunday dinner. The moment we opened the door the fragrance of the simmering corned beef hit us full force. What I now know as New England boiled dinner was a family favorite.

Unfortunately, Grammy Chapman died while I was still a newlywed. At the time, I was distracted with setting up housekeeping and earning a living and didn't really appreciate the memories the smell of corned beef could summon.

A few years later, Chuck and I were visiting Grammy's sister, Aunt Jean. She cooked us the family favorite: New England boiled dinner. The warm aroma of the cooking corned beef and vegetables permeated the entire house and brought with it happy memories of fun and fellowship around the table.

By then I wanted to capture that memory, so I knew I needed to learn to cook New England boiled dinner—not just the recipe off the corned beef package from the grocery store, but the way Grammy and Aunt Jean made it. Mom made it too, but since it was not my father's favorite, the memory, in my mind, belongs with Grammy.

Every St. Patrick's Day when corned beef goes on sale, I cook up a pot of the family favorite and bring back the memories of years past. As I am writing this, St. Patrick's Day is within the week and my mother is visiting. I asked what she'd like me to make for dinner and offered several suggestions, one of which was New England boiled dinner. Her face lit up at the thought. She has her own fond memories of this family favorite, and I'm blessed that by preparing a simple meal I can bring her joy. She passed the legacy on to me, and now I can thank her by returning the favor.

### Sunday Dinners

While my mom's family fare was simple, my dad's family had

I was blessed to have a favorite aunt everyone called Miss Flossie. She was the best cook in the world and inspired my culinary efforts. She wasn't big on formal entertaining. She didn't care if the plates matched. The "tools," as she called silverware, just needed to be somewhere close to the plate, but she definitely wanted her guests to love what they ate, so she worked hard at pleasing the palate! She loved preparing our favorite foods—nothing gourmet, just good, home cooking.

She often baked one of her delicious cakes and then called someone at the police station or the church to say, "I baked y'all a cake if you can send someone after it." She would have hand-delivered it, but she didn't own a car and had never learned to drive. Having tasted Miss Flossie's cakes before, they were more than happy to come and get it!

She was renowned throughout the town for her delectable cakes, her collard greens, and her turkey with dressing. Our church janitor once said, "When I get to heaven, I want my mansion to be right next door to Miss Flossie's so I can eat turkey and dressing for eternity!"

What a compliment to a lady who never saw herself as talented or gifted! She just did what she loved doing and shared it with others. As a result, Miss Flossie left a lasting legacy.

—PAT THOMAS

different food traditions. Every Sunday of his childhood, like many families, they had roast beef. My siblings and I all know the story of the family roast beef dinner. Everyone wanted the end cut—the pieces from each end of the roast with all the spices and flavor, crispy brown on one side and juicy pink on the other. Because these cuts were considered special, they often went to guests. As a young boy, my father felt he was slighted; he knew it had been weeks since he'd received the coveted end cut. So he could prove his point, he kept a chart detailing week after week of the end-cut recipients. He was right; he had been cheated out of his favorite part.

Though we didn't have roast beef every Sunday, we did have it on many special occasions. In my childhood home, roast beef was the signal for an important event.

When I was in high school, I was invited to my boyfriend's home for Sunday dinner. I was told they were having roast beef, and I pictured the beautifully browned roast smothered with seasoning and embellished with cooked rings of onions clinging—with the aid of toothpicks—to the top and sides. In my mind, I could smell its rich aroma and see the pretty pink of the meat, topped off with au jus. That was how roast beef was served at my house.

That wasn't exactly his family tradition. While both families called it roast beef, I learned that day that my family served prime rib and his served pot roast. I remember my surprise at the dry brown slice they placed on my plate that was then smothered with gravy. I was initially disappointed but discovered it, too, was good—just different. Both were wonderful meals, but very different.

In my home now, prime rib—cooked the way Mom taught me—continues to symbolize something special. Chuck always requests it for Christmas, and even though I see new recipes I'd like to try, I always use the family recipe for Christmas.

The draw to family recipes is also true for Thanksgiving. In October, *Bon Appétit* and *Gourmet* magazines feature pages and pages of terrific turkey recipes. I used to try them, especially after moving to New Mexico. Here, a Thanksgiving turkey with cornbread and green chili seemed like just the thing. It was good, but it just seemed wrong for the tradition of Thanksgiving. One year, Chuck and I visited friends for Thanksgiving. They cooked the turkey on a rotisserie over mesquite coals. It had great flavor, but it wasn't stuffed and had no gravy. It didn't feel right. Now I experiment with creative turkey recipes at other times of the year.

## SKINNIES—SIMPLE AS 1, 2, 3

(makes 12 crepes, serves 2–4)

1 cup flour

2 cups milk

3 eggs

1 tsp. vanilla (optional)

pinch of salt

Combine above ingredients in a blender and blend until smooth.

Heat a 10-inch frying pan over medium-high heat. For each skinny, made one at a time, melt enough butter to coat frying plan. Pick up the frying pan and, using wrist action, allow the butter to coat pan. Pour approximately half a cup of batter into the center of the pan, and, using the same wrist action, spread the batter to the edges of the pan so that the entire bottom of the pan is covered. Cook over medium-high heat for a minute or two, checking at edges to be sure the bottom side is browned. When nicely browned, slip a wide spatula under the edge and flip. Brown second side. Roll the crepe up loosely. Place rolled crepe on a plate and serve, or place in a heated oven until all crepes are made, adding each hot crepe to the plate in the oven, and serve. Top with butter and maple syrup as you would any pancake. They can also be topped with fruit or yogurt.

## Daddy's "Skinnies"

Most of my cooking training came from my mother, but my father was also a good cook—especially for breakfast. Our family favorite was what we called "skinnies." Each weekend morning we eagerly looked forward to "daddy's skinnies." As a child, I couldn't have told you what they really were, but now I know they're basically a crepe. Dad served them rolled up with butter and syrup.

Many years ago when my brother was single and setting up his own home, I got an early-morning call. He wanted to know how to make skinnies. I didn't know. That had been Dad's turf, a dish I didn't replicate in my own home, but rather looked forward to when visiting

Mom and Dad. I dug out some cookbooks and tried to help my brother, realizing I needed to capture that memory. Now skinnies are the standard weekend or special breakfast in my home, my sister's, and my brother's. Since my dad's death, Mom doesn't get skinnies at home, but I make them for her when she comes to visit.

A few weeks ago my friend's ten-year-old daughter spent the night with us. I taught her how to make the batter for skinnies and how to swirl it in the pan to get a light even coating. While I flipped them, she buttered the pan, poured in the batter, and swirled it. We have a new tradition she can look forward to whenever she visits.

## BURNT FINGER CAKE BY PAT THOMAS

My aunt Flossie was such a magnificent cook! Everything she made was the best, and she made a banana caramel cake that was out of this world! The recipe was devised by her sister, Bernice, but Aunt Flossie made more of them than anyone and came to be known for them because they were so different.

The first time I tried to make this wonderful recipe, I was a newlywed. I was trying to make the caramel and talk on the phone at the same time. I have never been too good at talking and chewing gum at the same time, so that was my first mistake. I had called my mother (as it was long past Aunt Flossie's bedtime) to ask her what "soft ball stage" meant. She told me that when a drop of the caramel was dropped into ice water, I should be able to form it into a little ball between my thumb and forefinger. While still talking to her, I tried it. The only problem was, I skipped one step ... dropping it in the ice water! I poured the hot caramel directly onto my forefinger! From then on I remembered that cake as "Burnt Finger Cake."

Years later, a good friend of mine who is a wonderful homemaker wanted to learn to make the caramel my aunt was so famous for. She asked me if I thought Aunt Flossie would teach us. I was sure she'd be delighted, as she loved compliments on her cooking. It was the only pay she needed. So we planned a time to go and I decided to record the moment forever. I took my video camera with me! Aunt Flossie has been gone since 1998, but I have a video of her standing at her stove, carefully explaining every step of the process to Pam and me. I still don't make the cake. I just know that no one will ever be able to make it like she did. But I love the fact that I can watch her do it anytime I want and can remember how blessed I was to have her in my life.

## Cooking with Kids

It often feels easier to do the cooking yourself and keep the kids out of the kitchen—and it may be. By taking the easy way out, however, your children will not be able to capture your legacy to pass on to others. I (Marita) am grateful that my parents, grandmother, and great-aunt passed on favorite family recipes to me and that I can now in turn share them with my mother as I continue the traditions in my own home.

While I do not have my own children, I have always found cooking to be an excellent way to keep the little hands of my nieces and nephews—and friends' children—busy. Yes, I have to think through the meal plan and determine which parts they can do. I have to watch over them, so the food preparation takes longer. Involving them in the cooking is not something I want to do every day—nor will you. But it's a great way to spend time with the next generation and create a legacy they can savor.

I remember the time my mother invested in teaching me to cook when I was a child. When we got a recipe under way, I would open all the cabinet doors and drawers so I could easily see what I was after: measuring cups and spoons, spatulas, pots and pans, and fancy cake dishes. We both functioned best when we could find everything with the sweep of an eye. If Dad walked in while we were playing around with the food, he would immediately shut every door and drawer while explaining, "You can't cook with all these doors open like this. You'll kill yourselves." We'd say nothing, and as soon as he left, satisfied that he had saved our lives, we'd open everything up and get back to work.

Dad's warnings almost did come true when Mom and I were making Christmas cookies for the National Charity League one year. I had all of the five drawers under the counter open. To see into them all, I opened the bottom one the furthest and the others each a bit less, like a staircase. As I was beating the batter, the electric hand mixer slipped out of my hand. It flew out of the bowl, still beating, flinging batter into the open cabinets. Then the bowl tipped over, sending cascades of batter down over the open drawers like a waterfall. I screamed. Mom screamed. Dad came running to rescue us from whatever was attacking us only to find us staring at globs of batter dripping onto the kitchen floor. "I can't believe you did this!" he exclaimed in disbelief.

The three of us spent the rest of the evening silently scouring the kitchen floor, cabinets, and soggy drawers. Mom bought carefully and artistically decorated cookies for the underprivileged. We determined never to make Christmas cookies again, and we put this dismal disaster behind us—that is, until we got the National Charity League's letter disciplining us for sending store-bought cookies to those in shelters at Christmas. We had violated the principles of the organization that motivates more loving relationships between mothers and daughters as they serve the poor together. I turned to Mom and said, "I liked you a lot better before we tried to make cookies together."

Yes, cooking with children can be challenging, but the potential for great memories can't be beat!

## MEMORY-MAKING MEALS

Think back through your family's history. What meals were memorable to you? Do you have the recipes? Are there family members who can share them with you—and even teach you how to cook them if special techniques are required? Make an effort now to collect the recipes for your family's favorite foods before it's too late—preferably in the handwriting of the one who originated the recipe. As an added bonus try to get a picture or video of them making these signature dishes. Cook them for your family—telling the story that goes with them—and then take the time to teach others how to prepare the specialty dishes. This will be a lasting legacy for them!

**HEIRLOOM RECIPES KEPT IN PLACE**
Create a special file, notebook, or formal cookbook containing your family's favorite recipes. After each, write a memory of a time the recipe was used, or simply note who considered the recipe a favorite.

## FELLOWSHIP

While food may be what brings people together, the best times around the table are often because of the fellowship. Dinner on the table relaxes people and allows them to open up, be real, and share. It's not that the table is elegantly or perfectly set—though it may be. It may, however, be set with paper plates and plastic cups. It also isn't essential that the food is fabulous and flawlessly prepared—though it may be. It may also be take-out from a local gourmet shop or even Costco's frozen (now cooked) lasagna. There is something intangible that takes place around the table. I've observed many occasions of friendly fellowship cut off when the host or hostess suggests, "Why don't we move into the living room where it's more comfortable?" Suddenly the ambience changes, people look at their watches—shocked at the late hour—and declare that they must head home.

## DAD'S TABLE RULES

In my childhood home, we spent hours around the table, and my father had rules for table fellowship. As a child, I didn't like his rules. Now, as an adult, I appreciate their value and feel frustrated when others don't operate with the benefit of my dad's training. So I pass his rules on to you. Try them at your house and you will see their value, too.

Rule 1: Only one person talks at a time.

Rule 2: Everyone gets an equal share of the conversation.

I'm sure you've been at a table where several different conversations were going on at once—perhaps even one on each side of you. You wanted to listen to and participate in each, but you couldn't. You may have felt totally left out—or uncomfortable—as others were conversing around you. This kind of interaction does not make for memorable moments—or, as the Electrolux appliance ad states, "simmering conversation."

When several conversations get going around the table in your home, you can simply say to the second conversation participants, "Let's all listen to what so-and-so has to say." Doing this once or twice sets the tone and allows everyone to be involved.

Dad's second dinner rule became known to us as the "Percentage Principle": everyone gets an equal share of the conversation. He divided the number of people into 100 percent and came up with how many minutes each one of us could talk. For example, if there were ten people at the table, a frequent number, each one would be allotted 10 percent of conversation. Mom and I always had exciting stories to tell, and no matter what anyone else had to say, we felt we could always top it. Dad would nicely say, "Marita, you have used up your 10 percent. Let's ask Randy about what kind of people came into his coin store this week." Randy often gave his 10 percent to Mom, who loved him for his sacrificial giving. We were all happy when he married Lauren and continued to give Mom his percentage. One of his friends asked him, "How do you get along in that talkative family?" He replied, "I just sit quietly and smile. About once an hour when there's a slight pause, I speak up and say, 'Oh, that's great.' They all thank me, and then they charge ahead."

Dad had an uncanny ability to divide the people into the time available and keep us on task. Mom was able to remember those who gave her their percentage and invite them back.

This rule is important because some people—like my mother or me—are apt to monopolize the conversation. This rule prevents that. Again, you don't have to announce rules; just be aware of who has not had a chance to say much and invite them into the conversation.

**A THOUGHTFUL MEAL**

Take time to discover your family members' favorite meals and make them when they visit. For those who live in your home, be sure to make their most-loved foods from time to time, particularly when they need cheering up or there's a reason to celebrate an accomplishment.

I was recently at a dinner party where several of us knew each other and were comfortably verbose and opinionated, but one couple knew only the host and weren't quite as outspoken as the rest of us. On the way home, I realized I knew nothing about the quieter couple. I had asked her a few questions and tried to draw her out, but she and her husband had hardly said a word.

Some people are harder to draw out than others and may need prompting. For this reason, I suggest a book called *The Book of Questions* by Gregory Stock. This simple little book has one question per page that requires more than a yes or no answer, and allows you to get to know the person answering. I encourage you to flip through the book, pick three or four questions you feel comfortable asking, and keep them in your mind or on a note. When one person has taken over the conversation, at a pause, you can turn to the quieter person and say, "Tracy, we haven't heard much from you. What do you...?" Since you've already set the tone for one conversation at a time, you can easily focus the guests' attention and allow that quieter person to talk, preventing one or two people from dominating the evening.

## THAT'S ENTERTAINMENT! BY PAT THOMAS

I love entertaining—whether for two or for fifty! When I was just a kid, I loved looking through my mother's cookbooks at all the beautiful table settings. I could own fifty sets of dishes and never have enough! Whether just having our kids over for a casual supper on the porch or hosting a bridesmaids' luncheon, it's a joy to me to have people in my home and treat them to a special meal with all the trimmings.

I especially enjoy doing themed dinners for the holidays, decorating the tables with Easter bunnies or Christmas items or red candles and ivory doves for Valentine's Day. But I think the most fun table I ever decorated was for my daughter's eighteenth birthday—which came right at her high school graduation.

I hosted a surprise party for her and set up the tables in the carport of our home. Along the walk by the brick wall on one side, I made a "path" of butcher paper with the title above it reading "The steps of a good woman are ordered by the Lord." I started at one end with brown construction paper footsteps and photos, and chronicled the steps she had taken in her life. I showed when she had stepped into our lives at her birth, when her little feet paddled across the pool as she learned to swim, how those same feet learned to tap dance, how her little legs could run like the wind when she played T-ball, and how she traded in the running shoes for Converse because cheerleading had become her love. The "footsteps" went all the way through her high school years and up to her graduation—heading off to college.

At the party, when each guest arrived, he or she walked the path and read the stories. On each table I displayed a different period of my daughter's life. One centerpiece was baby shoes, a small baby photo, and a stuffed bear. Another had her tap shoes, a lunch box, and a picture from grade school. Another had her cheerleading shoes, a pom-pom, a stuffed high school mascot, and a photo. It was really a very special birthday, a time of transition in her life, and a day she will never forget.

It's amazing how theme parties, using decorations made from items around the house, and spending very little money can be a simple way to create priceless memories for those we love.

## AUNT GERTIE'S BREAD BY NALLEY T. OSLAND

I remember savoring the moments when Aunt Gertie would visit, leaving a lasting legacy in the form of her special bread.

"Aunt Gertie's here!" I heard my mother call out early one morning. My heart jumped with excitement, because I loved my aunt's visits. Aunt Gertie was happy, plump, and always smelled like roses. Her dresses were soft, silky, and had colorful flowers all over. Her hair was always neat and orderly. In fact, you could say everything about Aunt Gertie was orderly, neat, and in place. To me, she was just what an aunt should be.

Whenever she visited, I knew what would happen. She would put on her apron and call me: "Tommie, I'll get the money. You take it and go to the grocery store. I want a cake of Fleischmann's yeast to make some bread. Now hurry back so I can get started!"

"Yes, Ma'am." In my mind, I could already smell bread baking. Only when Aunt Gertie came did we have wonderful, fresh, hot bread that we could eat right from the oven. To me, it almost seemed like magic. When she wasn't around, we always got bread wrapped in paper from the store—and that was nothing like Aunt Gertie's bread!

I would always hurry, sometimes run, and when my legs grew tired, skip, so as not to keep Aunt Gertie waiting too long. I was almost afraid she would change her mind if I did not get back fast enough.

On that one particular day I was, of course, in a hurry, so I went quickly to the back of the store to the long meat counter. The butcher asked, "What do you want today, Tommie?" I pointed to the cakes of yeast wrapped in little silver packages that reminded me of small treasure chests. He could tell I was on a special mission. I told him, "Aunt Gertie is visiting, and she's waiting to bake me some bread."

Running and skipping, I made my way back home. I handed the change and the precious small silver package to Aunt Gertie. She was pleased that I had hurried and she could begin to work her magic. I knew that the heavenly aroma would soon fill the house, but I would have to be patient and wait.

At last the call came: "Hot bread! It's ready!" When my cousins and I opened the door and rushed into the kitchen, the delightful aroma greeted us. This aroma was Aunt Gertie's calling card. We all sat around the table with hot bread, butter, and jams. Soon all that was left were crumbs.

To this day, the memory of this special family time makes me so happy, and if I ever happen to smell hot bread anywhere, I long for those good old days when Aunt Gertie came to visit.

## FONDUE SUPPERS BY FLORENCE

When our son, Fred, was about ten years old, a friend asked him, "What do you like best about your mother?" Without hesitation he answered, "Her fondue suppers." I would have expected him to say her joyful spirit, her sense of humor, her ability to make every day exciting, but my son saw me as the lady who made fondue suppers.

## EQUALITY AND CONSIDERATION FOR ALL

Ensuring everyone is included in the dinner conversation can be difficult, but it helps demonstrate love for each individual. A few ways to encourage equal time in the conversation might be:

Play "tag" for a short time during the meal. After one story is told or a question is answered in full, the speaker then passes the conversation to the next person by asking a question. (This is best with younger children.)

Grant each family member a portion of time to lead the conversation. When they do, they must direct the conversation to everyone other than themselves.

Teach children, when guests are present, that the goal for the evening is to learn as much as possible about the guests and their opinions. After the guests leave, see who can share the most things learned during the evening.

Divide the time among family members, allowing time for each person to be the focus. This is a time to care about the things that matter to them.

As I thought about his choice, I realized that many of our family memories revolved around food—what we ate, where we ate it, and what people were gathered around our table.

In my childhood, eating was something you did to live. Because we lived in rooms behind the store, we always had canned goods on hand. We didn't sell meat or produce, so our diet consisted primarily of what came out of a can. If we didn't stock it, we didn't eat it. Our desserts were bread pudding and rice pudding, both made from leftovers—the bread pudding from the crusts none of us wanted to eat and the rice pudding from what was scraped off our plates the night before. It was never a real surprise to find two green peas in your portion of pudding along with the raisins.

The menu was no surprise, either. Saturday night was hot dogs, canned baked beans, and canned and steamed brown bread. Sunday was roast chicken, stuffed and put in the oven before church so it would be done when we returned. Monday was leftover chicken, and Tuesday was beef loaf. Mother didn't call it meat loaf because, as she said, "After all, it is beef." Wednesday was canned Franco-American spaghetti with the beef loaf leftovers crumbled into it. Thursday was creamed dried beef on toast, and Friday, whatever the fish man delivered that day.

Our mealtime memories were not of the food but the fellowship, since our father entertained with stories and challenged us to discuss the daily news and political personalities.

When I first went to Fred's home, I saw a whole different focus. The conversation was all business. Each brother reported how much income his millinery store had made that day. They often bemoaned that women weren't wearing hats as they used to and "if it weren't for the Catholic Church insisting women cover their heads, we'd be out of business."

At Fred's house, dinners were served quietly in the dining room (so different from my experience eating in the store amid the customers). Anna, their maid/cook from Germany, had always created something new and different, and we tasted each item carefully. Anna was then called into the dining room, where we all complimented her ability and often burst into applause.

When Fred and I got married, I began by preparing what I knew how to make. The first Saturday night I produced the universal hot dogs and beans. "What is this?" Fred asked. "Hot dogs belong in Yankee stadium." Fred was in the restaurant business, so he brought home recipes and a professional menu planner with pale green pages and fine lines. I was to plan each meal a week ahead and only

---

### MOTHER MARITA LITTAUER'S MOCHA[*] LAYER CAKE

Combine 1 cup Swansdown cake flour with 1 1/2 teaspoons baking powder. Sift 3 times.

In a separate mixing bowl, beat 3 eggs. Add 1 cup sugar while beating until light and fluffy. Add 1 teaspoon vanilla to egg mixture.

Scald 3 tablespoons milk and 3 tablespoons strong coffee. Do not microwave to heat; use stovetop.

With mixer on low, alternate adding the flour and coffee mixtures into the egg mixture.

Butter and flour two 8-inch pans. Use real butter. Bake at 325 degrees for 20 minutes. Cool slightly; then remove from pans and turn upside down on cake rack until thoroughly cooled.

Frost entire cake and fill layers with 1 pint heavy whipping cream, whipped and flavored to taste with sugar, strong brewed coffee, and vanilla. To decorate cake, make a glaze with confectioners sugar and coffee. Drizzle on cake top and sides and then sprinkle with chopped nuts.

*The traditional definition of mocha refers to a specific type of coffee. There is no chocolate in this cake.

---

go marketing once a week. I didn't know in the morning what I felt like having at night, plus I liked going to the store every day. Hadn't I grown up in a store?

Fred won out with the meal planning as I filled in the lines on those green pages, and he ultimately turned me into a gourmet cook. As we raised our family, we always had extra company and often some outsiders living with us. I produced creative dinners on preheated plates as Fred wanted, and I kept the conversations lively and current as we had done in the store.

Even dinnertime is a compilation of our varied backgrounds—the food, the flair, the fun, and the fellowship.

Have you ever asked your children what they will remember about you or about your cooking? Will it be the fondue suppers? What will their memories be? What will they say about you?

## COOKBOOKS BY FLORENCE

When I first joined the Littauer family, I was amazed that the presentation of the Sunday feast was anticipated all week long. Anna would put on her fresh uniform after church and get right into the food. When she called, we all filed into the dining room, where the appetizers were at each place, ready for us to begin. After grace we would pick up our forks in unison while Anna went back to the kitchen to decorate the Sunday roast with bunches of parsley.

In recent years, these dinners have become distant memories, but Fred's sister Marita has collected the family recipes and put them into printed form for each family member. She has passed down the Littauer legacy, lest we forget. The following is her preface to the book of her mother's recipes and on the previous page, a favorite mocha cake recipe.

There are now five family Maritas. Are there any recurring names in your family? 1. Marita Oelkers Littauer, my mother-in-law, the first Marita. Grandma said the name was from a romantic novel; Grandpa said it was from a racehorse he had won money on the day the baby was born. My son-in-law Randy researched in the New York Genealogy Society and found proof that Grandpa was right. He typed "Marita" into their search engine and came upon a newspaper article from the New York Times with the headline "Trotters and Pacers." The article said that "a colt by Stamboul and Marita was timed a mile in 2:16 at the Empire City track last fall."

2. Marita Littauer Faiola Trotter, my husband's sister and the one who put the cookbook together.

3. Marita Faiola Noonan, the second Marita's daughter.

4. Marita Littauer Noon, my daughter.

5. Lianna Marita Littauer, my son Fred's little girl.

*Memories from Marita: A Collection of Family Recipes*

*Who can forget Marita Littauer's succulent, mouth-watering roast beef dinners with the beef done to a turn, followed by the luscious mocha cream cake, or perhaps, the deliciously light snow pudding. The grandparents came every Sunday for dinner at one o'clock. We children would be down in the hall to greet them with a kiss, for which we received a quarter each! Sometimes they would bring guests, and I am sure we all remember the Feldsteins, who came with them this particular Sunday. Our father was carving the roast, and when asked what cut of the roast beef she would like, Mamie Feldstein replied, "I'll just take both ends." All of our faces fell, because the end cut was the special treat we all died for.*

*While going through my mother's memoirs, letters, pictures, and clippings, I found a packet of recipes. Some were formalized on recipe cards; some were on snippets of paper. Some were her own in her handwriting, and some had been contributed by family members and friends. I thought it would be a good idea to memorialize these recipes for all of us to have copies. The collection has expanded a bit insofar as other family members have contributed.*

*I am reminded of Christmas and Thanksgiving dinners. I think we had photos every year of Anna bringing in the turkey in her special white apron. Dinner was at one o'clock, games of bridge and poker followed, and then the Smith family arrived around five o'clock, and out came the turkey, cranberries, and rye bread for sandwiches, and we all gathered at the table for another feast.*

*I hope this collection brings back memories of the wonderful times we all shared around the dinner table in our childhood and later on with our own families.*

The families from the five Littauer children are scattered from California to Florida and back again to the original family home in Larchmont, New York. We are all grateful to have this cookbook, so that in spite of our distance we can still enjoy the same Sunday dinners!

# 5

# FAMILY TRADITIONS
## $\mathcal{L}$AUREN

$S$ometimes the phrase "family traditions" can feel a bit over-whelming. We think "traditions" have to involve elaborate planning, or they have to have originated from our great-great-great someone or other to be valid or real. Traditions can be as simple as having a certain meal every Christmas Eve, stopping for a milkshake with your kids every August after school shopping is done, or even playing music every morning to wake up the family.

## MUSIC IN THE MORNING BY RANDY BRIGGS, JR. (AKA JIMMY THE ROBOT: THE AQUABATS)

As early as I can remember, I awoke to the sound of classical music every morning. We had speakers in each room of the house, and when my dad went to make the coffee, he turned the local classical music station on in all of our bedrooms. My dad discovered a jazz station that played polka on Saturdays, so whenever we needed to get up for a soccer game, he would turn on that station and my brother Bryan would rush out of his bedroom to shut it off! I can't remember a time when there wasn't music playing in our home.

I started piano lessons when I was six, and I really liked my teacher. I worked hard and learned fast. By the time I was in sixth grade, I was playing simplified Scott Joplin rags.

Mom and Dad took me and a friend to a local triple-A baseball game one evening. They were having an amateur talent competition, and my classmate kept encouraging me to enter. I finally acquiesced, just so he'd leave me alone. I was escorted to the announcer's box, top and center of the stands. My name was announced as well as my age. I guess no one expected much from an eleven year old, but as I began Joplin's "Maple Leaf Rag," heads began to turn. Before long, the entire stadium was staring up at me. I had never enjoyed my piano recitals— but this was different! Much to my surprise, I won!

I was in my seventh-grade music appreciation class when I first heard my teacher, Mr. Barton, play his saxophone. I remember think-ing, *That looks like it could be fun!* Apparently he had noticed my musical ability—even on the Tonette. (Remember those little plastic clarinet-like instruments?)

He approached me like a minor league talent scout saying, "Instead of playing Wiffle ball, you should pick up a real bat and ball." He invited me to join his beginning band, saying he would teach me to play the saxophone. I loved the way the saxophone felt in my hands, the sound it made, and even how the pads closed and sprang back open with my touch.

The following year, I auditioned for advanced band and made it. I was also in the marching band and was exposed to a whole new musi-cal experience. When it was time to move to the high school for my sophomore year, again I made it into the audition-only wind ensem-ble, earning the position of first chair!

Throughout my high school years, I played in every ensemble I could, including the marching band, jazz band, and wind ensemble.

I even played in symphonic band to learn other instruments. I would often spend my lunches in the band room practicing. I would play and play, my goal was to get better. I went to as many concerts as I could to watch ska and punk rock bands. I always thought, *Wouldn't it be cool to be in a band?* But I never thought I could be playing in front of hundreds of people each night.

Toward the end of my senior year, my friend Brian Croxill asked, "Would you like to be in this band with me?"

It certainly sounded like fun! I'd never heard of the band, so he gave me their CD. I listened to the songs, and they sounded good, so I went along with him. Within the month, I was invited to join The Aquabats as their saxophone player. Today, I've been traveling with The Aquabats for more than nine years. I not only play saxophone and keyboards, but do the back-up vocals as well. I've crossed the United States at least ten times, lived in tour buses for two months at a time, and played more than five hundred shows in better than 150 cities. The venues have included House of Blues; Los Angeles, Las Vegas, Chicago, New Orleans, and Anaheim; The Universal Amphitheater; Disneyland; Knott's Berry Farm; B. B. King's Club in New York City; and the Warped Tour. The Aquabats have produced five albums, which have sold more than 160,000 copies.

I never thought I would write songs or even be in a band. Now I have composed half the music on our new CD *CHARGE!* Every time I write something, I discover what works and what doesn't. I've listened to and played music all my life. I always have music flying around in my head. There are just twelve musical notes, but I keep reorganizing them and tapping out rhythms. I do whatever it takes; I whistle, I hum, I tap, I write, and I play. I can't imagine doing anything else.

Recently our fans were asked, "Who's your favorite Aquabat?" The following is a response we received:

*The Robot! [my stage name] Back when I was twelve, I was pretty good at piano and cello, but I was learning the sax and I hated it. I couldn't breathe correctly, and I felt like I never improved over the entire year and a half I had already spent trying to learn it. I was just about to quit when I went to The Aquabats concert. I saw the Robot play, and I fell in love... with the sax. The entire time I was listening to him play, I wanted to be as good as he was. My oldest brother took me to meet the Robot after the show. I told him about my dilemma, and he gave me some tips for sax playing. Let me say, to this day, I live by those words, and I tell every student I teach sax to what he told me. The Robot inspired me to continue playing the sax. Without his influence, I probably wouldn't be a diehard musician. He allowed me to broaden my musical perspective. I would have never been able to teach music to others, and I seriously have no clue where I might have been today without his inspiration.*

**SHARING YOUR VALUES**

Think of the values that were taught to you as a child. Did your family participate in regular activities that reflected these values? How can you continue these activities? Decide what values you want to pass along and plan some family events that encourage those values. For example:

- If generosity, serve at a shelter for those in need.
- If thoughtfulness, spend time once a month with a lonely friend or neighbor.
- If servanthood, do yard work for a widow in the church.

I'm thankful for this fan's comment on the few minutes we spent together that she feels brought new direction to her life. I'm grateful for parents who kept music running through my head from my birth, and who taught me to teach others. I guess my legacy has begun.

Our oldest son had a poster on the wall that read, "One God" and showed a man's arm and his hand fisted with the index finger straight up. Somehow, we always interpreted it as "One Family under God."

When my son left for college for the first time, we all stood together as he drove off and each held an arm up in the air, with our hand in a fist, and with our index finger pointing straight up. He rolled down the car window and returned the same gesture. We held our fists like that until he was out of sight. It has become our family salute.

We have continued this for each child, spouse, or friend as they leave our home from a dinner or a visit. We raise our hands and point to God.

Last year our middle son died suddenly. As the casket was lowered into the ground, our family stood there with our last salute to Vincent as he disappeared from our sight.

Now, in Vincent's memory, when we leave our children's homes, and as we leave our grandchildren, it is still our family salute until we are out of sight. It has become a "family friend" that will last for generations—even after my husband and I are "out of sight," we will still be "one family under God."

—*RICCI VERQARA*

## A BIRTHDAY GIFT

What do you give your father—a man who seemingly has everything—for his sixty-eighth birthday? This particular year, I (Lauren) was trying to come up with just the right thing for Dad when an idea hit me. I would replicate the typical Sunday dinner he loved as a child!

I served standing rib roast and potatoes made just the way his mother did. ("Always select the first three or four ribs from the small end of the roast. Roast at 325 degrees for twenty minutes per pound. Sprinkle the roast with salt and pepper. Stick sliced onions on with toothpicks. Add potatoes to pan juices for the last hour.") I also served crinkle-cut creamed carrots with fresh parsley and Yorkshire pudding.

## THUMB COOKIES

1 cup butter (Mom's handwritten note says, "use less butter")

2/3 cup sugar

2 egg yolks

2 cups flour

Cream butter and sugar; add egg yolks then flour. Beat until blended well. Form little balls and put on ungreased baking sheet. Make small indentation in each ball and put jelly in. Bake in a 375 degree oven until light brown, about 15 minutes.

The final treat was Grammy Littauer's Mocha Layer Cake, prepared with her original recipe. (See chapter 4 for the recipe.)

While I didn't give him a sweater, a shirt and tie, or a leather binder, I did give him a gift of childhood memories complete with tasteful delights.

## RECIPES FROM NORMANDY LANE

As a child, I loved pressing my thumb into the little round ball of dough when making "thumb" cookies with my mom. I remember the feeling of reaching into the bowl, scooping out enough dough to fit in the palm of my little hand, and rubbing my hands together over and over, rolling the dough to make a small ball. Once the cookie sheet was filled with perfectly rolled little balls, I could push my thumb into the dough. When every cookie had my thumbprint in it, I got to put a tiny spoonful of strawberry jam in each divot.

The recipe for my favorite cookies came from a fabric-covered, six-ring notebook filled with handwritten recipes. It was a perfect size for my four-year-old hands.

Now, holding it in my fifty-year-old hands, I have a greater

**M**y husband and I are professional circus clowns and have performed in the US, Canada, and Japan with Ringling Brothers Barnum & Bailey Circus and various other shows.

Someone once said, "You can shake the sawdust off your shoes, but you can't shake it out of your heart." Being a circus performer is not a job, but a lifestyle—like Christianity is not a religion, but a relationship. I frequently speak on circus history, our experiences, and how they have helped us grow spiritually.

Now I am handing this heritage down to our children ages three, four, eleven, and twelve. They can feel the heart of their parents' passion as we pass along the legacy of the clowns!

—*BARBARA VOGELGESANG*

appreciation for what this little recipe notebook means. It was a wedding gift to my mom and dad. The first page reads, "Recipes from Normandy Lane for Fred and Flo. With love from Anna." The pages are aged with brown edges, turned down corners, and food splats on our favorite recipes. Each recipe was handwritten with a fountain pen, and the penmanship has a European look, making it quite hard to read. Anna, you may recall, was Dad's housekeeper and prepared many of the family meals when he was a little boy. She was from Germany and lived with the family on Normandy Lane most of Dad's childhood. She only spoke German to Dad, so during his preschool years, he spoke more German than English.

One Christmas, I was invited to a cookie exchange that Mom would also be attending. As a surprise for Mom, I prepared "thumb" cookies—what I now know to be tea cookies. I scanned the original recipe into my computer and reproduced recipe cards to attach to each package of cookies. I also typed the recipe so it would be easier to read. I don't know if anyone else has made the cookies, but I have passed on the legacy.

## Cook Night at Jon's by Jonathan Briggs

While I was growing up, dinners were a special time for me, and the preparation was as important as the meal itself. When Mom or Dad was cooking, it was an extension of dinner. The television wasn't on, just as it was never on during a meal. We always assisted in the preparation, and it took years for me to work my way up from prep chef to sous-chef. Now that I have my own apartment, I am finally the head chef, and I love it!

I don't remember going out to dinner, but I do remember cooking. My parents exposed me to a wide variety of foods, and we were expected to eat everything on our plate. Whining wasn't tolerated. I think an appreciation of various foods is gained by experiencing a mixture of styles, textures, and flavors. I remember not liking certain vegetables or preparations as a child, but I think that was because it was new or different. I knew I had to eat it anyway, so I just got over the hurdle and ate it.

We searched for new recipes in cookbooks by noted chefs or in magazines like *Bon Appétit* or *Gourmet*. The point is we never made a meal that was just so-so. We looked for a way to use one more ingredient to make a dish more interesting. Even Mom's meatloaf was extraordinary.

Many children do not get exposed to great food and the joy of cooking as I was. I remember families who brought hot dogs for their children to eat at our house, because they wouldn't eat our burgers or our steaks. Boy, did their kids miss out! I was in the marching band at UCLA, and during the summer of my third year, many of my friends complained about the dorm food. Since I had an apartment, I suggested, "Why don't we make it a thing where I cook every Friday night?" My fellow band nerds were excited by the possibility of a "home-cooked meal," and that's when the tradition of "Cook Night at Jon's" began.

## EMILIE'S TEA PARTIES BY FLORENCE

It didn't take long for Emilie Barnes and me to become "best friends." As soon as we met, we discovered how much we had in common. We both grew up living behind a store—a coincidence that drew us together in humor and in our mutual legacy—we both taught Bible studies, and we both love to entertain. We decided we should help other women who hadn't learned the art of hosting fancy dinners and the other household skills. So with our husbands' help, we started "Feminars," seminars for women. We showed women how to make tablecloths and napkins from inexpensive sheets and how to organize their handbags so they could find their keys. Soon we were training women all over Southern California, and this ultimately led us into writing books that, between our two families, now number about one hundred titles.

Recently I asked Emilie what legacy she was leaving her family. I assumed it would be related to her home management skills, which she has passed on to thousands of women all over the world. Instead she replied, "I think it's tea parties for my granddaughter." I didn't know about these, so Emilie shared the following story:

*When Christine was two years old, I started having little private tea parties with her. We used real china cups, placed doilies on the table, and picked a few flowers for decoration. As she grew older, her two little brothers became the waiters. I put white shirts and ties on them and showed them how to pass the plates of cookies. Christine could invite some friends, and the boys, on their own, would give each girl a cookie and a kiss on the cheek. Grammy's tea parties were a big hit.*

*The year before Christine's sixteenth birthday, I began shopping for teacups in antique stores around the country. I gave myself a budget: no cup and saucer could cost more than five dollars. Then, for her birthday, I put on a tea party for her. Each girl could choose which cup and saucer she wanted to use from my year's collection. What fun it was for me to watch the girls giggling over their selections.*

*I couldn't resist making a lesson out of the cups, so I told them the teacups mirrored life. Each one was different. Some were prettier, some were bigger, and some had little cracks or chips. They weren't perfect because life isn't perfect. The chips represented problems in life that they were overcoming with God's help.*

*At that point one girl said, "Oh, I'm so excited. Look, I have a chip in mine."*

*They all examined their cups to see if they had any chips. After my little sermon, I told each girl she could take her cup home to keep.*

*"To keep?" they cried out.*

*"Yes," I answered, "as a reminder of this day and that God heals the broken pieces of our lives."*

*Christine is now twenty-two, and one day she asked me, "You know what I remember best about my childhood?"*

*"What?"*

*"It was those tea parties, especially my sixteenth birthday with the chipped cups."*

As Emilie finished this touching story I asked her, "Did anyone ever have a party for you as a child?" She paused for a moment, and then replied, "I hadn't thought of this before, but my mother would surprise me once in a while. Mama was so busy as a widow trying to raise a family while living in that dress shop. I was very shy, and when I'd come home from school, I'd head right into the back room. But when Mama had a pot of tea ready and some cookies, I knew we were going to have a tea party. We'd sit at the little table, and I felt free to talk. Mama told me later that those tea parties were the only time I really shared my feelings. Maybe that's why I relax over a cup of tea, and why I've passed on a legacy without realizing what I was doing."

Emilie has not only passed on this tradition to Christine but to so many others who have read her book *If Tea Cups Could Talk.*

Like Emilie's experience, were there any special times with your mother, grandmother, or other adult that started a pattern or tradition you've followed? What party times have you enjoyed with your children? What will they remember about you?

> **TIME WELL SPENT**
>
> Consider ways to spend time with family members enjoying each other's favorite pastimes or interests. You might:
>
> - Learn to golf with your uncle who is an avid fan.
> - Ask your grandmother to teach you to knit, which is her expertise.
> - Teach your daughter the fine art of playing hostess by having her friends over for tea (or punch) and having her make finger sandwiches and miniature tarts.
> - Show your grandson how to build a model car.

## WHAT LEGACIES DO COLLECTORS LEAVE? BY RANDY BRIGGS, SR.

I guess I can blame my dad for my interest in coins. He began collecting stamps when he got out of the service following World War II. On his semiannual trips to the local stamp and coin store—the store I now own—I would sit at the counter and wait for him to bring his collection up-to-date. Mr. Coops, the owner, let me look through trays of old coins, which I found much more interesting than Dad's stamps.

One day, when I was about nine, my father went to the bank and brought home a bag of five thousand one-cent coins. He dumped them onto the living room floor and told me to sort them by date and mint mark—the tiny letter denoting the place of issue. My mom was appalled when she came home from work, but she let me finish since I was making headway. Ultimately, I built a complete set of Lincoln cents from 1934 to 1958. Not bad for one day, but the worst thing was, I was hooked and wanted to do it again. I loved looking at the coins, separating them, and putting them in tubes. I even began going through my parents' change every night looking for treasures. My fascination has never stopped.

While in high school, I developed a love for history while taking World History from Mr. Burke—also a collector! He not only made history come alive, but he had several three-ring binders filled with genuine historical items and coins he passed around in the classroom to help illustrate the history he was teaching. There were items like authentic Civil War money, a piece of wood from Ford's Theater where Lincoln was shot, a coin produced from George Washington's silverware, ancient Greek and Roman coins, and so on. Today, I'm amazed he managed not to lose any of it. What a revelation—history and collecting things all wrapped up in one neat package. Now all I needed was to find something historical to collect.

I searched for months until one day I saw the movie *Khartoum*, starring Charlton Heston and Sir Lawrence Olivier. It was the story of an individual soldier, General Charles Gordon (Heston), sent in 1884 to the Sudanese city of Khartoum to battle the "forces of evil" embodied in the person of Mohammed Ahmed, the Mahdi (portrayed by Olivier). Gordon's orders were to evacuate all Europeans from the city and leave it to the Sudanese, who would certainly be overrun by the Mahdi's rebellion. Gordon's Christian beliefs would not allow him to abandon the Sudanese, so he decided to stick it out until relief arrived from England. Besieged in Khartoum for nearly a year, Gordon failed in his mission to put down the Mahdi's rebellion, was himself martyred, and the town was taken. Two days later, the relief column arrived, too late. It was a fascinating story, but was there anything connected with Gordon that I could affordably collect?

Within a couple of weeks I happened to get a catalogue from a coin dealer in the East and amazingly, he listed one solitary piece of paper money—a siege note from Khartoum! I didn't even know Gordon had made any. How exciting! Here was the chance to start a collection. I phoned the dealer, ordered the note, and waited. The package arrived a few days later. My excitement quickly turned to frustration when I found that the note was printed entirely in Arabic except for a seal in French and what appeared to be Gordon's signature. Since no catalogue pictured or even told about this historic paper money, there was no way of knowing whether this really was a piece of money from the siege or even if it was authentic currency.

I spent the next few months researching the siege of Khartoum and the paper money Gordon had produced. During the many months of containment within the battle-torn city, money ran out due to hoarding, and the local economy ground to a halt. Sensing the myriad problems that could arise, General Gordon created an issue of paper money, personally guaranteed by him and the Egyptian government. Once the Mahdi conquered the city of Khartoum, the currency was declared illegal to possess, and anyone found with it would be killed, thus making the paper money extremely rare.

The next major step came when a good friend of mine who was a paper-money dealer purchased a huge collection from a famous collector. He received many large boxes over the next few months, and we unpacked them together. The paper money was packed loose in the boxes without any organization. We found out later that when the collector had died, he'd left no information or instruction for his wife. She and a young neighbor boy gathered up the notes, stuffed them loose in the boxes, and shipped them to my friend. Out of one of the boxes came a Khartoum note. I was ecstatic, of course, and as we unpacked the rest, we found nine more. I came to find out this was a complete denomination set, so I bought it.

Over the years I have accumulated the world's only privately held complete set of the siege notes (eighteen in all), including all the denominations and signature varieties. I've also gathered dozens of books, prints, autographed letters, statues, and newspapers—the list of items goes on and on. I have become a noted expert on this subject and was even invited to speak at the International Banknote Congress in London.

My three sons all are very aware of my love for military history, my Gordon collection, and the hobby in general. As they wander through the house, the pictures, statues, maps on the walls, books in the bookcases, and the coins and paper money in albums constantly remind them that I am a collector. I never miss an opportunity to teach them the stories behind the items, and they often ask me to show them something or share from my knowledge. They even tell their friends about things I have. Collecting is a major part of who I am. I do not believe that my collections merely reflect history, they *are* history, and I have tried to expose each of my boys to the joys of collecting.

Children need to know what makes their parents "tick." Sharing your passions with your children is a lasting legacy.

## PIXIES AND PHANTOMS BY JUNE DURR

When our children lived at home, every Sunday, no matter what our budget, we ate at our dining room table, set with whatever "best" we had and spread with foods the entire family looked forward to eating.

We practiced using our "restaurant" manners and etiquette—my husband pulled out my chair for me, and our son pulled out the chair for his sister. We said the blessing out loud, and together we laughed and shared joys.

The surprise came after dessert, when the four names in the little bowl were drawn and "The Pixie of the Week" began. Each person kept the name they drew secret, and throughout the week had to do their "pixie's" chores without getting caught and other kind or supportive things that would make the person happy. The next Sunday the pixies were revealed at dinner.

We all had so much fun sneaking around doing chores, pinning notes to pillows, and blessing each other with inexpensive or handmade gifts.

The other treasured family game was "The Phantom Family." At dinner, we would discuss people who were in need of cheering up or kindness. We'd agree on a family or person and then bake cookies or other treats, wrap them beautifully with a ribbon, and enclose a card that read,

**PERSONAL TIME MATTERS**

Do you allow yourself time to enjoy your own favorite activities? It's hard to share your favorite activities with others if there's no time to do them yourself. Set aside a few moments each week or a couple of times a month when you can indulge in the things you enjoy. This is the perfect time to invite your children, younger family members, or friends to join you. You might have your five-year-old niece over to create a finger painting while you paint with oils, or ask your son to join you with his favorite instrument as you play the guitar. Just have fun with the results, and don't expect perfection.

*With love from the Phantom Family.* We'd leave our gift on the doorstep, ring the bell, and run. We'd hide and watch to see who opened the door. If we got caught, it didn't count, and we'd have to repeat the gesture with someone else. The goal was to teach our children to do good deeds in private without getting recognition.

Our circumstances have changed over the years, but our family remains interlocked in our hearts because each member knows they are loved and treasured.

## CEMETERY FLOWERS BY BONNIE SKINNER

Always fascinated by beautiful flowers, as a child I looked forward to Decoration Day, now called Memorial Day. It was a family tradition to visit the cemetery and put flowers on the graves. I knew the "country" flowers—those picked from our garden—would soon wilt, but the "city" flowers from the florist were very special and lasted much longer.

One Decoration Day when I was a young girl, as I walked around the graves and identified the flowers, I noticed a small baby's grave with no flowers at all. So, I "borrowed" some pink carnations from a nearby grave and more pink flowers from other graves to completely cover the small mound. As I stood admiring my handiwork, I noticed other barren graves, so I decorated them as well. Some I decorated in a solid color, such as the pink baby's grave; some with a mixed variety of flowers, and others with fancy greenery.

Satisfied with my work, I scanned the cemetery, expecting to see it carpeted with flowers. Instead I was horrified to see gaping holes of missing flowers in the larger arrangements. It was obvious that in my eagerness to work with the flowers, I'd made an absolute mess. I had to borrow and balance as much as possible so that my rearrangements would not be so evident.

Satisfied that I had tidied up the cemetery sufficiently, I picked up the large bouquet of long white gladiolus with enormous stems that I had reserved for myself. Clutching the massive glads, I walked around singing, "I come to the garden alone, while the dew is still on the roses… and he walks with me and he talks with me, and he tells me I am his own!" As I sang, I realized I really belonged to Jesus. I felt he was pleased to hear me singing and that I had made sure each grave had equal amounts of flowers.

Feeling somewhat spiritual, I knew Jesus wouldn't mind if I took "my own gladiolus" home with me—so I did. I walked down the short road between our house and the cemetery, carrying the flowers as if I were a bride. At home, I placed them in Mother's best vase on the dining room table and went off to play with my little brother, satisfied that I had contributed to our home décor.

It wasn't long before I heard Mother's voice yelling, "Who brought these flowers into this house?" Seeing me, it was clear she needed to look no further. She literally dragged me down the road, yelling, "Now, you put those flowers back where you got them!"

I clutched my glads with frightened hands. With a wild look of disbelief, Mother surveyed my damage to the cemetery. "What have you done?" she screamed. She couldn't believe one of her "precious children" had made such a mess of the entire cemetery. Even I realized there were still large empty spaces in most of the arrangements. Her next words were, "Bonnie Jean, get me a switch!"

That ended my redecorating days, but the beauty of that expanse of flowers and of my personal arrangement is a picture I keep in my mind that still brings a smile to my face.

Throughout my adult life, I have made it a family tradition to take my children—and now my grandchildren—to the cemetery on

Decoration Day. Each year my grandchildren say, "Grammy, tell us about when you changed all the flowers around at the cemetery." They love to hear about their grandmother getting into trouble, and our shared laughter binds us together like nothing else can.

## TRADITIONAL OR NONTRADITIONAL

Recipes, collections, activities—almost anything can become a family tradition. You're the one who knows your family best, so if you're beginning a tradition, start with something that appeals to the majority. Maybe that's sharing cinnamon rolls together (homemade or store bought, it doesn't matter) the first Saturday morning of every month. Maybe it's attending the opening game every year of your local minor league baseball club. Maybe it's collecting rocks from every trip you take. Whatever you choose, you're strengthening a family bond that will only grow stronger over time.

# 6

# HOLIDAY TRADITIONS
## MARITA

*I* have always felt that the Norman Rockwell and other similar picturesque scenes we've all seen on Christmas cards and in magazines add to the stress and tension so many people feel during the holidays. We look at these harmonious homes and feel guilty that we're the only ones not having that representation of happiness. They create a sense that we need to work hard to create that perfect presentation—or the holiday will be a complete failure.

When I quit decorating for Christmas, I felt a great sense of freedom. I didn't have a Christmas tree for ten years while we lived in a house too small to accommodate one. I left all the Christmas decorations in storage. But this doesn't mean I was a true Scrooge. I had Christmas parties at my home—after all, I like to cook and entertain. I just put on the invitations a line that advised my guests, "Dress festive; you are the decorations!" Most came dressed in red and green. The women wore sweaters with sparkles or images of Santa, and once my guests filled the room, it took on a festive, decorated quality—and all I had to do was cook!

While my personal stories will not be the ones that inspire you to create wonderful holiday memories—though I may free you from some guilt—I offered to be the lead in this chapter because I have a wonderful Norman Rockwell-like memory I want to share with you. Between my story and those from our readers, I hope you will get many ideas of what you can do for your friends and family during the holidays. I'm sure that as you read the following pages, you will appreciate even more the importance of making these special memories.

## THE NORMAN ROCKWELL THANKSGIVING

When Chuck and I had been married just a few years, I got the idea that I wanted the traditional Norman Rockwell scene for Thanksgiving. We have no children of our own, and at the time we didn't live near either family. Chuck had never been to New England, where I grew up. New England is where the first Thanksgiving took place, so surely, if one wants to experience a real Thanksgiving, Massachusetts is the place to go! (Massachusetts is also where my favorite aunt resides.)

I suggested to Chuck that we take a trip to Boston and then go to Aunt Jean's for Thanksgiving. Chuck loved the idea, so we began to make plans. Aunt Jean was thrilled that we would be coming. She and I discussed cooking the Thanksgiving dinner together. As both of my grandmothers were no longer living and as Grammy Chapman's sister, Aunt Jean, is the closest thing I had to a grandmother,

**PRESERVING THE MEMORIES**

Consider the holiday activities or events you loved as a child.

Have you passed on these traditions? Think of one you'd like to include in your holidays this year. What will you do to make it happen?

Write down at least three of your favorite childhood memories of the holidays to share with future generations. Begin by thinking of the things that made the holidays special, whether in your immediate family or from stories you've heard about previous generations.

I could just see Norman Rockwell showing up to paint the picture I had in my mind. This would be the most perfect Thanksgiving ever.

When the time for the trip came, Chuck and I packed up and flew across the country. We landed in Boston and rented a car. We spent several days touring historic sights such as Beacon Hill and the path of Paul Revere's ride. This really put us in the mood for Thanksgiving. We were thankful for the sacrifices others made to make America free!

Wednesday evening, the night before Thanksgiving, we drove halfway across the state to Aunt Jean's little house. We pulled up after dark, and lights from every window of her cottage-like home welcomed us. With eager anticipation, I bounded up the steps to her front door—which she threw open before I could knock. She had been as excited as I was—perhaps even more so—and had been sitting at the front window, watching for us to arrive.

After the initial hugs and kisses, we all moved into the kitchen, where I saw pies lined up on the windowsill. When I commented about them and expressed that I'd planned to help her, she exclaimed with her hands on her hips, "Well! I've been cooking for days. If you wanted to help, you needed to get here sooner!" (In my childhood home, we did not start cooking for Thanksgiving until Thanksgiving!) I assured her I was looking forward to helping her with all the last-minute preparations the next day.

On Thanksgiving morning, Chuck and I were still snuggled in bed when I heard pans rattling in the kitchen. I groggily plodded into the kitchen to find her struggling to get the big pan filled with a large turkey into the oven. I helped her with the heavy load. And so began my Norman Rockwell Thanksgiving in New England. We worked side-by-side in the kitchen throughout the day. When dinnertime came, we were joined by her son and his wife. The five of us squeezed in the little breakfast booth I remember from my childhood. We had a beautiful turkey, mashed potatoes, mashed turnips, green beans she had canned from her garden, Jell-O salad, cranberry relish, fresh rolls, and apple pie, pumpkin pie, and mincemeat pie—the fruit of days of cooking.

While the process of cooking with Aunt Jean did not play out exactly as I'd envisioned, the result was something even Norman Rockwell would have been proud of. That Thanksgiving in New England is one of my most treasured memories—bringing a smile to my face even now.

What about your family and friends? Are there holiday traditions you treasure? I hope that reading the following stories will bring memories out of the cobwebs and into the forefront of your life. I encourage you to write them down and share them with your family. But even if you only think about them as you read, may they bring a smile to your face as sharing my story with you has done for me.

Perhaps you do not have warm holiday fuzzies from the past. As they say, there is no time like the present. Read through the memories shared here and adopt and adapt the ideas that feel comfortable for you and your current place in life. Don't feel guilty that you haven't done these clever things in the past, and don't get mad at your childhood family because you don't have happy holiday memories. Instead, start now to create some family legacies—even if they are only for you. Maybe they will be as simple as inviting some friends over and requesting them to "dress festive"!

## WHO CAN CARVE THE TURKEY? BY LAUREN

My dad passed away just a month before Thanksgiving, and all of us kids gathered at Mom's that year for the holiday dinner. We were careful to prepare all the typical family recipes in our attempt to keep the holiday as normal as possible and minimize the gaping hole we knew my father's absence would create.

The time came, and our beautifully bronzed bird was removed from the oven. We prepared the gravy, set the food on the buffet, and placed the turkey on the rosewood carving tray. My husband, Randy, now the senior statesman of the group, was handed the carving knife. He dutifully took the knife and began to carve. He was sure he was doing it "just like Father Fred," when some of the moist, tender meat fell off in chunks. My brother quickly surfaced to lend his expertise. He met with little success. Soon, Marita and I were hovering over the men giving suggestions and instructions. Knowing I should have done the carving all along, I took the knife and set out to "do it the right way"! Much to my amazement, I had no more success than my husband or brother. By the time we completed our butchery, we were left with a jumbled mess of big chunks and tiny slivers of meat, two whole legs, and a despicable carcass. We realized that, while Dad had always carved the turkey and made it look so easy, none of us had ever carved "The Turkey."

## LITTLE THINGS MAKE THE DIFFERENCE

Make holiday tasks memorable by adding small touches that are repeated every year, such as:

- Drink hot cocoa while setting up the Christmas tree.
- Sing Christmas carols while baking cookies.
- Drop cookies off at a nursing home when you are out shopping.
- Pray together for some of your friends as you address their Christmas cards.

Turn tasks, like carving the Thanksgiving turkey or placing the star on the Christmas tree, into a reward for the most generous act that year. (Be sure to have enough "rewards" and activities for each family member to earn one.)

Dad's absence left a huge void in our Thanksgiving and the massacred turkey was the tangible evidence of our loss. I'd like to tell you that we learned our lesson and that subsequent holiday turkeys were carved with great finesse, but the reality is we'll never do it just like "Father Fred"!

Is there a task in your family that someone always does? Does he or she make it look easy? Take the time and extra effort to identify the task and learn how it's done. We must first learn from our heritage before we can pass it on as a legacy.

## TOGETHER FOR CHRISTMAS BY RAELENE SEARLE

My husband, Chip, comes from a large family. With siblings getting married and having children, getting everyone together for Christmas was becoming more and more difficult. Suddenly, family members' parents and their own Christmas traditions had to be considered.

But we are a close-knit family. We just couldn't let the holiday season pass by without trying to get everyone together to celebrate. My father-in-law, Ron, came up with a great idea that has worked well from year to year.

Each year we have our Searle family gathering on the Saturday two weeks after Christmas. This approach has worked well, especially for those who need to travel more than a few hours. It also allows each family to have its own celebrations without feeling pressured to see everyone.

The host plans an easy menu for a late afternoon meal and assigns each family items to contribute. Chip and I hosted this event for years because our home was generally an equal distance for everyone attending. Since we've moved, his brother, Stephen (who moved down the street from our old house), now hosts the gathering.

For gift giving, we drew names for several years. Eventually we decided our gift giving would be more fun as a white elephant exchange (with a price limit) for adults, while the kids would continue drawing names with their cousins.

Every year we choose a theme, and each couple creates a gift basket that reflects that theme—and their own creativity. For example, one year when we did nursery rhymes, the couple who had "Mary, Mary, Quite Contrary" put together a basket of gardening items. Other themes have included "rooms or areas in and around the house," "colors," "seasonal fun," and "geography."

The Searle family Christmas is an event we all look forward to year after year. Creating extended family memories—and giving and receiving fun and unique gifts—make this a gathering that's rarely missed by any of us.

## CHRISTMAS TREE BY PAT THOMAS

I grew up as an only child and, since my mother was the youngest of ten, all my cousins were much older than I. Our extended family was not close, with the exception of my aunt and uncle who lived next to us and had no children. My aunt was Mother's oldest sister, and had practically raised both Mother and me; she was more like a second mom than an aunt.

My family wasn't big on traditions; they never had any growing up. However, the one tradition I remember most as a child was cutting down the Christmas tree with my uncle. We trekked through the woods behind the house and looked for just the right one. Of course, it had to touch the ceiling! Then we would drag it back to the house where I decorated it. As he grew older and developed emphysema, this adventure became more and more difficult. Yet when I went away to college, he wrote that he could hardly wait for me to come home so we could go get the tree. Oh, how I cherish those memories!

When my husband and I married, we continued the tradition of cutting down our own Christmas tree. And when our children came along, they went with us. Somewhere along the way—I think it was when I was experiencing back trouble one year—I began to let the three of them go by themselves. Then the year our son went to college, the tree-cutting group was down to our daughter and her dad.

I remember shortly after our daughter married, her dad remarked sadly, "Well, I guess I'll have to get the Christmas tree by myself this year."

When Christmas approached that year, our daughter said to me, "Tell Dad he'd better not get the tree without me! We'll just have to get two this year!" You can just imagine how excited he was to hear that. The tradition has expanded now to include our son-in-law, and we hope that one day it will include grandchildren as well.

Not only has the tradition of *getting* the tree continued, but the tree still has to be *huge!* Their first tree was so large, there was room in the dining room for nothing *but* the tree!

There is another Christmas tradition I started the first year we were married. We didn't have much money, yet I wanted to remember friends and neighbors with a gift. So I made cookies and candy and wrapped them in gift boxes, and my husband and I delivered them. When our son was old enough, he helped cut out and decorate the cookies. A few years later, our daughter joined the process. We made it a family affair to deliver the boxes each Christmas. It was one of my favorite parts of the Christmas season.

## The Guest of Honor by Karen R. Kilby

A Nebraska winter chill filled the air as David put down his briefcase, closing the door behind him. "What's for dinner, Karen? It smells wonderful—are we having company?"

I greeted David with a kiss and slipped my hand in his, gently leading him into the dining room to receive his first Christmas present.

"It's beautiful!" he exclaimed. "I love it! But it's only December first!"

The dining room table, set with the lovely white damask cloth handed down from his grandmother, instantly brought back childhood memories of special dinners in David's grandparents' home—just as I knew it would. The sterling silver flatware given to my mother as a wedding gift graced two place settings of our fine white china adorned with deep-green salad plates and matching colored-glass stemware. Monogrammed sterling napkin slides given to David's mother and father by his grandparents added the finishing touch to the napkins. The flickering flames of the candles cast shadows on the silver candelabra and glimmering serving pieces we had taken pleasure in discovering together on our antique treasure hunts. Strains of Handel's *Messiah* filled the air as we enjoyed the first of many candlelight dinners throughout the month of December.

"We're starting a new Christmas tradition," I said. "With only the two of us and no family close by, I'd like to make the holiday special, just for us."

David looks forward each year to our continuing tradition where he is the guest of honor, whether we're enjoying a five-course dinner or a simple bowl of soup.

It has become, however, much more. As we set aside time from the hustle and bustle of the holidays, we are able to better focus on the "reason for the season," making Jesus the true Guest of Honor.

## A New Tradition by Diane Baier Spriggs

Our children, Bobby and Trina, were married the same year—six weeks apart. (Now, eleven years later, I'm still working on forgiving them for that!)

Although it was a trying time, especially since they announced their wedding plans about halfway through our home remodeling project, we survived in relatively good form. We love our "son-in-love," Keith, and our "daughter-in-love," Jennifer, and are pleased with the choices our children made.

That we also love and get along well with both Jennifer's and Keith's parents is an added bonus. They're wonderful Christians who have raised their children to be fine, upstanding adults.

So, when the weddings were over, and the dust settled (literally) in our home, we were looking forward to "happily ever after" and a life of peace and calm. That was until Thanksgiving rolled around.

As always, I began making plans for Thanksgiving lunch at our house. After all, it was our family tradition. I called the kids with the details, and that's when I first heard those dreaded words: "But *they* want us to come to *their* house."

Although all three sets of parents tried to be gracious about the situation, I knew our four children were being torn apart in their efforts not to hurt anyone's feelings. To be honest, I don't remember whose house they went to that Thanksgiving, but I do remember that I determined right then and there that they would never be put in the position of having to choose between families again.

Long before Thanksgiving arrived the next year, I shared my plans with the kids for a new family tradition. They liked the plan then, and they still like it today. This is the way we now "do" Thanksgiving at our house.

Each year, our kids and their families go to their in-laws for lunch and enjoy the traditional Thanksgiving turkey and dressing with all the fixins, as we say in the South.

That night they come to our house. So they will have plenty of time with their in-laws, I do all the cooking. But we keep it simple—usually spaghetti, tacos, enchiladas, or whatever they have chosen for that year.

When they arrive, the Thanksgiving decorations are still up, but the Christmas tree also is set up in the living room with just the lights on it. The ornaments we've collected through the years, and that our children grew up with, are also set out.

While I put the finishing touches on the meal, the children (and now our grandchildren, too) begin putting ornaments on the Christmas tree, in no particular order. The only exception is that, traditionally, I'm the only one who can put the "mobile" ornaments on the tree. These are the ornaments that were made from the figures on the crib mobile I used on Bobby's and then Trina's cribs when they were babies. They are little wooden animals with babies riding on their backs and are very special to me.

When dinner is ready, the decorating stops, even though the tree is far from being completed. (We finish it the next day.) And everyone gathers around the table for a light meal.

After supper, we all go back into the living room, turn off all the lights but the ones on the tree, and find comfortable places to sit. Then we go around the room, and, one at a time, each person shares what he or she is thankful for. This special time is usually filled with a few tears and a lot of laughter. (I remember the first year we started the tradition, I told them I was thankful that, when they were teenagers and I wanted to kill them, I didn't. For some reason, they thought I was joking!)

To keep Christ in Christmas:

Make attending Christmas Eve services an annual event.

Include those without family and friends nearby in your plans.

Read the Christmas story as a part of Christmas Eve activities.

Purchase an advent wreath and advent devotional; use them every night during the season.

Read a few verses from Matthew 1 and 2 and Luke 1 and 2 each day or week of December.

For adult family members, consider giving in their names to charity, particularly to an faith-based organization, as a gift.

Find an aspect of the Christmas story to research and study in the Bible during the holiday season, such as the wise men's gifts, the city of Bethlehem, angels, or the lives of ancient shepherds.

---

After everyone, including the grandchildren, has had a turn sharing "thankfuls," we go back around the room again, this time sharing our prayer requests. Then we pray together.

Finally, we give each child and grandchild an ornament chosen especially for them. Their ornament will then be added to the collection that began the Christmas before they were married. As we removed the ornaments from the tree after Christmas that year, we divided them into three boxes—one for us, and one each for Bobby and Trina. Someday, when our grandchildren are ready to get married, I'm sure their parents will divide their family ornaments with them, and the tradition will continue.

When the ornaments are given out, the Christmas season has officially begun for our family, and what could've been a day of "tug of war" between in-laws has become a magical night full of love—just as it was meant to be.

## COLLECTING MEMORIES BY BETTY WINSLOW

Our family loves Christmas and keeps many traditions, but one of our favorites is our Christmas memories collection. To outsiders, they look like Christmas ornaments, but our family knows they're more: They're memories. Decorating the tree each year means telling once again the stories they represent.

Matt's pig ornament was crafted the year he sang "Old McDonald Had a Farm" endlessly, mentioning only pigs verse after verse. His soccer player reminds us of his soccer-playing days. The strawberry-gelatin-eating mouse? That represents his favorite dessert flavor!

Mike's tiny wooden bat is painted with season stats, team name, and his jersey number from his Little League team's championship season. The ribbons are in team colors. The engraved brass heart was added the year his daughter, Kendall, was born. Kendall's own collection, to be given to her when she is older, began that same year.

Amanda, the family artist, left a trail of paper scraps the year she learned to cut snowflakes. The tiny artist's supply basket she received that year included a few of them. They're still there, twelve years later, too. Last year's ornament commemorated her new love—emergency medicine—and her first solo trip on an airplane.

Then, there's Lisa's collection. She's the oldest, so her collection holds many memories. The year her braces came off and she could chew gum again, her celebration was marked with a miniature, old-fashioned bubble-gum machine. A tiny nutcracker represents her first trip to see *The Nutcracker*. A clothespin ballerina dressed in scraps from her very own costume reminds us of her first *Swan Lake* performance. In 1990, she was appointed to the Naval Academy and left home, the first child to spread her wings. To honor that year's biggest event for all of us, we each hung a patriotic ornament.

In 1993, Lisa died in a car accident several weeks before Christmas. That year we started a new tradition. A small tree stands in the dining room, displaying her collection, where its presence triggers many Lisa stories during Christmas Eve dinner with our extended family. Now, her stories are still a part of every Christmas.

For our family, decorating the Christmas tree has always meant sharing memories, laughing, crying, and remembering. And someday, when the children's ornaments go with them to new homes and new lives, my husband and I will decorate an "empty nest tree" with our own memories—of places we've been together, inside jokes, and things we love about each other. We'll add new ones each year. Our collection of memories, like our family, will continue.

As you have read through this collection of holiday legacies, I hope your heart has been warmed by the experiences shared here. Perhaps they made you smile, or maybe made you cry. Maybe they've brought up memories from your own life—or pointed out shortfalls. Whatever your reaction to these stories, please allow them to serve as triggers for creating your own family legacies. After all, as you have seen here, there is joy in family legacy!

# 7

# HOLIDAY TRADITIONS
# WITH CHILDREN
### *Lauren*

*I*'m so blessed to have many warm childhood memories of the holidays, and because of those memories, I've made a point of creating the same for my children. It is a delight as parents to share the things that mean so much to us with our children, and doing so is part of establishing our legacy. But perhaps your childhood wasn't particularly happy and you can hardly bear to think of it, let alone recall a pleasant holiday experience. If so, this might be the year to create new memories and change the legacy of your family. Whether cherishing old traditions or creating new ones, you can help ensure the children in your life have joyful memories to treasure. Sometimes it's as simple as a piece of straw or a few cranberries.

## DID YOU KNOW CRANBERRIES FLOAT?

Our New England Thanksgiving dinner always included fresh cranberry orange relish. Since I was the oldest—and the most responsible—I was allowed in the kitchen at a very early age. The day before Thanksgiving, Grammy Chapman and I would make our cranberry relish.

## ORANGE CRANBERRY RELISH

1 12-ounce package fresh cranberries, rinsed and drained

1 unpeeled orange, cut into eighths and seeded

1 cup sugar

Place half the cranberries and half the orange slices in food processor. Process until mixture is evenly chopped. Transfer to a bowl. Repeat with remaining cranberries and orange slices. Stir in sugar. Store in refrigerator.

Makes about 3 cups.

After donning aprons, we emptied the bag of cranberries into a sink full of water for rinsing and sorting. I loved to swish my hands in the cold water and see the cranberries float to the top. I could splash around all I wanted and not get in trouble! My little fingers were the perfect size for examining each berry. If I found a squishy one, I threw it away; if I found one with a stem, I pulled off the stem. Then I carefully placed all the rinsed and now perfect berries in the colander to drain. While I was preparing the cranberries, Grammy Chapman got out the old-fashioned meat grinder, tightened it on the cutting board, and cut an orange into eighths.

Now the exciting part really began! Grammy turned the crank and I plopped the cranberries into the opening of the meat grinder. The juice bubbled up, and the cranberries floated on the top of the opening. It was lots of fun to add more berries and watch them pop back up. (Grammy was careful that my fingers didn't get too close to the grinder.) Now and then, we'd insert a piece of orange and watch the color change as the fruit came out. Once all the fruit had been put through the grinder, we poured sugar over it, and I got to stir it all together. Then Grammy spooned the relish into jars and put them in the refrigerator for the next day.

I still have Grammy Chapman's antique food grinder and have even purchased two more at antique stores so each of my three sons will have one for their own household someday. By then, I'll be the grammy coming over to make cranberry orange relish with their children!

This past year, my sons couldn't be home until Thanksgiving Day. With no one home to help, I made the relish by myself. Rather than create the mess the grinder makes, I decided I'd just throw everything into my food processor. It was much quicker and neater—but it just wasn't the same. It was ground too fine and had lost the familiar texture I prefer. From now on, I'll find the old grinder and do it the old-fashioned way—even if I have to do it myself.

## THE REMOVABLE BABY JESUS

Randy and I own a retail store, and Decembers are especially busy. If we're not careful, all our conversations will center on sales figures, cash flow, and inventory needs. From our desire to keep Christ in Christmas, we've made a special effort to maintain a spiritual focus during the holiday season. I attended a holiday seminar put on by Emilie Barnes, and one of her ideas in particular struck a chord with me.

The first thing we needed was a nativity set. I didn't realize that finding the set I wanted would be so difficult. The first requirement was that it had to have a removable baby Jesus! Why would that be important? I set my decorations up for the entire month of December, and since Jesus was not born until Christmas (traditionally, anyway), I wanted the manger left empty to create a sense of anticipation and understanding of what we were celebrating. Second, I wanted it to look nice while remaining practical. I keep the nativity set on my living room coffee table, and I wanted little hands to play with it all season. Ultimately, I

## A FEW OF THEIR FAVORITE THINGS

A few fun activities to try with children:

Use holiday recipes the kids can help with. Be sure to consider ahead of time what their tasks will be.

Consider old-fashioned decorations the kids can help make, such as popcorn or cranberry garland, paper snowflakes, or candy cane reindeer (made with pipe cleaners for the antlers, "google" eyes from the craft store, and little red pom-poms for the nose).

In addition to purchased gifts, ask the children to create a gift for each family member.

Walk or drive around your community searching for holiday lights and decorations. Have the children leave a thank-you note at their three favorites.

Go caroling with friends and their children.

Do the activities mentioned in various Christmas carols: roast chestnuts or walk in a "winter wonderland" and make a snowman.

Have the children make the centerpiece for Thanksgiving with pinecones and colorful leaves, construction paper pilgrim hats, or turkeys make from their handprints.

found exactly what I wanted, and when we put out the nativity set, I wrapped up the baby Jesus and hid him until December 24.

On Christmas Eve, I made a pot of spaghetti sauce, and the boys helped me make homemade pasta. We baked a pan of brownies and then decorated them as a birthday cake for Jesus. We even put candles on the cake and sang "Happy Birthday." Randy and I reminded the boys (and ourselves!) that the reason we give gifts at Christmas is to remember the gift Jesus gave us.

After dinner we all went in the living room where I read the Christmas story from Luke 2.

When we finished reading the Christmas story, I gently unwrapped the baby Jesus and asked one of our sons to place the baby Jesus in the manger.

We never opened presents on Christmas Eve, and we never discussed business. The evening was all about celebrating the birth of our Savior.

This past Christmas we went to my brother's home in Nevada, so I carefully wrapped up our entire nativity set—which now includes more than thirty pieces—and took it with me. At their home, we unwrapped each figure, and two-year-old Lianna and I arranged the nativity. But, of course, there was no baby Jesus to be found. I already had him tucked away. Christmas morning, after breakfast, Lianna put the baby Jesus in the manger, and we read Luke 2.

A tradition that started with my family has now been passed to my niece! Think of the traditions that have passed down in your family as you read the following stories.

## THE ANGEL TREE BY DIANE BAIER SPRIGGS

Someone once said, "The reward for surviving your children's troublesome teenage years—when they hate you for no reason and wouldn't talk to you if your hair was on fire—is that someday those same children will grow up, get married, come to realize you are wonderful after all, and present you with grandchildren!" That prophecy came true in our family, and we now have three wonderful grandchildren: Baleigh, eight; Hunter, five; and Savana, one.

The Christmas we knew our first grandbaby was on the way, we started a new tradition at our house. Each year, we set up a small artificial tree in the foyer in addition to the big tree in the den.

As we all gather around the small tree, which is already set up with white lights on it, the expectant mother gets the honor of adding little white angel ornaments to the tree and an angel topper. It's our way of welcoming the baby to the family. Of course, the most important part is that we take plenty of pictures to show the babies later so they'll know they were loved and wanted long before they were born.

Our grandbabies were all born in the spring, so we knew the

Christmas before that they were on the way. But if the timing hadn't been right for the Christmas before their birth, we already had plan B in place. We would set up the angel tree for their first Christmas and let their mommy help them add the angels!

Although our children tell us there won't be any more grand-babies, the angel tree is still upstairs in the attic—waiting for our great-grandchildren—when the tradition will continue.

## STRAW IN THE MANGER

Young children have the mind-set that "it's all about *me!*"—especially at Christmas. One way we've (Lauren and Randy) promoted good will and selflessness in our family during the holidays is by displaying a small, empty manger.

We always cut and decorate our Christmas tree on the day after Thanksgiving. The house is then ready as we begin our preparation for the baby's birth.

When our boys were still living at home, on the first Sunday of Advent, I read the explanation of Advent as one son lit the first Advent candle. Then I placed an empty wooden manger on our kitchen table and read the following explanation:

*With excitement we anticipate the special Christmas morn,*

*Rejoicing daily that our Christ child soon will be born.*

*We'll spread our love throughout our home by preparing a cozy bed—*

*A bed of straw to place his tiny little head.*

*As each day passes throughout the month,*

*We'll add a piece of straw for special love we've spread to one another,*

*Special little gifts or deeds and fun surprises to each other.*

*What fun our family will enjoy as we spread our love around.*
*On Christmas morn with joy and glee,*
*We'll celebrate the Christmas tree.*
*But most of all rejoice and praise*
*The birthday of our King!*

Then I put a basket of straw next to the manger and reminded the boys how we use it. Every time one of them did something good without being asked, he got to put a piece of straw in the manger. When he did something nice for someone else, he could put another piece in the manger. As the month went on, the manger gradually filled up with straw, and before they knew it, because of their kindness and good behavior, the baby had a thick bed of hay to sleep on!

Then, when we read the Christmas story on Christmas Eve, one son got to place the baby in the manger. This is a very simple, visual way to teach children about doing kind things for others while anticipating the birth of the baby Jesus.

## GINGERBREAD MEN COOKIES
## BY LOU WORKMAN SOUDERS

My first memory of making cookies is rolling out gingerbread dough on my grandmother Workman's cupboard. It

### HOLIDAY ACTIVITIES TO STRENGTHEN THEIR FAITH

Have younger kids set up an unbreakable nativity while they tell the story.

Ask kids to share in reading devotions during Advent.

Decorate solid-color or glass Christmas bulbs using paint pens from the craft store. Write the year and one way God blessed your family that year.

Watch "A Charlie Brown Christmas." Over cookies and milk, talk about the true meaning of Christmas and why Charlie missed it.

Give a gift to Jesus. As a family, find a way to serve someone else over the holidays.

was fun standing on a stool with an apron on, sifting the flour that was stored inside the flour bin. (That cupboard now has a home in my breakfast nook.)

Several years later, my mother began the Thanksgiving tradition of blessing her family with a wonderful dinner. "Family" meant my mother's three sisters and their husbands, Granny and Bo, her parents,

---

## LOU SOUDERS'S GINGERBREAD MEN

**Mix Together**

    1 cup (2 sticks) margarine

    1 cup sugar

    1/2 teaspoon salt

**Add**

    1 egg

    1 cup molasses

    2 tablespoons vinegar

**Mix in**

    5 cups flour

    1-1/2 teaspoon soda

    1 tablespoon ginger

    1 teaspoon cinnamon

    1 teaspoon ground cloves

Chill dough (I chill the dough overnight.)

Preheat oven to 375 degrees.

Roll out on pastry cloth with small amounts of dough and lots of flour. Keep the rest of the dough in the refrigerator, or it can become very sticky. Don't roll dough too thin. Cut shapes and place on cookie sheet. Decorate with raisins, candies, or colored sugar.

Bake for six minutes, just until edges begin to brown and they smell yummy. Remove from pan immediately.

Makes 5 dozen.

---

El (her unmarried aunt), and all the nieces and nephews, as well as Daddy, my three brothers, and me.

Dinner was wonderful, but as children, our favorite part was the gingerbread men with raisins for eyes, mouth, and buttons.

As the years went by, the family grew, adding sons and daughters-in-law, grandchildren, and great-grandchildren. We had grown to forty-plus people when Mama gave up the Thanksgiving ginger-bread tradition. I remember asking Mama what I could do to help. We decided that making the gingerbread men was the most time-consuming task, so the cookie cutter passed to me thirty-seven years ago.

Now we carry on the tradition in my home with my parents and my brothers' families. It isn't a small event though. I make sixteen to eighteen dozen because my sons, Brooks and Harry, eat them by the handful.

Each person likes them a different way. Brooks and Harry like them in quantity. My daughter, Helen, likes a raisin with every bite, so raisins are placed at the tips of arms and legs. Katelyn, Beau, and Brooks Barron, my grandchildren, want no raisins. No matter the preference, these cookies just wouldn't be the same in any other shape.

When my "nest" emptied, I taught Mary Madeline, a friend with five children, to make them. We set up the gingerbread-man assembly line and made all of hers and my eighteen dozen in one morning. Now those children are growing up, and my grandchildren are taking over the Gingerbread Man Factory.

Through all these years, I've used the same cutter. I was worried that if it broke, the tradition just wouldn't be the same. One day, while shopping for my business, I found another cutter just like my old one! I was so excited I nearly jumped up and down! Now we are assured that our cute gingerbread man will go on for a few more generations.

## THE CHRISTMAS EVE GIFT BY RAELENE SEARLE

I have always been a picture-taking fanatic—even before the scrap-booking frenzy began. The camera was in my children's faces from birth and, even as they got older, they never complained when I took their picture, even in public.

Christmas is my favorite time for taking photos, and although most of my picture taking is spontaneous, I do quite a bit to ensure good-looking pictures. Past years attest to my efforts. I'd move around the room to find just the right angle that includes the decorations in the background. I'd take surprise shots when the kids were laughing to ensure good smiles, rather than simply saying, "I'm going to take your picture—smile." We've even posed the dogs with their Christmas gifts, so the whole family was included.

Wanting my Christmas-morning pictures to be of a good-looking family—not of people who had just dragged themselves out of bed with rumpled pajamas and tousled hair—I decided to buy the kids new pajamas to wear for pictures.

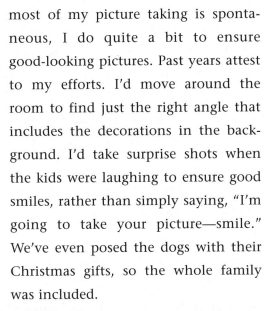

**KEEPING IT SIMPLE AND FOCUSED**

At the beginning of each holiday season, list the traditions you want your children to experience, what lessons you want them to learn, and what you will do to reinforce them. (For example, if you want them to learn selflessness, you might have them provide gifts for Angel Tree or Samaritan's Purse.) On your calendar, schedule a few days when these activities will occur. Be careful not to overbook yourself, or the holiday bustle may crowd out these important events.

Once we had gathered around the Christmas tree, I handed Megan and Aaron their first package to open—the boxes with their new pajamas. The pajamas didn't excite them, especially when I told them to stop opening gifts, put their pajamas on, and brush their hair. My insistence on "cleaned up" kids wasn't received well that year.

Not wanting to abandon the idea of children in crisp, new pajamas for Christmas morning pictures, I came up with a new idea the next year. On Christmas Eve we had the kids open one present—their new jammies, of course. I thought they would enjoy having something new and clean to sleep in. They were excited to open one gift—even if it was a "squishy" gift. They loved their new pajamas, and when I explained that I wanted to do this every year so we had great pictures, they thought it was a neat idea.

Every year since, Megan and Aaron have looked forward to opening their Christmas Eve gift of nightwear. Sometimes it's received after dinner, other times it's at midnight after we get home from a Christmas Eve church service.

As they've grown older, the pajamas have turned into shorts and T-shirts, or sweats—whatever they like to sleep in at a particular age. And every year I take my Christmas-morning photos from willing models.

Now I look forward to another tradition that resulted from my photo efforts: each Christmas morning we have fun looking through our "Christmas only" scrapbook at all those great-looking family photos of Christmases past.

## IMPORTANT LITTLE THINGS

The things you remember and treasure the most from your childhood are probably not extravagant gifts or elaborate activities. Rather they are probably uncomplicated but meaningful moments, such as making gingerbread cookies with your grandmother or sharing what you are thankful for at Thanksgiving. The same will be true for your own children. So, don't let your bigger plans, such as having a beautiful family picture, steal the delight of the holidays. Focus on making the little things meaningful. Those pajamas you give them on Christmas Eve might just be one of their fondest memories.

# 8

# FAMILY GATHERINGS
## *Lauren*

*F*amily gatherings and reunions blend the joy of being with those you love the most and, at the same time, being with the very people who can drive you up the wall. There are moments when the idea of getting loved ones together seems intimidating. The planning, the conflicts (schedule and otherwise), and the simple challenge of keeping kids entertained can make you want to avoid family get-togethers. And yet, these moments together can be both meaningful and memorable. These are also the times when we learn more about our own history and times when we can begin to pass on our own legacy to younger generations. For these reasons, time spent together as an immediate family and as an extended family is vital. And in the end, it is often more fun than we ever expected.

## ROCK CANDY BY RANDY BRIGGS, SR.

Annual summer vacations have always been a highlight of my life. As long as I can remember, the onset of summer has heralded a time for family trips. These adventures were not just a week at the beach or a trip to the mountains, but real treks to the Canadian Rockies, Yellowstone, the Pacific Northwest, and the New York World's Fair in

1964. As I look back on the thousands of miles traveled, I remember learning to drive the car, reading maps, and visiting numerous historical sites and museums. Boredom never seemed to be a problem.

Now, as a married man, I've tried to pass this great tradition along to our three sons. Most summers have been spent traveling by car, motor home, or plane to wonderful destinations all over the United States, Canada, and Europe, and I'm sure that if you asked any of our kids to tell you the best times they remember most about their childhoods, they would say "vacations."

Having three young boys in a vehicle at the same time was a recipe for vacation disaster, unless their behavior could be controlled. One of the most successful techniques that Lauren and I found to curb bad behavior involved rock candy. Now you might think this sounds like bribery of the most tooth-decaying kind, but it really wasn't.

When traveling in uninhabited areas, we offered a reward of two or three pieces of rock candy (the kind that looks like little pebbles) to the first person who spotted a wild animal. Subsequent confirmed spottings were rewarded with single pieces. We didn't count sightings of ordinary animals or birds such as rabbits or sparrows, unless they were a species unique to the area in which we were driving. This contest kept everyone's eyes glued to the scenery and the interior of the car relatively peaceful.

I remember one particularly beautiful day in the Canadian Rockies when we had ventured out into a serene meadow for a picnic. Sitting on a blanket, we started to unpack lunch. Lauren and I were concentrating on making sandwiches and weren't paying a lot of attention to our surroundings when one of the boys said, "Look! There's an elk." That was immediately followed by another sighting and then another. Suddenly, we were being approached by a herd of twenty or thirty very large quadrupeds intent on sharing in our feast. We hastily gathered our food and retreated to the safety of the motor home and highway, greatly relieved that our boys had learned to watch for wild animals. "Rock candy for everyone!"

## THE FAMILY GATHERING BY RAELENE SEARLE

My husband, Chip, is the oldest of six children. All the siblings are very close, even with the addition of five sisters-in-law and one brother-in-law. Everyone gets along amazingly well.

As each child married and moved away, we found it increasingly difficult to get together regularly. As a result, we worked to think of a way to have a yearly family gathering that didn't put a financial burden on young, growing families.

We decided to plan a vacation that didn't require hotels, amusement parks, or eating out. Camping was something we all enjoyed, so it became our solution.

Each year we rented a cabin for five days in Yosemite National Park. It was just the right size for each family to have their own room. We shared the cost of the rental and took turns cooking and cleaning up. With lunches on our own, each family was

### STARTING SMALL FOR BIG RESULTS

If you can't plan a full reunion, consider:

- planning "regional" reunions in several spots— one area a year. It can simply be a long weekend, and since fewer people will attend, the planning can be as easy as a hotel and restaurant reservation.

- combining a vacation and reunion. Invite everyone to join you at a specific location. It could be a cabin in the mountains, a major theme park, or your childhood hometown.

- making it a point to visit at least one geographically distant relative each year. Try to vary who you see, and be sure to keep in touch with those you are likely to visit throughout the year.

only responsible for one meal. Each family's supply list was simply what was needed for that one meal, sandwich items for lunches, and a few other odds and ends assigned to them such as cleaning supplies, condiments, or paper goods.

We spent the days hiking or swimming in the river. Evenings were spent doing family devotions (each head of household was responsible for one night) and playing group games such as Taboo or Scattergories.

We not only saved a lot of money by dividing the costs of this trip, but we created many memories as an extended family. We still talk about Chip and his cousin Rob climbing Half Dome in a "dusk to dark" trip. They each spent more than six months of intense weightlifting and running to prepare for this strenuous hike and climb. The rock is 4,882 feet above the valley floor, and the last 900 feet is a very steep climb straight up the east face of the granite dome. Ascending this enormous rock is not recommended for the average tourist—only those in prime physical shape. We have great pictures of the cousins climbing up—taken by each other—and then at the top. What great—and painful—memories Chip and Rob have every time they wear their awarded hat, which reads "I made it to the top."

Then we remember when Chip and his youngest brother, Stephen, ignored the falling snow on one of their hikes. The snow eventually covered their trail, and they got lost—wearing only shorts, sweatshirts, and hiking boots. They struggled to find their way back to the cabin, choosing to simply head downhill and hoping to end up somewhere near where they had started. Fortunately, they found their way home and spent the evening thawing out next to the fireplace.

I have scrapbook after scrapbook full of the memories we have created as an extended family through inexpensive and stress-free gatherings. Making these family times part of our vacation planning every year has been the greatest blessing to each of us and has built endless memories as a legacy for our children and grandchildren.

## HOW TO MAKE A FAMILY REUNION FUN IN SPITE OF EVERYTHING! BY THE REV. JAMES W. CHAPMAN (FLORENCE'S BROTHER)

I have been involved in seven large family reunions. There are two wonderful things about such heart-warming and nostalgic events. I'll tell you the second later, but the first is when everyone arrives and you see smiling faces that you haven't seen in decades. There are Cousin Henry and Aunt Mabel. Grandma and Grandpa Abercromby have made it, which relieves the worry that they wouldn't be up to the trip. And then there are hosts of little children you didn't even know existed swarming all over the reunion site.

It is a joyous scene that makes the months of preparation worth every minute. You forgive the people who cancelled two days ago, leaving you with two hotel rooms and no one to put in them. You aren't even bothered by the two second cousins who somehow got wind of the event and showed up uninvited. (That solves one of the empty rooms!) Finally, you decide to ignore the fact that Cousin Leonardo has shown up with a new girlfriend whose garb and manner

### THE SPIRITUAL SIDE OF LIFE

Take time when visiting relatives to discuss your family's spiritual heritage. Some questions might be:

- Did Grandma believe in God? Why or why not?
- What were Sundays like when you were growing up?
- Describe the church you attended as a child and the church you are attending now (if applicable).
- If your relative isn't a Christian and practices a different faith, ask why he or she chose that path rather than Christianity. (Tread carefully here. This isn't the time to argue the virtues of either faith.)

make you certain she has been in some unnamed profession, possibly an old one. Furthermore, they show no signs of sleeping in separate quarters, in spite of their not having had "the benefit of clergy," which seems true in all imaginable interpretations of that phrase. And so we begin.

But much has already happened. First, *you* had to have the idea, since no one else seems to have been moved to gather this now scattered clan. And so you write to all the family members you can think of and ask if they would like to attend a reunion about two years away. Always make it that far in advance so that no one is booked already.

This is usually a fairly simple step because people are willing to commit to about anything that's two years away! ("A year from next July? I think I'm free!") This, of course, does not mean they will come.

Another of the joys of running a reunion is hearing the reasons different relatives have for bowing out. They range from the indisputable (death, usually reported by someone other than the deceased) to the understandable (expecting a baby or moving overseas) to the absurd (the Red Sox are playing an important series with the Yankees that weekend). But through the months that stretch before you to the actual happy event, the list will go through a metamorphosis that would put the caterpillar to shame. When all is said and done, however, you have a beautiful butterfly before you, ready to spread its wings all over your carefully laid plans

Now several questions arise.

### Where Will You Gather?

If you can avoid it, never have it at your own home unless you're looking for a good excuse to redecorate (after the reunion, not for the reunion). A much better choice is some neutral spot such as a resort or hotel near your home or the old family homestead, hallowed by the joyous memories of Christmases past. For the reunion of my mother's family, the MacDougalls, we roomed at a hotel and then Saturday morning all sixty-two of us met on the lawn of the old family homestead and read a letter our grandmother had written about the house in 1899. I was interested to note that though the woman who now lives in that house had welcomed me warmly some months before and showed me around the familiar rooms without hesitation, on this day of days, there was no one in the house, and it was as secure as Fort Knox. Apparently it had something to do with our numbers. At any rate it was a wonderful morning, and we met the neighbors as they slowly and cautiously emerged from houses that hadn't existed in our memories. They were naturally curious about this invasion of their neighborhood by a suspiciously strange (in the sense of unknown, not odd!) group.

After reading all the assigned letters and listening to ad lib remembrances of various folks whose main wish was to be heard, we all piled into multiple vehicles and headed for the cemetery. This, of course, is sacred ground. Everybody that was anybody in the MacDougall clan was buried there. From Grandfather James Ellis MacDougall (whom none of us had ever known, but after whom a significant number of us were named, including me), down to the latest aunt or uncle who had fallen before the eschatological scythe of time. My father and mother are there. He died in 1948 when we children were thirteen, seventeen, and twenty-one. My mother died more than thirty years later in 1984.

## Where Will You Eat?

That evening we had the inaugural dinner at a restaurant I had never seen. The caterer, whom I had never met, had recommended it. All had been done by phone from Ohio. I don't recommend this way of planning a reunion. For example, when we got there on the appointed afternoon, it was about ninety degrees outside. We entered the stifling hall our caterer had lined up and learned there was no air conditioning! We were appalled. When we extrapolated what the temperature would be when we added sixty-two sweaty MacDougalls to the room, it was not a pretty prospect. However (and I promise this is true), at four o'clock a violent but benevolent thunderstorm roared through, cleaned out the humidity, and dropped the temperature about twenty degrees.

It was delightfully cool in there that evening. Aunt Jean was able to don her MacDougall plaid suit and address the assembled tribe as our elder stateswoman. To say I was relieved is akin to saying Isaac was relieved when the ram appeared in the thicket! So where you have your reunion has to be carefully researched, because there is no guarantee of a fortuitous storm.

### Where Will You Worship?

One needs to take care of Sunday morning. For us, who tend to be a religious group, this meant church in the old family church. I called to see if we could, by chance, take over the Sunday morning service for that day. Again the reunion gods were smiling on us. The new minister was due to begin the following week, and they had nobody to preach that day. I modestly volunteered my service and that of the entire family. The secretary of the church was audibly relieved.

Originally there were seven MacDougall children, including my mother, and one of the descendants of each of those siblings did a part in the service. My daughter Laurie, who is also a minister, had the pastoral prayer. We were told that it was their custom to ask for prayer requests before the prayer in case someone was sick or had died (before the service, not during it.) People called out, or more precisely muttered out names of stricken family members. This, coupled with their New

England accents rendered their reports all but incomprehensible despite Laurie's best efforts to grasp who had been struck down with what. For example, one of the requests was, "Nawmer has a tuma." It sounded as though this could have been something about a sandwich. Laurie decided to lump all the requests together and pray generically for those who were sick or may have died, as the case may be.

Our aunt Sadie had been a giant figure in our Pantheon. She had lived in Merrimac all her life, conducted a kindergarten in the homestead, and taught piano to uncounted students. Before the sermon I asked how many worshippers had been to her school and how many had taken piano lessons from her. Almost every hand went up for one or both of these roles. She had had a great influence on that little town.

### When Will You Get Paid?

After the service we enjoyed a catered brunch in the church hall. This brings us to the answer to the fourth question regarding running a reunion: Get the money up front! Some fifty-five people had told me they would stay for the brunch at eleven dollars each. I, being the trusting soul that I am, assumed they would (a) all come and (b) all pay. I am now a wiser and less idealistic man. A significant number of the esteemed MacDougalls told me they had to leave early and sadly couldn't stay for the brunch. Even more sadly,

---

### A FEW HELPFUL HINTS FOR REUNIONS

When at family reunions or while visiting loved ones, take pictures and encourage family storytelling. As everyone reminisces, be sure to record what you're learning. Keep a notebook handy so you can write down the memories during a quiet moment later that day. You might choose to use a tape recorder as everyone is speaking, or keep the video camera rolling off to the side. Keep in mind that the best conversations for gathering information are often those that are unrehearsed and casual.

they didn't pay for the brunch I had ordered at their request. My brother-in-law, Fred, and Aunt Jean chipped in some money to help me cover the cost of the escapees.

### The Joys of Farewells

Back at the beginning of my tale, I said there were two happy moments in running a reunion. The first was the joy of seeing all the faces from the near or distant past. The second happy moment is when they all drive away on Sunday afternoon. After you have greeted Cousin George and enthused over his new comb-over, you discover that the obnoxious habits he had as a kid have been preserved like fossils in an archeological dig. And as cute as all the little children were who appeared in glorious array on Friday, by Sunday their cuteness had faded away, and only your own grandchildren have survived with reputations intact—and not even all of them!

Despite all of this, the effort is well worth it. I realized that I would never see some, if not most of these people again. That has proved to be true. The two matriarchs of the family, Aunt Jean and Aunt Frances, have died, as well as several others who were there.

Are memories worth resurrecting, even if they are unpleasant? They are indeed. They are part of who we are and what we have become. In the tangled web of life, they are threads woven close to our own, and each influences the others. We are, like it or not, a family, and as we grow older we have that indefinable desire to see how everybody turned out and how they're all doing.

So have your reunion. Watch out for the pitfalls I have mentioned. Nail it down as firmly as you can, and be sure to get the money up front. You will be happy you made the effort and even happier to see it pass into the pages of history. A significant part of your past will be illuminated again, and you will understand that families are not random people thrown together, but a band of brothers and sisters who share a heritage, a host of memories, and perhaps most significantly, a set of genes. Knowing from whence we have come can help us chart where we are yet to be. Thank God for what has transpired in our past that has brought us to where we are today.

# 9

# TREASURED TRIPS
## *FLORENCE*

The Christmas after my husband died, my brother Ron and his wife, Nance, invited me, my brother Jim, and Jim's wife to go on a cruise from Rio de Janeiro to Antarctica. He had an apartment on the cruise ship, and he got extra accommodations for the rest of us. We traveled from the middle of December to the middle of January. Each day gave us a story of a lifetime—starting with our trip to the huge statue of Jesus at the top of Corcovado Mountain where we were marooned when a tree fell on the power lines and the cable car could not come up to rescue us. I sensed that day, as I sat at the feet of Jesus and a hurricane swept upon us on the mountaintop, that if I lived through this experience, I would write it all up as an adventure story.

I know from my writing background that if you don't grab the moment when it comes, you will never get the emotion back again. You can write from memory later, but you'll never experience the same passion, the same excitement, you had when the event happened. Because of this, I disciplined myself to write each day. Although I missed some family fellowship, I knew in my heart I would never remember the thrust of each emotion at a later time. Could I ever again feel the fear that came over me as I saw the little rubber boat I was to get into for the ride under the Iguazú Falls in Brazil? Could I really grasp at a later time the thrill of dancing tango in Buenos Aires? Could I ever again call to memory the humor of attending a lavish reception for an ambassador who did not come, the solemnity of the walk on the Falkland Islands that Margaret Thatcher saved from capture, the thunderous crack of the icebergs breaking apart, and the joy of walking amid more penguins than I knew existed in the whole world? Would I ever get a full feel for Christmas on *The World* and my opportunity to present "Silver Boxes" in the ship's theater?

Memory is great, but recording vivid experiences as they happen is unbeatable. I am so grateful for my desire to pass my experiences on as they happened and my discipline to do it. We later printed up my writings of this trip of a lifetime and sent them out as our "annual greetings" to our CLASS Christmas card list.

Shakespeare wrote in *Julius Caesar* (Act IV Scene 3), "There is a tide in the affairs of men, which, taken at the flood, leads on to fortune; Omitted, all the voyage of their life is bound in shallows and in miseries... We must take the current when it serves, or lose our ventures." From here on, may each one of us be looking for the tide, and know the current when it lifts us, so we will never lose our ventures.

Think about some of the family

**SOMETHING A LITTLE DIFFERENT**

Consider various types of trips.

- A region of the country: northwest states, the southern part of your home state
- A type of sight: national parks, state capitols, Civil War sites, historical places in a specific city
- A type of activity: best fishing holes, top ten places to ski, major museums to explore
- A repeat of a favorite childhood vacation

adventures you have enjoyed—or endured! Besides my stories, in the following pages you'll read about those escapades of several of our contributors. So sit back, relax, and take a trip with us that won't even cost you airfare!

## FROM SEA TO SHINING SEA by LARISEE LYNN STEVENS

Dad had an insatiable curiosity about this country, and we explored the length and breadth of it. Whether natural or man-made, if something was of historical interest, we saw it. His hobby was visiting state capitol buildings. By the time I was in high school, I had walked the rotundas and chambers of thirty-five of them. (My husband and I continued this tradition with our children, who now are doing it with our grandchildren.)

Vacation was a wonderful learning time for us. As he mapped out our route, Dad read about and researched the things we would see. He knew all about the crops, flora, and fauna of the areas we passed through, as well as the cities, rivers, and sights. Even as a small child, I never slept in the car for fear I might miss something. My sister and I made scrapbooks of each trip and sang songs containing the name of the places we were as we drove along. We sang "Wabash Cannonball" when we crossed the Wabash River and "Tennessee Waltz" as we traveled through Tennessee. Silly, but fun, and thinking of and singing the songs passed the miles.

On these trips, Daddy taught me of the magnificence of this country. I saw firsthand the majesty of its creation, the mix of its cultures, the magnitude of its possibilities, and the wonder of its freedom. Daddy not only taught me to be proud to be an American, but to be awestruck by the country and its people.

## AVOIDING "ARE WE THERE YET?"

Use your children's interests to keep them busy. For the math lover, how many miles left to our destination and what percentage of the distance have we gone? For the reader, write a story about the place we are going.

Listen to books on tape or read aloud as you travel.

Play new praise songs and learn them together.

Play simple games on the plane such as tic-tac-toe or hangman.

Before leaving, discuss the areas you will travel to or through. Offer ideas of things for the children to look for as you drive.

Prepare a sack of their favorite toys, and have a few new items such as coloring books to bring out later in a long trip.

Give older children their own maps to follow. Have them mark the places they see and the landmarks you pass.

In addition to visiting state capitol buildings, we helped our children make scrapbooks of our trips. Before each trip, I bought each child a spiral notebook and several colored pens. Each time we crossed a river, they wrote its name in the notebook. When we saw something interesting, they noted what they saw—be it a rail fence, Pike's Peak, or kudzu. We even wrote down interesting street, highway, and town names. When they were younger, we purchased postcards for their scrapbooks, and when they grew older and could handle a camera, they took pictures of what we saw.

When we listed the rivers we crossed, we added where the river began and where it emptied, other rivers that fed into it or that it fed into, large cities that it flowed through, where we crossed it, and what it looked like (full and wide, small and sandy, and so forth). When listing the states we crossed, we included major cities, border states, and interesting things we saw in it. When listing interesting place names like "Two Gun Road," we added educated guesses as to how the place had received that name.

These guesses turned into some interesting stories! Once home we looked up what we had seen in reference books, and sometimes one of the children drew a picture to include in the scrapbook.

Our children are grown with children of their own, but they are carrying on the family travel traditions. I can picture my father beaming as my three-year-old granddaughter shares her awe at what she sees by batting eyelashes over her big blue eyes and saying, "Nana, that is amazing!"

Our family has learned that a trip is much more valuable when we prepare for it, give each child a notebook, encourage them to take notes, and review the material when we get home. Instead of voicing "Are we there yet?" questions, children happily noticed everything they saw. Then, as they are growing up, they enjoy rereading these family trips and showing their pictures to their friends. A little preparation and a few supplies can turn a long trip into a fascinating excursion.

## DAD ON TOUR BY MARY ANN REMNET

My childhood memories of my dad were of his long work hours and late nights. He worked as an aerospace mechanic during the height of the NASA moon launches, and his working hours did not allow him much presence in our lives.

About ten years ago, however, I decided to take a four-day mini-vacation to Washington, DC. On a whim, I asked my dad to join me. Much to my surprise, he agreed. It was an enlightening and enjoyable visit. He shared the family history with me and talked about his struggles to support us. One afternoon, as we excitedly crisscrossed the Smithsonian National Air and Space Museum, I finally realized the value of his sacrifice and the fruits of his labors.

He showed me every bolt of every space capsule he had helped manufacture.

My tour of the museum, through his behind-the-scenes eyes, was unforgettable. Sharing his part of history brought us both great pride. It somehow made his absence during my childhood seem insignificant. Now I understand why we always woke up to the dull blue flicker of the television as he awaited Apollo splashdowns. Consequently, I am able to share the memorable time with my children—noting his contributions to space exploration. Because of our tour-from-the-heart, his sacrifice for us will never be forgotten. He left a legacy I almost missed.

## WEEKENDS WITH GRANDMA BY KATHLEEN M. EDELMAN

Have you ever felt invisible? Coming from a large family, getting the attention I wanted and needed was difficult. There were five children in my family. My two older sisters are only one year apart in age. They became close playmates for each other, and it didn't help that my mother frequently dressed them as if they were twins. Less than two years after I was born my baby brother arrived. He was my parents' dream, my father's namesake. The birth of my younger sister, six years later, became the center of my older sisters' attention. They thought she was a real live doll for them to play with—and they did.

I was the middle child, the one psychology often calls the "invisible child," and invisible is exactly how I felt growing up.

I vividly remember the day my parents brought my baby sister home from the hospital. I was eight years old at the time. I went outside, cleaned out our front garden, prepared the soil, and planted some flowers my mother had purchased but hadn't had time to get in before leaving for the hospital. Just as I was finishing this big surprise project—expecting my parents' praise for my efforts—they pulled in the driveway. I stood, smiling proudly, as they got out of the car—sure they would shower me with accolades. In slow motion, I watched my smiling parents carry this bundle of joy straight up the walk, past my hard work, and into the house without a word. I truly felt invisible.

My mother's parents lived close by, and we often spent time with them. My mother spoke to them nearly every day, but always toward the end of the week, my grandma would ask to talk to me. I eagerly waited for the words I loved to hear: "Kathleen, would you like to come spend this weekend with Grandma?"

I started packing my things immediately. When Friday finally came, I sat on the porch and waited for my grandma's car to turn down our street. When she rounded the corner in her big green Pontiac Bonneville, my heart danced! To this day when I think of that moment, I can see her smiling face, her hand waving out the window, and her gray hair fresh from the beauty shop.

I was in her car before she could put it in park.

The first stop was always Ben Franklin, a five-and-dime store near my

## GO AHEAD AND DREAM

Plan two vacations, one that is simple, practical, and can be done within the next year. This may be as easy as an inexpensive weekend away somewhere nearby. Make the other a once-in-a-lifetime experience. Although this trip may not be possible for some time, think through some of the things you'd like to do. For each trip, start researching the places you'll see, the local landmarks, the geography, and the history. Let your children help with some of the planning. Start early and let the preparation be part of the fun.

grandma's house. There I chose my very own paint by numbers—one I would not have to share with anyone. From there we headed over to the grocery, where I picked out my favorite foods and drinks, which always included cream soda and barbecue chips. (My parents were great and very loving, but with five children, we seldom got all our favorites at once.) Oh, how special I felt to have my own stuff! If Grandma bumped into one of her friends as we shopped, she would introduce me as if I were the new queen in town.

After that, it was home to Grandma's house. We ate dinner and talked, then settled in for a Friday evening of television and painting. I painted while Grandma watched her favorite show, *Jeopardy*. After that program was over, I grabbed the cream soda and chips, and together we watched my favorite show, *Mission Impossible*. I knew my family was watching *The Carol Burnett Show* at that same time. At home, everyone had to agree on the Friday shows, but not at Grandma's.

At home, I shared a bedroom with my two older sisters. Most of the time it wasn't too bad—until they became teenagers, and their friends were over all the time. They would kick me out of my own room! I really didn't care to stick around anyway; all they talked about were boys, boys, and boys. At Grandma's, I had my very own room to sleep in—it was great!

In the morning I woke up to fresh donuts my uncle had picked up at the local bakery. The smell of my grandma's coffee and the donuts lured me to the kitchen. He always bought my favorite nutty, glazed chocolate donuts, and a powdered sugar one for Grandma.

I felt so important at Grandma's house. I was able to do everything I wanted all weekend. It was like being a princess. During the day, Grandma and I went for walks, talked on the porch, and played games.

Although we had no money for vacations, my father planned one day each summer when he, my brothers, and I would go to Boston on the train. The month before the one-day trip, we could suggest things we wanted to see. Since it was a "history trip," we could not choose parks and zoos unless they had some historical value. Once we chose a few possible destinations, we had to read about them and send for information. I remember climbing up Bunker Hill Monument and riding peacefully in the swan boats at Boston Commons. Perhaps my favorite time was visiting the statehouse with its shiny gold dome. As a guide showed us around, he asked if we would like to meet the governor, Leverett Saltonstall. We had never met anyone important, so we went wide-eyed into his office with the guide. "These children would like to meet you," he explained to the governor who came around from behind his desk and talked to us.

To this day when I go to Boston, I look at that statehouse and remember not only the governor, but also a father who cared enough to plan and prepare for our once-a-year history trip to Boston.

---

She liked card games the best, since she was a master bridge player. Grandma taught me all the games she knew, and we had so much fun!

My mother became chronically ill when I was ten years old and died when I was twenty-one. My relationship with Grandma grew even stronger after my mother's death.

As the years passed and I had my own apartment, I still went to Grandma's for dinner and a sleepover now and then. When I met my husband, Brad, I made a point of taking him to meet her. With my mother gone, it was very important to me that they meet each other— the two people I loved so dearly. I knew how my Grandma would talk to him about me. She would share with him how she saw me and how special she thought I was.

Grandma died shortly after their meeting. I was crushed. Today, when I think of her or look at her picture, I realize it wasn't the favorite foods, paints, or drinks that made me feel special. It wasn't the television program or having my own room. It was her smile and wave when she picked me up in the driveway. It was the smell of her night cream and holding her hand as we walked. It was when I looked up from playing cards and saw her looking at me, smiling. Most of all, it was her strong loving embrace when she dropped me off back home.

My grandma, without words, said to me, "I see you and I love you!"

Knowing that the person you are today is built on yesterday's memories, I believe those weekends with Grandma helped shape who I am today.

Since my mother isn't here to pass along the kinds of wonderful memories my grandma gave me, I make it a point to spend time with my children and let them know they are an important part of my life. I also make sure they know I recognize their talents and gifts. Most importantly, I teach them they are fearfully and wonderfully made by God.

As I sit on their beds at night to pray, I thank God that out of all the moms in the world, he picked me to be their mom.

In my personal prayer time, I thank God for my grandma and all she gave me during our time together. I will always love my grandma for making me feel special, loved, and most of all, for truly seeing me. I am not invisible.

## HALF THE FUN IS GETTING THERE BY WENDY STEWART-HAMILTON

I possess the same traveling gene as my dad, who started the "Sunday After-Church Drive" tradition in our family. We wandered down the back roads and side roads of southern West Virginia to "see what we can see." Upon returning home to his cheerful "home again, home again," we would head to our rooms to take our Sunday afternoon naps that got us rested for that evening's church services and the coming week.

My dad inherited that same traveling gene from his father, Harry Zickafoose, who took his family on many road trips. Harry ministered as an interim pastor for struggling churches in North Carolina.

As far as I can tell, our family traveling gene began in Germany when five brothers came to America in the early 1800s.

This rich heritage of family trips has inspired me to make traveling with my kids special and unique. In addition to trekking from Texas to West Virginia and Virginia at least twice yearly to visit family and friends, my husband and I have enjoyed creating new travels for our children.

Some of our family favorites are "namesake trips," "foreign lands in domestic places," and "big and unusual journeys."

## Namesake Trips

"Namesake trips" are trips we take as a family to cities that share a name with a member of our family. For example, we journeyed to Hayden, Arizona, a small suburb of Phoenix, which shares our son Andrew's middle name. With our daughter, Kayleigh, we have had many options of places to visit that have her middle name "Elizabeth," such as Elizabeth City, North Carolina; Elizabeth, Illinois; and Elizabeth, Colorado, to name a few.

For our family, namesake trips must follow a couple guidelines to be "authentic." First, the spelling of the name has to be exact, though I've been tempted to steer journeys toward the "windy city" (Chicago) in honor of my name, Wendy, which means "wanderer."

If, however, you have a uniquely spelled name like our daughters, Kaile and Kayleigh—both pronounced "Kaylee"—exceptions can be made to visit a street with the same name, such as "Kaile Lane" in Escondido, California. Second, the name of the city to visit can be the same as your first, middle, or last name. Third, the journey can be anywhere in the world. We've even planned a variation of a namesake trip for our family, to visit Scotland and Ireland to see Ceili dancing (Ireland) and then Ceilidh dancing (Scotland) in their traditional settings. When spoken, Ceili and Ceilidh sound exactly like "Kaylee." So this trip will honor the pronunciation of our daughters' common name.

By searching out places that share their names, we are showing our children firsthand that a great name really is to be desired both in people and in vacationing spots. Beyond this, we are not only honoring our children in the present but also giving them a connection to something that began in the past.

### Foreign Lands in Domestic Places

These trips involve visiting places locally with the same name as cities abroad that you would like to visit as a family.

For example, although you may not be able to visit Paris, France this year, the trip to Paris, Texas, or Paris, Kentucky, may be manageable for your family. Although the Parisian sites vary from city to city, your family will enjoy sipping lattes and eating croissants together regardless of which Paris you're in.

For fun you might take art canvases and paint when you and your family visit Venice, Florida, or search for souvenir windmills from Holland, Michigan while you visit their annual Tulip Festival, or ask the locals where the best bratwurst is in Frankfurt, Kentucky.

## Big and Unusual Journeys

As the name implies, these "big and unusual" family journeys involve traveling to and seeing sites we don't normally see. Some examples are the many places that feature the "World's Largest Things" (www.worldslargestthings.com), or catching up to the Traveling Roadside Attraction and Museum called the *World's Largest Collection of the World's Smallest Versions of the World's Largest Things* as it moves throughout various cities in the United States.

From the "World's Tallest Man" in Alton, Illinois, to the "World's Largest Can of Fruit Cocktail" in Sunnydale, California, big and unusual journeys are definitely journeys families can remember fondly for a lifetime.

If you don't know where to begin creating big and unusual journeys, check out www.legendsofamerica.com. Our family has received useful information from Kathy Weiser, owner and editor of Legends of America, as we plan trips to see ghost towns, learn more about historical people, and investigate folklore and legends across the United States and Canada.

Sometimes as parents, we cringe as we think about traveling in a car with kids or we anticipate every imaginable scenario of "what can go wrong, will go wrong." When we let that stop us, we miss out on the joy of the journeys.

I love to use this quote by Babs Hoffman when combating obstacles in traveling with my family: "Stop worrying about the potholes in the road and enjoy the journey."

So whether you fly, drive, sail, travel by rail, or hike a trail, family trips are fundamentally fun, and half the fun is just getting there. Family journeys are foundational to leaving a lasting legacy as your children and grandchildren remember "the trip when...."

# 10

# A Legacy of Faith
## *Florence*

W hen I was growing up, there was no such thing as "I don't feel like going to church today." We all knew that on Sunday we got up, put on our go-to-church clothes, and walked across the street to the Riverside Memorial Church. By the time I was twelve years old, I was assisting the teacher for the Sunday school kindergartners, and at fifteen, I became a full-fledged teacher of the fourth grade Sunday school class. I look back and wonder what I was teaching at that point, but I do remember the attendance in my group held up, and at the time, that was the gauge of whether or not you were a good teacher.

My brothers and I sang in the junior choir, were in all the pageants, ate all we could pile on our plates at the yearly Strawberry Festival, and got sunburned at the Sunday school picnic at Lake Attitash. Our only social activities were sponsored by our church.

When I went away to college, I joined a local church and was a faithful attender—in contrast to most of my sorority sisters who slept in on Sundays.

After college graduation, I returned home to Haverhill. My father had just died, and my mother needed me to help with the store. Once again the church became my social center, and I took on leadership positions. When I met Fred, I could tell he was a moral person and a church member. He studied God's Word and lived accordingly. What I didn't realize until after I was married was that his church was different from mine. They believed in the Bible, but also in another book they perceived to be of equal value. Plus they accepted a specific human leader as equal to Jesus. We attended this church for many years before I discerned that it was a cult.

In the process of losing our two sons to a fatal condition, we gave up on God and church. "How could a good God let something like this happen to people like us?" we asked ourselves. We didn't know that Jesus loved us, even though we had sung that song in Sunday school. Nor did we know experientially that God had power to change lives. Both Fred and I, at separate times within months of each other, prayed and asked Jesus to come into our lives and change us—to take away the pain of grieving and give us new joy. As we did with everything, we tackled our new spiritual life with zeal and excitement.

## FAMILY PRAYER TIME

Once Fred and I decided that we were going to start raising Christians instead of just children, we had to change our lifestyle. We were already focused on living lives that honored God, so we didn't have to adjust our morals, just our priorities. Sunday went from being tennis tournament day to church day. Since Fred was the tennis champ at the country club and was always ready for an exciting match, his partner couldn't understand why Fred said he wouldn't play until one o'clock on Sundays. "Littauer's got religion" was the word that went around the club.

The Lord must have known how difficult it would be for us to change and grow in our old surroundings, for we hardly knew the plan of salvation before God called us to California and moved us into "Bungalow One" at the headquarters of Campus Crusade for Christ. I went from being a social pacesetter to becoming a Bible student. In Connecticut each of our children had a separate bedroom; in California they were stacked into two rooms with bunk beds. Instead of being able to go to our rooms, we all were together—almost on top of each other— all the time. What initially seemed the big step down on the ladder of life, in retrospect became a leap to new heights in our family relationships.

The first change we made spiritually was to start a prayer time with our children. When Fred first mentioned that I was to have dinner ready at 5:30 and in a condition that it could be put on hold for fifteen minutes while we prayed, I said, "That's impossible!"

We had never done anything on schedule or by routine in our home before. Fred's arrival time in the evening had never been consistent, and I had usually fed the children early, so the idea of scheduled togetherness seemed hopeless to me. Since his office was now in the Arrowhead Springs Hotel and we lived next door in Bungalow One, Fred determined that he would come home each night on time. The preparation was left to my creativity and control.

## THE DIFFERENCE ONE PERSON MAKES

Is there someone in your life who has had a particular impact on you spiritually? Consider:

What was it he or she did that made such an impact?

Did she or he have an influence because of something big the person did for God or a relatively small act of faithfulness?

Who else has this person influenced?

What about this person's attitudes or behaviors contributed to his or her ability to touch your life?

The next challenge was getting children who had never prayed more than "Now I lay me down to sleep" to want to pray. Fred and I had to establish a purpose for our prayer time. Were we going to pray because it was a good Christian thing to do or because the children needed to know God answers prayer? The latter was the obvious answer, but the next question was how? How would we show our children that an unseen God hears and answers them?

The first night, we asked the children whom they would like to pray for. Amazingly, they got excited about choosing, and we established several categories. Fred, being the organized one, got out three-by-five cards and wrote titles on the top of each card such as "Family Needs," "Friends," "Church," "Missionaries," and "School Friends."

That night, we set up the system and Fred prayed. The next night we chose one card, "Family Needs," and wrote down our requests. Next to these were two columns: Date Asked and Date Answered. We entered the date asked and then each of us, including four-year-old Freddie, gave a sentence prayer for that particular family need.

Each night we started our prayer time with requests for additional items to be placed on the cards. The children liked coming up with a new item, and began thinking about prayer requests during the day so they would have something to add. After the new requests were on the cards, one child each night chose which card he or she wanted us to pray about. By keeping them involved in the process, we maintained their interest in our prayer time. We made sure we did not pray long, overwhelming thoughts but only simple requests.

Some of the items the children wanted prayer about would not be worthy of including in Scripture, but they were of importance to them. Freddie brought up little preschool requests, and we never said, "That's not worth praying about," even though we may have thought it at the time.

One request was for Erica and Valerie's behavior. We wrote this on the School Friends card, and when Freddie prayed that night he said, "Dear God, forgive Erica for lying, and forgive Valerie for tattling, for if Valerie hadn't tattled, nobody woulda knowed that Erica lied."

As prayers were answered, we recorded the date. Although God doesn't need records of our little petitions, we needed to see results to teach our children that God does respond. As we saw answers, we thanked the Lord for these blessings, and later we added the steps of confession and praise.

For us the prayer card system achieved the goal of teaching our children that God hears and answers prayer. An unexpected benefit was the discipline I learned in having dinner ready on time and that Fred learned in making himself come home each night consistently on time; we didn't realize how much the children needed to have this new stability from their parents. Another plus was that they knew dinner was waiting and, therefore, our prayer meeting wouldn't go on forever. This removed the fear of endless, pious platitudes from parents that so often keeps young people from wanting to participate in family devotions. Keeping the children active in the requests and in the selection of the nightly prayer card gave them a feeling of control and saved them from dreading our prayer time. They were never bored, and as adults they now know and use the power of prayer.

## FAMILIES WHO PRAY TOGETHER...

We asked several of our friends what they've done to make family devotions interesting and meaningful. The following is a sampling of the answers we received.

Sally, a single parent, wrote, "When school began last year, we started a new schedule, which has helped get our day off to a good start. I get up at six, have some quiet time, and wake the children up at six thirty. By seven, everyone is to be dressed, beds made, and in the kitchen for breakfast. We all sit down together and talk about our upcoming day. Then we pray for specific events or people we'll be facing (tests, problems with friend or teachers, schedules to be met, and so forth). We keep a notebook, so the next day we can see how God answered the day before. This has been a good way for our family to see that God cares for every need and how he works in our lives. Anytime they want to mark off an answer, the prayer book is in easy reach."

Darrell wrote from Pennsylvania, "We have devotions at the same time Monday through Friday. My wife and I have found the consistency and discipline of it to be a positive influence on our children. Our devotions are not long, drawn-out discourses, but short readings—sometimes only two or three verses of Scripture—with an emphasis on how we can apply the truth in our lives. And in our prayer time, we express our sincere and deepest feelings to God."

Mike told me he said to his four-year-old, Joshua, "You, Joshua, have to learn to obey your parents when you're small so that when you become older and Jesus talks to you, you will know to listen to him and obey him."

It's never too early to train a child to hear God's voice. As we make prayer a part of everyday life, we show our children that prayer is a normal function like eating and not just a boring religious ritual.

Betty and Greg gave me some thoughts on how they taught their children to pray. "One of the ways we encouraged our three children, even as toddlers, to have a 'God orientation' in their everyday lives was to involve them in the prayer requests that frequently came into our home. Whenever we received a prayer request via the phone or in person, we gathered everyone and immediately prayed about the need. The children accepted this as a part of everyday life, so when a family crisis occurred, our natural response was to gather in the living room and cry and pray together. When an eleven-year-old cousin drowned, God became our comfort as we came together in this way. Answers to prayer were treated in the same way with praises given to God."

We all know that our children grow up reflecting what they have seen in us, for we serve as daily examples. If you want your children to pray and believe in God, make sure they see you living what you're teaching.

Jan and Don recall what they did when their two daughters were young to instill Christian principles into their little

## AN EVERLASTING LEGACY

Read Hebrews 11, the "Hall of Faith."
- Pick one or two of the people listed and study their stories in depth.
- Was faith ever difficult for them?
- Did they ever sin?
- What did simple faith help them to accomplish?
- Do you think they were confident about the outcome of the events mentioned in Hebrews?
- How does this passage define faith? How did the person or people you chose live this definition out?
- Is there a particular area of your life where God is asking you to have faith? How will you answer him?

girls' lives and to teach them Bible verses and hymns. They instituted a method of prayer for the family. They all sat on the floor and prayed that God would speak to each one of them. After a period of silence Don closed in prayer. One day he noticed tears in six-year-old Heather's eyes. He asked what was wrong and the child replied, "You didn't give God enough time to talk to me."

At bedtime Jan sat down with Heather on the side of her bed and prayed again that God would speak to her. They waited quietly, and after a while Heather lifted her head with a smile.

"Did God speak to you?" Jan asked.

"Yes," Heather said softly.

"What did he say?"

"He said, 'I love you.'"

What a lesson for a little child to be helped by her parents to hear the voice of God and know God loves her.

As I considered these stories from my friends, I was struck by how important a parent's influence can be. Our responsibility—our privilege—is to train our children in the Christian faith. While the examples shared above offer some creative ideas, the stories that follow remind me that the influence of a parent or family member on a child's spiritual life can be a powerful thing.

## HERITAGE OF FAITH BY RUTH E. CROW

Saying, "I love you, Mother," no longer brings a response when I visit her in the nursing home now that ten years have passed since her Alzheimer's diagnosis. She doesn't sing or speak anymore. However, the heritage of faith she and my dad passed on continues. So many beliefs I hold dear and now have shared with the next generation began with the faithfulness of my parents.

According to my mother, I started going to the church I currently attend nine months before I was born. Mother's attitude about going to church is engraved deep inside me. She always insisted that going to church was an opportunity and not something to dread. If I was too sick to attend church, then I was too sick to play or even watch television. In fact, I had nine years of (almost) perfect Sunday school attendance. The only problem was that I could not seem to sit still and be quiet while Miss Emerson told the Bible story.

An important part of the legacy I cherish is a love for the music that moves my soul. For me, music was a significant part of learning to understand God and his plan for me. I spent many hours waiting for Mother while she participated in the adult choir practice, and I can still hear her singing louder than anyone in the choir.

It always seemed to me that the piano would walk and talk when Memaw Burns played "When the Roll Is Called Up Yonder." The songs and Bible stories inspired my questions about heaven and how to know Jesus as my Savior. My parents made sure I found the answers. I learned that Jesus loves me and died to provide forgiveness for what I have done wrong. At an early age with limited understanding, I prayed and asked Jesus to forgive me and become my Savior.

Returning to live in my hometown and attending the church of my childhood has motivated me to assess my parents' legacy. And I strive to share my cherished past, blessed present, and hopeful future with my children and grandchildren. Although my dad has passed away and my mother can no longer speak or sing, their legacy continues as it is shared with future generations.

## AT MY KNEE BY SANDRA SCHOGER FOSTER

When our sweet daughter, Kristin, was born in 1966, my husband, Ray, and I were of course delighted. One evening we were hovering over her and saw her first smile. Suddenly I wondered, *Will she choose to accept Christ as her personal Savior and Lord and live for him all her life? And what if she doesn't?* I had heard distraught older women at church talking about their teenagers who weren't walking with the Lord. I'd hear them say, "I don't know if my child ever accepted Christ." I determined right then that I would give our children plenty of opportunities to accept Jesus into their hearts at my knee. I didn't ever want to wonder.

When Kristin was three years old, she showed me a picture of Jesus knocking on a door that she had colored in Sunday school. Under it were the words "Open your heart and let him come in." We talked about what it meant for Jesus to knock on our heart's door and for us to let him in. She said, "I want to let Jesus in my heart, Mommy." I was thrilled when she prayed and asked Jesus to be her Savior.

In 1969, we welcomed our son, Bradley, into the world. One evening as we three cuddled him, Kristin looked at us and asked, "Is this boy a Christian?" We wanted to laugh because it was so cute, but we sensed her sincerity. "We hope he will be someday," we told her. "Let's pray and ask Jesus to *make him* be one," she said forcefully. She prayed for him and we did too.

One Sunday evening, when Bradley was four years old, we watched a movie at church. It started with the birth of Christ, then went into his ministry, his death on the cross, and his resurrection. The next morning our son crawled into our bed saying nothing and looking upset. I sat up, gathered him in my arms, and asked what was wrong. He asked, "Did that really happen to Jesus like in the movie, and did he really do it for me?" We talked about it, and he said he wanted to ask Jesus into his heart and then did so without hesitation.

Whew! My highest goal had been achieved, and both were safely in the fold along with me, Ray, and other family members.

Throughout their growing up years both kids loved Jesus and

I visited my sister-in-law, Katie, just weeks before she died of cancer. She was in acute pain, and yet each day she wrote in a book she had titled her "blessings." If she received a call, a visit, a flower, a gift, or a grandchild's picture, she wrote it down as that day's blessing. She had an uncanny faith as she prepared to meet her Maker. Instead of focusing on her pain, she recorded her blessings.

Her family now has the written legacy of this mother's ability to trust the Lord and rejoice in her blessings during adverse circumstances.

wanted to attend Sunday school, church, and youth activities. I watched them, sometimes holding my breath at the antics of the young, but I always knew they had anchored their souls in Jesus' nail-scarred hands. Ray and I shared our faith with them at home and talked about what the Lord had done for us in general family conversations and in individual discussions. Praying together over concerns made us grow closer. We prayed for our children continually, and for the person they might meet someday and marry.

Kristin and Bradley are still strong Christians today, and their spouses are as well. They have families of their own and are active in their local church. They have carried on the legacy and watched for those special moments that might give them the opportunity to be the ones to lead their children to the Lord when their little hearts were tender. They won't have to wonder if their children ever accepted Christ as their Savior.

Yes, there were shouting matches, slamming doors, groundings, tears, and hugs. We had misunderstandings and ups and downs just like anyone else, but we got through them with God's grace and help. I trusted God to do what we couldn't do as parents, and always remembered the special life-changing time when they came to faith in Christ at my knee.

## FOOTPRINTS OF FAITH BY WENDY LAWTON

Who would have guessed from looking at the water-stained pasteboard box that it contained a priceless treasure? As I examined the faded family photographs, a brittle piece of lined paper dropped to the floor. The script was faint, but I read the words of her handwritten prayer: "This day, July 10, 1912, I hereby sign and give my son Robert over to the Lord, for the Lord to redeem his soul from sin and to make him an earnest Christian...." Suddenly, a shared faith connected me to a great-grandmother I had never met.

I had discovered something more valuable than gold—a footprint of faith in a family that had seemed singularly godless. My father faintly remembered his grandmother, Elizabeth McKelvey Coats, as a godly woman, but this scrap of paper confirmed it.

Elizabeth Coats was a woman of vibrant faith. Her prayer, committing her thirty-five-year-old son into the hands of the Lord, communicated a vital witness. The act of relinquishment and the faith that it embodies speaks across the years. My great-uncle Robert chose to live his life without acknowledging the God of his mother. Indeed, each of Elizabeth Coats' children fell away from the Lord. But God honors prayer in ways we often don't expect, and he honored my great-grandmother's prayer on behalf of generations she never met.

My grandmother, Elizabeth Coats' youngest daughter, married into a Jewish family, and my father was raised with one foot in the synagogue and the other in nominal Protestantism. He ultimately chose neither.

As I was growing up, my mother faithfully took my brother, sisters, and me to Sunday school and church even though my father didn't attend. One Sunday, when she couldn't go, my father dropped us off. That morning I heard the plan of salvation so clearly that at the age of seven, I asked Jesus to come into my heart. The Lord accepted that childlike request and the repentance that came with it. Our children's church leader asked me to stay after church to talk. My father, who had come to pick us up, patiently waited and afterward, listened to all I had to tell him. Three years later my father, Elizabeth Coats' beloved grandson, found Christ. He served the Lord with enthusiasm and energy for the remaining seven years of his life.

Years later when I found my great-grandmother's prayer, I affirmed a milestone on our family's spiritual journey. Just as the Jews of the Bible recalled God's faithfulness generation to generation, our family story reminds us that the Lord keeps renewing his covenant.

## FAITH OF OUR FATHERS BY LAUREN

I was a thirty-nine-year-old mother of three sons when, for some reason, I was lagging a few steps behind all my men as they climbed the front steps of the Pilgrim Church in Merrimac, Massachusetts. It was

### WHAT YOUR LIFE'S ALL ABOUT

Create a mission statement for your life.

Begin by considering the purposes God has for all of his children and for you individually.

Think through the various ways God has uniquely designed you. What gifts, talents, interests, and opportunities has he put in your life?

Determine the ways your unique design can be used to fulfill the purposes God has for you.

Create a mission statement based on what you have just discovered. It might read something like: I will use my technological skills to bring others closer to God and to assist them with their practical needs.

Finally, find a way to make this statement a part of your life. In the above example, it might be offering to help someone keep their computer maintained or running the projection system for the worship service.

a warm Sunday morning, and we were all in town for the MacDougall Family Reunion.

As I watched my husband and sons mount those steps, I was immediately awash in emotion. Those were the same steps my great-grandfather, James Ellis MacDougall, had faithfully climbed with his family for decades, Sunday after Sunday. Now on this day, some seventy years later and four generations past, his descendants were ascending those same steps to that same sanctuary to worship together.

Struggling to hold back tears, I took my place in the choir and prepared to sing the opening hymn. I only got through the first three notes before I could sing no more. As we sang, "Faith of our fathers, living still..." I looked out over the congregation filled with my relatives, and realized that we were actually living the words of that hymn. The faith of my ancestors was "living still"! My great-grandfather was probably a common man, but I know he was a man of faith. The branches on our family tree have taken various spiritual paths, but I realized, sitting in that church on that day, our differences were insignificant. The single unifying factor was our acknowledgement of the saving grace of Jesus Christ our Lord.

That was a day of spiritual rebirth for me. I reflected on the sacrifices my husband's ancestors had made to experience the religious freedom found in this country. I pictured James MacDougall lagging behind for a moment as he watched his five daughters and son climbing the front steps of Pilgrim Church. I recounted the faith I saw lived out in his daughter's life, the impact his grandchildren had made in the world and surveyed the hope that lived in the faces of his great-great-grandchildren.

The faith of my great-grandfather was truly a "holy faith"! I pray that I "will be true to thee till death"!

## Forgiveness by Michelle Diercks

What do you do when your heart has broken and your dreams have shattered? Many people give up and choose a destructive path. That was not the case with my grandmother. Her husband left her and their young children to fend for themselves. It was during a time when divorce was not the norm, and people whispered about families who had suffered its devastation, often treating them like social pariahs.

Grandma raised her children to work hard and never give up. They survived on little, and how they managed to stretch the meager dollars she earned is a miracle from God.

Grandma also chose to forgive her husband and not to grow bitter. She chose the higher path, the road less traveled. Forgiveness is never easy, especially when you have been hurt so deeply. God gave her a forgiving heart and helped her to press on. A mother's love raised two wonderful children, who went on to marry and have children of their own.

A mother's love brought Grandma to family gatherings where she would have to be in the same room with the man who had betrayed her. She was kind, and because we were so young, we didn't understand how much that meant to our mother. How easy it would have been to stay away or to say angry things. Our family gatherings were peaceful; we were able to experience the love of both of our grandparents.

I learned a lot about forgiveness from my grandma and the way she lived her life. As I have grown older, I've realized that one of the greatest gifts I can give my children is to live in peace with family and friends. Life is too precious to spend it living with bitterness.

## SPIRITUAL BIRTHDAYS BY PAT THOMAS

While growing up, I struggled with feeling secure in my salvation for a number of years. I think one of the main reasons was that I heard so many preachers say, "If you can't remember the date and the time, you are not saved!"

No one told me to write down the date I had asked Jesus to be my Savior, so I didn't know, and that haunted me.

Finally settling that issue several years after I was married, I determined that my children would never go through that struggle. I had heard of celebrating your "spiritual birthday," and I thought it was a wonderful idea. Therefore, when each of my children came to know the Lord, I had them write down their testimony in their own words, including the date.

Oh, how precious those are to me today, written in their elementary words and childish handwriting, but so innocent and sincere from their little hearts.

Each year on their spiritual birthday, I gave them a gift and a card—something small—to help and encourage them on their spiritual journey. When my daughter married, her husband was amazed at this, and he, too, began to celebrate her spiritual birthday. It becomes a time of earthly celebration and spiritual renewal. What a joyous legacy!

## A LEGACY OF FAITH BY LOU WORKMAN SOUDERS

We called my grandmother Ma. She was tall, slim, and graceful. I loved being with her because she always had time for me and made me feel special. I remember her sitting in church wearing soft dresses, gloves, and beautiful hats. When I hear the old hymns, I picture her hanging clothes on the line or feeding the chickens, singing "Love Lifted Me" or "What a Friend We Have in Jesus." While I was growing up, she was the only person I knew who wrote in her Bible. She lived a godly life, and her love for her Lord was evident.

Recently, while moving my parents, who bought and remodeled her house years ago, I found some pages in Ma's handwriting tucked inside a Bible. They contained a prayer she had written:

*My prayer for all my children and grandchildren is that they will make the sixth chapter of Deuteronomy their lifeguard and prayer. Read a portion of it every day in prayer and meditation. Remember only one thing in this world counts—that is preparing for life eternal. Now these are the commandments, statutes and the judgments commanded to teach you. Fear the Lord thy God and keep all His commandments and statues and teach them diligently unto thy children. —Ma*

I am having this prayer copied for all of my cousins and brothers and our children. We were prayed for before we were even born!

## ABOVE ALL

There is no more important legacy to leave than a faith in God. The family heirlooms will break, Grandpa's love letter to Grandma will fall apart, and the Christmas trees will eventually end up in the trash. As much as these things are treasured, and rightly so, how much more valuable are the very souls of those we love? As family history is shared and preserved, it's important to pass along the thing that matters most: your relationship with Jesus Christ. As you read this chapter, I trust you've been inspired to share your faith with your loved ones. Teach your children about prayer and the other disciplines of the Christian life, show them what you believe through the way you live, and tell them the gospel story. There is no greater gift you can give.

# 11

# SEARCHING FOR UNTOLD STORIES
## FLORENCE

W hen I first wrote the outline of this book, I did not even think of this chapter. I was simply anxious to share the value of passing on a legacy. I wanted to share about the value of personal effects, pictures, furniture, and traditions. As I was putting together stories of my own life, however, I discovered a lost legacy.

Since childhood, I have known I had a brother who died, but I did not know any details; my mother wouldn't talk about him. I knew he was named after my father's brother, Arthur, but that was all Mother would say. By the time I was a senior in college and was old enough to be really curious, my father died. He *couldn't* tell me what Mother *wouldn't* tell me. Once I was married and had given birth to two brain-damaged sons who both died, my mother-in-law clearly stated, "There were no brain-damage problems on the Littauer side of the family." This comment meant the problems must have come from my side.

Was it my side? Did the death of my sons follow the pattern of my brother?

"What did Arthur die from?" I asked my mother. "What was it?"

"I don't know," she sighed. "The nurse came in one day and said, 'He's dead.'"

"Didn't you ask? Didn't you want to know?"

"Once he was dead, it didn't seem to matter why."

No matter how often I questioned my mother, the discussion always ended the same way: "It didn't seem to matter why."

Long after my mother died, with my brother's death still unexplained, I thought of asking my aunt Jean.

When I questioned her, she sat up straight on her chair and said, "Well!" Aunt Jean started every important sentence with a "Well!" It seemed to establish authority.

"Well, I've never told this to anyone before because your mother didn't want people to know."

"Know what?" I asked.

"How sick she was. She was consumptive you know." Aunt Jean liked to add insider information to any conversation.

I didn't know she had been consumptive. I was told she was in poor health when she got married. She'd weighed ninety-two pounds, and my father took her to the White Mountains for their honeymoon, where she "could breathe fresh air."

"Well, it all boiled down to your mother was too weak to have this baby, and he was too weak to live. They should have never had him in the first place." Her opinion was always strong, and in her mind, always right.

"Was there any diagnosis?" I asked.

"No. They told her from the beginning that he wasn't very strong, and when he was three days old, they told her he just died."

I wondered why my mother had been so secretive about Baby Arthur. There didn't seem to be anything disgraceful about the death.

"Why wouldn't she talk to me about him?" I asked. "There doesn't seem to be anything she could have done."

"Well, it wasn't the death. It was what happened afterward. You see, it was the Depression, and your father had no money for a funeral. You know our family has always been big on funerals and going to the cemetery on Memorial Day." I did know that visiting each grave and putting pots of geraniums by each stone was a yearly family ritual.

"What happened to the baby? What was the problem?"

"We had little Arthur brought to our local cemetery, but with no money for a plot, they just put him in a box and buried him in a pauper's grave."

"A pauper's grave? What's that?"

"It's the part of the cemetery where poor people are buried. We never let anyone know, but the whole family held it against your father that he couldn't provide a proper burial place for his son." I knew my mother's family had something against my father, but I never knew what it was.

"How did my mother take it?" I knew in my heart how my proper mother felt, but Aunt Jean was ready to talk.

"Well, she was mortified, and your grandmother was so humiliated. The family let her know that this incident was a blot on the

**TELLING THE UNTOLD STORY**

Consider carefully whether it is worth pressing into an issue that may be touchy for some family members.

List the reasons it might be beneficial to tell the story. Would it help answer medical questions? Would it help foster understanding among feuding family members?

Begin by talking with trusted family members who might have the full story. If they are unwilling to discuss the issue, find out if there is a point when they might share, such as upon the death of a family member involved in the untold story.

If your reason for asking is simply curiosity, try researching through public records and through other methods before risking family conflict.

MacDougall reputation in town." The MacDougalls had prided themselves on impeccable behavior. They were looked up to in the church, and Aunt Sadie, who made the rules, was the church organist and choir director.

No wonder I remember a sadness about my mother during my childhood. Now I had an explanation of why the family never seemed to accept my father. They had held a grudge against him for bringing shame to the family name. No wonder Mother could never talk about the death of her infant son. *"Why didn't the family buy a plot for him if it was such a problem?"* I wondered but didn't dare ask.

As I thought these revelations over, Aunt Jean added no touch of remorse for the family's behavior: "It was always hard for your mother to go to the cemetery on Memorial Day. She couldn't put flowers on little Arthur's grave because none of us knew where it was."

A few years ago, when I told this story to my brother Jim, he set out to find the grave. He went to the cemetery and talked to the caretaker who seemed as old as the cemetery itself.

Jim and I wanted to place a stone marker in memory of our brother, but the caretaker said, "You can't have a stone for the indigents when you don't really know where they are."

My grandparents are in that cemetery with a spacious plot and a granite tombstone. My mother and father are in an adjacent lot, my husband is next to them, and there's even a space for me. But somewhere in Pauper's Field in Locust Grove Cemetery, there's a box with no marker—only our memories of what should have been.

Aren't we grateful to know where they end up—in heaven with our Lord! My mother has a new strong body and is holding her baby who was just too weak to live.

## What Happened to John A.?

One day I told my daughter-in-law, Kristy, the story of Baby Arthur. "Do you have any untold stories from your family?" I asked.

"I don't think so," she replied. But then she suddenly had a thought. "There was my great-great-grandfather John A. McDonald."

"What happened to him?'

"He disappeared."

"Disappeared?" I asked. "Like Mary Poppins, into thin air?"

"That's the funny part," Kristy said. "Nobody knows."

"What *does* anyone know?"

"The family has his birth record from the state of Maine, a record of his marriage to my paternal great-great-grandmother, and information on his son Leslie Earl, and then there's nothing. It's as if he just blew away." Her eyes grew big as she thought of this family mystery.

"Has anyone ever tried to find what happened to John A.?"

"Oh yes," she replied, "and the answer is always the same. 'We just don't talk about it.'"

The family continued without the knowledge of John A.'s demise. From him came Leslie Earl, then Harry Alonzo, down to Kristy's father Robert McDonald, and then to Kristy herself.

"I didn't think I had an untold story," Kristy added thoughtfully, "but now that I have a daughter, I guess I'd like to know what happened to her great-great-great-grandfather John A. I'd just like to clean up the family record, but what should I do?"

What should she do? Will she ever know?

## Tell Me the Story

When I decided to share the story of Baby Arthur, Marita sent out an

## TELLING WITH TACT

Ask God for wisdom regarding how to handle sensitive information.

It may be best to remain discreet regarding who the story is told to.

Consider writing it down in the family history, but not sharing it publicly. The information is preserved, and family harmony may be too.

At times, the difficult issues in our families can be used to show the power of God to bring us through—or out of—difficult situations. The stories can also be used as warnings against sin or illustrations of a life without God.

e-mail asking if anyone else had any untold stories in their life. We received several examples. I found many families have secrets, things they never wanted to tell, but as the aunts and others age, they seem to be eager to leave a lasting legacy. If you ask, they might be glad to tell the family's untold stories. The following examples tell tales of secret siblings and starched shirts, of outlaws and in-laws. Enjoy!

## SECRET SIBLINGS BY PAMELA SONNENMOSER

The summer of 1977 seemed as perfect as any Southern California summer could have been. My little brother and I spent endless days at the beach near our home, rode our bikes down freshly paved streets in our subdivision, and walked to Thrifty's Drugstore for double-scoop rocky road ice cream cones. I was ten; my brother, Robbie, was six. I loved being the oldest. Robbie thought I could do anything. He was right. I could run faster, ride farther, and bake better easy-bake cakes than any big sister on the block. After all, I was the oldest.

The Fourth of July was about to burst into a spectacular celebration when my mother began reminiscing about a fireworks stand she and my dad owned the year I was born. That was *way* back in Missouri. She was nine months pregnant with me and tripped over a guide wire from the tent. Laughing at the thought of a *very* pregnant lady toppling head over heels, she pointed to a scar still evident on her shin. Still laughing, she spoke the words that changed our life. She said, "Larry was so worried about his baby sister or brother; I think the next few weeks of waiting were harder on him than they were on Daddy and me."

As soon as the words were in the air, hanging thick and dangerous, no one willing to grab at their meaning, she wished she could take them back. Robbie didn't notice. But I did. Who was Larry? I desperately wanted to know. After all, I was the oldest. Or was I?

Mother's shooing us into the yard to check the temperature of chilling watermelon didn't stop my curiosity. I was about to burst when Daddy came out and asked me to help him get chairs from the garage. He pulled out two folding lawn chairs and put them face-to-face. We were about to have our first serious father-to-daughter talk.

Daddy told me that day that Mommy wasn't the first lady he married. He had been married two times before he met my mom. He told me he wasn't a very good dad back then and that he was so happy he met Jesus before he met Mommy. After I was born, his ex-wife didn't want him seeing his other kids. He said it was complicated and that it wasn't really her fault either. But it hurt him so much that they left Missouri and moved to California when I was eleven months old. They hadn't spoken to any of his other children in nine years. I couldn't imagine not seeing my dad for nine days, much less nine years.

Still the only question on my mind was "Who is Larry?"

Daddy hung his head in sadness and regret. "Larry is one of your big brothers. He lived with your mom and me when you were born." He couldn't stop himself now that the secret had been exposed. "You have six half brothers and three half sisters."

I sat still, trying unsuccessfully to fight back the tears that were stinging my sun-kissed face. "Where do they live? What do they look like? What are their names?"

My ten-year-old mind spun as I fired question after question at my broken and saddened father. My dad spoke quietly. "I'm so sorry you don't know them. I love you and Robbie, and I love my other kids. Please forgive me, sweetheart; you deserve to know who they are."

As my confusion changed to compassion, I reached around my daddy's strong neck and hugged him tightly. I didn't understand all I had just heard, but I knew my daddy loved me. It was not just the Fourth of July, it was "Independence Day" for him. In telling me the secrets, he'd been set free.

Company would be arriving soon for hot dogs, watermelon, and fireworks, so we took the chairs to the backyard and set up the picnic table near the grill. Mommy and Robbie carried out supplies and condiments. The other siblings weren't mentioned again that night.

There was so much mystery revealed throughout the rest of that memorable summer. Daddy found his already-adult children from his second marriage. His son and daughter from the first marriage seemed to have vanished without a trace. No one knew where they had gone.

Robbie and I instantly loved our new brothers and sisters and lingered over every picture they sent. We found out we had nieces and nephews our ages. Daddy shared stories about his life when his other families were growing up and told us he wished he had known Jesus then. Incredibly, we found out later that each of them had met Jesus (and much later we learned their families had as well).

Years later, as my dad was dying of cancer, he received a phone call from Kenneth, his firstborn son. It had been almost twenty years since I'd found out I had brothers and sisters. Daddy talked to him for more than an hour. Then he handed me the phone. Kenneth and I talked and laughed as if we had known one another our whole lives. When he told me he was proud to know me, I had to fight back the hot tears stinging my eyes. He was proud of his little sister. I was so happy. After all, he was the oldest.

I'm happy to know where each of my brothers and sisters live. I know that I was born on my oldest sister's twenty-first birthday. I know that one of my brothers is a missionary in South America. We exchange Christmas cards and email. I have only met two of them in person, but I am happy to know that if I don't meet the rest here on earth, I will meet them in heaven. You see, even when our earthly father was lost in confusion, our heavenly Father had his eyes on each of my secret siblings.

## A TIMELY SURPRISE BY LINDA J. GILDEN

Growing up, one of my favorite Christmas traditions was carefully placing Mama's cross-stitched tablecloth on our dining room table. After being folded all year, the cloth was a checkerboard of lines that passed through holly leaves and bright red poinsettias. After running to wash our hands in the kitchen, we gently finger-pressed each crease and smoothed every little pouch and wrinkle. No one dared put an iron on this old cloth for fear it would disintegrate.

Mama knew how much my sister and I loved that tablecloth. So one recent summer when she and Daddy went on a trip, she found a sewing shop that sold similar cross-stitch tablecloth kits. Mama bought my sister and me our very own Christmas tablecloth kits so we could create our own special holiday linens.

We were both so excited! Not being a very enthusiastic seamstress, however, I stored mine in the closet until I was mentally ready to undertake such a task. I liked cross-stitching but had done very little of it since my children were born. And after all, it was only the summer… there was lots of time until Christmas.

Time passed quickly, and I suddenly realized if I was going to complete the tablecloth by the holidays I would have to start right away. After all, I knew exactly where it was… or did I?

When I didn't see the kit, I began pulling things off the closet shelves. I looked at all the piles around me, a chronicle of many years as a pack rat: The wooden "little people," honored with individual names during the years my children played with them, now still and silent in a blue plastic bucket. Framed pictures dating back to my mother's first dance recital, stacked and divided by frayed beach towels. Old 78 albums that once prompted my children to say, "Mom, these are awfully big CDs." Broken telephones and appliances that had challenged my son as he took them apart, confident they would be good as new when he put them back together. My daughter's Garfield collection, patiently resting in its marked plastic box, waiting its turn for display again. But nothing that even remotely resembled my tablecloth kit!

I'm the one in the family with the reputation of being Miss I-Can't-Keep-Up-with-Anything. Would I have to confess that the tablecloth had joined the ranks of the unaccounted for at my house? How could I be so careless with something destined to be handed down from generation to generation?

My sister had finished her tablecloth long before, despite being a full-time medical student. She has always been an overachiever and adept at multi-tasking. Several times when I had visited her apartment, she stitched while we caught up on the news.

For a while I could just say I'd been too busy to think about sewing.

But my deadline was awfully close, and I couldn't even find the table-cloth to get started.

Several more trips to the closet yielded no better results. I even invited a friend to come over and help with the search, but the table-cloth could not be found.

Fearing they would ask, I practiced my speech about what happened to it over and over in my mind. I tried several excuses that shifted the blame from me onto others—even the dog! But I really didn't want to lie. I finally decided the best approach was simply to say I hadn't had time to do it (which was true) and had put it in a safe place (I didn't have to say it was so safe that even *I* couldn't find it!). I didn't want to let on that I didn't know where it was—I knew I would find it before another Christmas season arrived.

Despite frequently visiting my house during the holidays, neither Mama nor Sister acknowledged the obvious absence of the new, cross-stitched tablecloth from my dining room table. When passing through the room, they just commented on how pretty the table looked. To my relief, I never had to use my carefully rehearsed answer to the dreaded question "Where's your new tablecloth?"

On Christmas Eve, the entire family gathered as usual at Mama's house. First, we came to the table for vegetable soup and the reading

### CAREFULLY CLEANING CLOSETS

Create a list of stories that have been left untold.

Compose a corresponding list of why you want the information and determine the importance of obtaining it.

Note the people who might know the story or the places where more insights might be available.

Some stories are exciting and fun, but just not shared. Others may be painful to those involved. Take time to think things through before charging ahead to get information.

Always proceed with love.

of the Christmas story. Then we moved into the living room around the Christmas tree.

Christmas was always Mama's favorite time of the year and it was not unusual for her ninety-eight-pound, type-A frame to be bouncing! But for some reason, this year she was really enthusiastic as we gathered beside the tree.

Our usual method was for the youngest child or grandchild to sort the presents. This took a while, so we sang carols as we waited. Then we began opening gifts together. Of course, the children and Mama always finished unwrapping their stack of presents first, no matter how orderly the process began.

But that year, as soon as we settled into our spots on the furniture and floor, Mama and Sister started whispering. They waited excitedly for the presents to be delivered to the intended recipients.

When that was done, they jumped up, grabbed one of the largest presents in my pile, and said, "This one! We want you to open this one first! Hurry up! Don't anyone open a gift until Linda opens this one. C'mon, Linda, open this one first!"

This was a little out of the ordinary, but they were so excited I obliged.

Carefully breaking the ribbon and tearing the paper, I teased them by taking my time.

"Oh, for goodness' sake, just open it," Sister said.

Finally, still puzzled by their enthusiasm, I exposed the box and lifted the lid. And there it was! My tablecloth! Each stitch perfectly crossed and each little rhinestone lovingly sewn in the middle of every poinsettia. My tablecloth!

A tear rolled down my cheek as I realized how much time and love had gone into this gift. Sister had finished hers and then stitched mine.

Mother added green stems and sewed rhinestones. On top of that, they kept the secret for months.

My tablecloth! My very own treasure, an heirloom for my children to one day enjoy.

All that work searching for the tablecloth and all along my mother and sister had snitched it out of my closet when I wasn't home so they could work on it! My friend even knew where it was and helped them get it. Then she dutifully helped me unload that closet two or three times as I searched for it, even though she knew it wasn't there! And it was no small closet!

Now when December rolls around, my children and I are the ones who carefully unfold the Christmas tablecloth, finger pressing and smoothing as we go. Not only is my tablecloth beautiful, it is a lovely reminder of a Christmas when one of my greatest frustrations yielded a precious, surprise gift of time from the best mama in the world and her accomplice, the best sister in the world!

Now, when Mama and Sister walk through my dining room during the holidays, they always grin and say, "Oh, what a beautiful tablecloth!"

And I wholeheartedly agree.

## THE RICHEST MAN IN MIDDLETOWN BY KAREN R. KILBY

He owned almost every penny in the state of Pennsylvania, all the tickets to ride the Tilt-a-Whirl, a roller skating rink, and his very own shiny, bona fide Hamilton Beach soda fountain milkshake machine! Not only that, Uncle Don drove a Cadillac that would fly if you closed your eyes and didn't peek.

Every summer from the time I was eight years old until I was almost sixteen, I rode the Greyhound Bus from the Motor City of Detroit to Harrisburg, Pennsylvania, and spent the entire summer with Aunt Orpha and Uncle Don.

Uncle Don owned dozens of the penny weight machines found in just about every drugstore and movie house, the ones that told your fortune as well as your weight when you stepped up on the scale. Traveling with him through the hills and valleys of the countryside was an adventure as we stopped in all the small towns to collect the bounty that poured from those gigantic machines. Pennies from heaven fell every morning as he gently pitched them onto my bed to wake me up. I soon learned that the longer I snoozed, the more pennies I got to keep!

And, if that weren't enough to dazzle an impressionable child, he owned an amusement park and it was in his own backyard. Uncle Don owned acres of land that ran along the Swatara Creek on the outskirts of Middletown. Every summer people thronged to play bingo, ride the rides, or escape the heat with a boat ride or swim in the refreshing, cool waters of the creek.

Uncle Don set me up—at the ripe old age of eleven—in my first entrepreneurial venture by taking the prized milkshake machine from its esteemed place in the family kitchen to the refreshment stand in the park. There I flipped hamburgers and made the best milkshakes in town before anyone ever heard of McDonald's. At the end of the summer I went home $300 richer, money used to open my first savings account.

My sister, Kate, and I believed Uncle Don was the richest man around. But, of everything he owned, his most prized possessions—in our opinion—were the memories he shared that brought my father back to life for us. Daddy had been a salesman for a large paint manufacturing company. He traveled during the week and was home on weekends. On one of his trips, he became ill from food poisoning and died three months later, leaving my mother a widow with my three-year-old sister to care for and me on the way. Mother kept her feelings and memories hidden, not wanting to expose herself to the pain of his loss. She rarely talked about my father, and it didn't seem natural to ask.

Uncle Don, on the other hand, was brimming with stories of childhood antics with my father and their sister, Beryl, whom they loved to tease. My father, Coy, was the oldest. I learned he was the apple of his parents' eyes and much admired by his younger brother and sister. He ran track in high school, enjoyed golf and tennis, and was an accomplished horseman. His yearning to explore the world sent him on a freighter to China before he settled down to married life. He had a wonderful sense of humor that expressed itself in practical jokes and was a budding inventor. Best of all, Uncle Don repeatedly showed me and told me how much my father would have loved me.

My father's legacy continues in countless ways. Kate has become quite the world traveler. My youngest son, Keith, inherited my father's build. My son Michael resembles the portrait in the family gallery. My oldest son, Kurt, is the avid golfer; my daughter, Susan, has recently discovered her love of tennis; and my grandson Tyler's favorite sport is track. What a joy it is to see my father's life celebrated through our children.

## OF OUTLAWS AND SIX SHOOTERS BY LARISEE LYNN STEVENS

Because I had taken a two-week vacation from work to be with Daddy when my mother died, it fell to me to clean out Mother's things and, at Daddy's request, give them to various family members according to the list she had made.

I always knew my daddy had a hunting rifle, but as I searched the closets for the items on mother's list, I came across an old gun—a cowboy-style six-shooter. My first thought was that it had been my mother's father's gun because he had been a U.S. marshal. He did his best to keep law and order at the great Land Run of 1889 that opened Oklahoma Territory to the white man. He was half Choctaw, and his family had come over the Trail of Tears. His grandmother was sister to one of the great chiefs of the nation. Oh, Mother had told me many stories of her family, but I had never heard one about a six-shooter.

"Daddy, do you know anything about this old six-shooter I found in the box up in the closet?"

"Yeah. That was Clyde Barrow's gun. My dad took it from him."

"*The* Clyde Barrow of Bonnie and Clyde fame?" I asked incredulously. My father's parents died before I was born, and my daddy never talked about his family.

"How on earth did your father take Clyde Barrow's gun?" I couldn't believe I'd never heard this story!

"Well, he was city marshal at Caddo [Oklahoma], and Bonnie and Clyde were on the lam. They were tracked and cornered in a shootout near Caddo. Daddy was the arresting marshal, and he took them to his jail and locked them up. He put Clyde's gun in his desk and locked it. When Bonnie and Clyde were busted out of jail by their fellow outlaws, Clyde just left his gun behind," Dad said.

I was astounded! Mother had told me many stories of her father chasing famous outlaws, but the only stories my Daddy ever told me about his childhood or his parents were about his one-room school and how his daddy was hit by a car and killed. I had always thought my grandfather was a farmer!

Daddy passed away two years after Mother. We children went through his papers and found several letters written by my grandfather to the family, and one official letter on city stationery to the warden of a nearby prison inquiring about the upcoming release of a prisoner who would be on probation. My grandfather signed it with the title "City Marshal." Now I have proof of his position from the letters left behind, and I will always treasure the six-shooter from the infamous Bonnie and Clyde!

## THE LESSON OF FORTY-THREE SHIRTS BY LARISEE LYNN STEVENS

As a kid growing up, I found my mother was most willing to tell me family stories when she was ironing. Standing for hours using a hot iron made the task seem to take forever. Telling me stories helped to pass the time for her and gave me undivided attention from my mother and a sense of our family's history.

While I have six brothers and a sister, I came along as an "oops" twelve years after my nearest sibling. My sister was the last of my siblings to leave home; I was six years old at the time. Having a twenty-five-year span from my eldest brother to me has had its challenges and its rewards. While it's true I'm the youngest of eight children, I actually was raised as an only child with seven fathers and two mothers!

These brothers were raised during the tough years of the Depression, which I knew little about. After I got old enough to iron my own clothes, I discovered how much I hated to iron blouses. While complaining of how hard I thought ironing was, it occurred to me that as I was growing up, Daddy wore a long-sleeved white shirt six days a week and a blue one on Saturdays. Mother prided herself on Daddy's well-ironed, starched shirts. That put me to thinking about ironing for six boys. With Daddy's shirts taken into consideration, I did some quick math and figured Mom must have ironed forty-three shirts a week as the boys were growing up. In my eyes, that was cruel and unusual punishment!

One day some time later, as I watched Mom toil over Daddy's white shirts, I asked her if she indeed ironed forty-three shirts a week when my brothers were young, or if she made "the boys" (as she called them) each iron their own as she had made me do.

Laughing, she reminded me that "the boys" grew up during the Depression. They were lucky that Daddy had a job, but money was still very tight. She explained, "Each boy owned only two shirts: a yellow one and a blue one. Each morning I would wash (by hand on a scrub board) the clothes they wore the day before."

She continued. "Remember, your daddy worked very hard to house and feed us, and it was important to me that my boys not look needy to the community. To keep the shirts from seeming worn and faded, I had a secret little trick. Each time I washed the shirts, I added a little fabric dye to the final rinse water. Then when I starched and ironed each shirt, it looked like new."

I had never thought of that myself. As I listened to Mom, I recalled working in a five-and-dime store as a teen. People in the community who knew my brothers or who went to school with them would sometimes stop and inquire about them. They would usually tell me a story about themselves and my family, then comment on what clean, well-dressed, industrious, and well-mannered young men they had been growing up.

My mother's story was a piece of the puzzle of who I was. My family was not high profile in our town in the ways one usually thinks of community leaders, yet I knew I had a well-respected family name to live up to. It was then I understood the value of hard work, good manners, care in one's appearance and conduct, and what it meant to be from a "good" family. I also understood what my mother meant when she would say, "Being poor doesn't mean you need to be dirty or helpless." I had never been in want, but I understood for the first time that during the Depression, my family had been short on money, but not on dignity, ambition, or industriousness. They may have had only two shirts each, but they were wealthy in good manners, good character, and good repute. Isn't it amazing what a drop of dye can do?

## No-Nonsense Christmas

The "Lesson of the Forty-three Shirts" brought my (Florence's) mind back to the year my father bought my mother a new iron for Christmas. We had little money, and Dad knew my mother was constantly burning holes in his shirts because her old dented iron had no controls. When my mother opened up her one present that Christmas and saw it was an iron, she burst into tears.

As a child, I didn't understand why she didn't like an iron she really needed. My dad also was stunned by her reaction. Mom wouldn't say a word, but we opened the next few presents in silence. Our Christmas excitement was ruined.

That night after the store was closed and we children were all in bed, I heard my dad ask my mom, "Now Katie, what was all this fuss about?" Mom cried again. She hardly ever cried, so I sat up and listened.

"Are we so poor you couldn't buy me a real present?" my mother asked.

"I thought you'd like an iron that wouldn't burn," Dad said. "You've been complaining about the old iron for a long time. I thought you'd be happy with an iron."

"I was hoping for a real present this year," Mom sobbed. "Something soft and pretty, like maybe a blouse."

Dad told me later, "I'll never understand women. You buy them what they've been complaining about, and they cry for something they don't need."

From then on, Dad and I bought Mom's Christmas present together. We didn't consider what she needed; we just bought something impractical and pretty.

## DON'T FORGET ME by ROSE SWEET

I glanced at the calendar. The second anniversary of my mother's death was last week, and I had forgotten. There are some things in our lives we may choose to forget, those things that, when mentioned, can take a pleasant family gathering to the depths of sorrow and regret.

Mom was beautiful: tall, slender, and pale with rich henna hair and big green eyes. In the 1940s she was in her early twenties and the first female chemist to work for TWA in Kansas City, Missouri. Howard Hughes, her boss, asked her out to lunch once and said he'd call her later. He never did. She loved to tell that story and many other adventures—such as meeting Errol Flynn and other Hollywood types—including the one about the dashing mechanical engineer from California who swept her off her feet with a dozen red roses each week for a year. Mom's single life ended when she accepted the engineer's proposal, kissed her parents good-bye, and drove her Nash Rambler to California to marry Dad.

Life was a fairy tale for a few years: a new husband, a new home, and a *most* beautiful new baby (me). But "after every wedding comes a marriage," and for Mom and Dad at least, that meant more babies, bottles, and bills. Dad was away at work more than Mom could stand—she was frustrated being a stay-at-home mom—and I remember hearing some of their arguments. All I knew was that "money was tight right now" so Mom could not go out to lunch with her girlfriends as often as she did before. There was no doubt my parents deeply loved each other—even as a child I could see it in their eyes—but they didn't know how to resolve conflict. So, my dad chose to stay later at the office to avoid the heat, and Mom became bitter.

In the book of Hebrews, bitterness is described as something that takes root and grows, hurting you and poisoning those around you. That's what happened in our household. In between all the genuine good my parents did and the authentic love they showed us, there was an ever-present undercurrent of quiet anger. Our parents—two educated Christians—could not resolve their conflicts: Mom buried her frustration in intellectualism, and Dad stuffed himself with another piece of pie. Almost every week Mom raged at the boys, taking her anger at my dad out on them. The girls took turns receiving Mom's long, angry lectures or the hairbrush across our legs. Dad was rarely home, didn't know what was happening, and never seemed approachable. Our large, happy family was turning sour, and by the time we were all in our teens, we were scrambling over each other to get to the front door first and move away from home.

No one ever knows all the intimacies of their parents' marriage, but the fruit of it can never be hidden from the children. While we longed for our parents to be happy, none of us was able to help Mom and Dad overcome their distance. They had disappointed each other, but my mother's bitterness kept *all* of us away from her.

She had so much to give and to share, but no one could stand being around her for more than a few hours because she would criticize or condemn them. Thus, there were few holiday meals and no more Christmas visits.

As adults, my siblings and I matured and faced our own human weaknesses. One by one we went to Mom, sought her forgiveness for our own attitudes, and learned to love her just as she was. It still wasn't pleasant to be around her and visits were short. The older she grew and the more deeply enmeshed in her alcoholism she became, the more her bitterness showed on her once lovely face—corners of the mouth turned down, rheumy eyes tinged with arrogance, hands wrinkled and cold.

At the end of her life, our family traveled from around the state to be together. Like reunited members of the MS *Bounty*, we shared a tyrant mother whom we once had admired and longed to serve, a parent we'd been forced to defy in order to survive. It's not a warm and fuzzy bond, but one that nonetheless brought us together around her hospital bed. Was she aware she was dying? Did she know we loved her? Did she even care? Mom could talk but chose not to. She died withered, shrunken, and bitter to the end.

At her funeral, we tried the best we could to remember only the good, most of it from our early childhood. We laughed and celebrated the gift of her life without anyone bringing up the pain that had scarred us. I asked my sister, Barb, if she had seen any soft side of Mom at all in the last few years. She and I were the oldest and have the clearest memories of the early years when we had the "good" mom. Barb told me that a few weeks before Mom's death, Mom had suddenly grabbed Barb's hand and looked up into her face, pleading pitifully, "Please… don't forget me."

"That's all she said," Barb told me. "I was shocked. I assured her I would not and tried to soothe her. A second later she was her old self, kind of turned off and not available—like she'd never even said it."

While Mom's life is not a secret to those of us who lived with her, we will try to keep her downhill path away from the younger ones. The weakness of her life will remain an untold secret, and we will share the legacy of her early life of beauty and joy.

I am sad for such a life lost—a life that I can never forget but sometimes wish I could. Will your family forget you? Will they *want* to forget you? Or worse, will they have to forget you to escape painful memories?

Forgive, seek reconciliation, and forgive again. Don't let bitterness be your legacy.

## COMPLETING THE PICTURE

Take a minute to go call an older aunt or other elderly family member. Ask about the family secrets or untold stories. They may be as exciting as some of these, or they may simply be a piece of history. In either case, they are apt to be like finding a lost piece to a puzzle. Once it is slipped into place, it helps complete the picture of who we are and our place in the family.

# 12

# ADOPTION
## *Lauren*

*L*ove transcends genetics and genealogy. True love and affection bridges the biological gap created by adoption.

I was five years old when my six-month-old brother, Frederick Jerome Littauer III, was diagnosed with unexplainable brain damage. He would awaken in the middle of the night screaming and convulsing. My aunt Virginia recently reminded me that when she came to visit us and Freddie would awaken crying in the night, she would get up to tend to him so Mother could sleep, only to find me already at his crib rubbing his back, attempting to soothe him. Ultimately, Freddie needed continual medical care and was placed in a children's home where his needs could be met. He died a few days after his second birthday.

Mother gave birth to a second son, Larry, just before I turned seven. I doted on him, watched over him, and cared for him just as I had with Freddie III. Larry was only six months old when he was diagnosed with the same condition. I was devastated when he was placed in the same children's home a few months later. But I kept these hurts inside not wanting to add to my parents' heartache.

I was nine when my parents adopted my third brother. His foster mother called him Jeffery, so they named him Frederick Jeffery Littauer, giving him Dad's initials.

## MAKING A CHILD FEEL AT HOME

When a child is adopted into your heart and home:

Share adoption stories from the Bible with your child and explain the concept that God's children are adopted into his family.

Keep a journal of your long wait for the child.

Celebrate the day of official adoption with a small but special gift or an activity your child loves.

If the child was adopted from another culture, honor that culture in small ways such as in your decor, by learning about it, and by enjoying some if its cultural events.

Tell your child the story of his or her adoption with an emphasis on God's hand in bringing you together as a family.

I thought of Fred not only as a brother but also as my own flesh and blood. He was a part of me. The fact that his biology was different than mine played no part in the way I loved him. For the past forty years, I have been his cheerleader, confidante, protector, supporter, sounding board, and advisor. I look on him today with tremendous pride.

On September 9, 2002, Fred and his wife, Kristy, had their first child, Lianna Marita Littauer. What a joy it was to be standing in the hospital hall as they moved Lianna from delivery to the nursery and to get my first peek at my niece! Her birth was not without concern, and I was a nervous wreck. How thankful I was to hear that she would be fine.

A few weeks later, when I was visiting with Kristy and Lianna, I said to Kristy, "You know I couldn't love Fred more than I do, and I couldn't love Lianna any more if she were my own flesh and blood. But I have to admit, a little part of me is sad that she has nothing of me in her."

Kristy quickly and lovingly responded, "Oh, she has a lot of you in her! Everything you've poured into your brother is a part of who he is today, and that becomes a part of who Lianna is as well."

I am so thankful Kristy feels that their children will have a part of me in them. I'll treasure and hold those words close to my heart forever. Fred—and now his daughter—really are a part of me, regardless of biology.

I was talking about adoption and parenting with Fred one evening, and he commented, "Your parents are who tuck you in at night." Genetics has nothing to do with parenting. I know beyond any doubt that I could not love my adopted brother Fred more than I do. Adoption is a way to create a legacy of love.

## LEGACY DETERMINED BY CHOICE BY JOY HUSTON

I was so very flattered to be selected to train for my new career as a flight attendant—an "air hostess" in those days. Following graduation from the training school, I accepted the invitation to share an apartment with four other airline hostesses. I recalled all the appropriate memorized Scriptures to validate this decision: "With Christ all things are possible"; "I can do all things through Christ who strengthens me"; and perhaps the longest but certainly one of the first verses I completely memorized, from 1 Corinthians 10:13: "There hath no temptation taken you but such as is common to man, but God is faithful and will not let you be tempted above what ye are able but will with the temptation also make a way for you to escape that you may be able to bear it."

My upbringing as the eldest of four was with Christian parents and included regular church life and plenty of the usual Christian activities. The restrictions my parents put on us and their failure to live in the real world, however, were not qualities I chose to emulate when I became a parent. There was such control that my father even chose my first job for me!

But I did memorize Scripture, and I was finding it useful as I started living in an apartment with a few friends—this was a new situation for me. It was not long before I realized that I had no control over who entered our apartment. This was not just my home but also the home of my fellow air hostesses, and they had as much right to have their family and friends visit with us as I did.

My Christian friends visited, but increasingly more and more of my fellow residents' friends were hanging out. Upon returning home after a flight duty, I would come upon a party in full swing!

On one particular occasion I had been "grounded," medically unfit for flying with a middle ear infection and laryngitis so severe I could only whisper. Everyone else was on flying duty, and I was alone to answer the door to the apparent friend (someone who was passing through the city) of one of the girls, so I welcomed him to come in and wait for her to come home.

I returned to my bedroom and shut the door. Suddenly the door opened and the unknown man walked in. He sat at the end of my bed talking sweetly to me. When I asked him to leave, he threatened me with a sheath of glass and the sharpened hook from a coat hanger. I offered him my "pay packet" if he would just leave! Instead he came closer, and despite my resistance, pinned me down, told me, "You'll enjoy this!" and raped me. I tried to scream, but no sound would come out. He slapped me across the face, told me to tell no one, and grabbed my money on the way out the door. I ran to the bathroom and locked myself in, but it didn't matter. He was gone!

I was devastated and in pain. What could I do? I didn't even know his name. The shame came over me in waves as I tried to put this attack behind me. What worse thing could happen to a naive Christian girl?

A few weeks later, I found out what was worse—I was pregnant! What would I do? I couldn't go home; my father would kill me. The family would be so humiliated. What would the good church people think of us? But I had no other choice. I took a leave of absence, left this loose group of friends, and went home.

My mother was in a state of shock. Her first words were what I'd predicted, "What will people think of us?" Her concern was for her reputation, not for my pain and shame. "Your father will kill you. He will."

Mom wanted me to run away—anywhere—but I was frozen in that spot in the kitchen and couldn't move. "We'll get your brother, that's what we'll do. He's big and strong and he'll protect us from your father." When my brother arrived, I was still standing in that same spot—glued to the linoleum.

"How could you do this to us?" he screamed at me. "We can't let anyone know." My father burst in right then and headed straight for me with his fists already in knots. "I'll kill you, you slut!" My brother grabbed him and wrestled him to the floor as Mom and I both shrank back in horror.

My baby sister peeked out from her room, wide-eyed over the battle in the kitchen. Finally, my brother got him calmed down, but my father would not look at me. Instead he grabbed my mom, shook her, and said, "We can't let anyone know." Mom agreed and murmured, "What will people say? What will people say?" Here I stood in the midst of a family fight. No one looked at me, no one said they felt sorry for me; they just got to work on how to cover this up and save the family reputation.

Abortion was not a choice in those days, and the family wouldn't consider it even if it had been an option. Staying in town and letting people see me pregnant was an even worse choice. "Send her away," my father bellowed. "Get her out of town." My brother opted, "Give the baby away. Surely we don't want it." "Maybe a foreign country would be better," my mother added.

They all agreed I had presented them with a scandalous situation, and the faster they could dispose of me the better. No one asked how this happened. They refused to talk about it and just assumed the worst—whatever scenario considered by each one of them to be the worst.

I wasn't let out of the house lest someone see me, but Mom did help me make some larger dresses. Then she packed me up and said good-bye as if I were heading for prison.

When I got off the plane, there was no one to meet me, even though I had made arrangements with the "unwed mother welfare agency." I checked into a nearby motel for the night and went to the agency office the next morning. They assigned me to wash pots in the agency kitchen. Once I was given a caseworker, he decided to make me into a "mother's helper." His wife, a former English teacher, was bedridden, and he needed help caring for his little daughters, two-year-old Rebecca and six-week-old Deborah. Suddenly I was a mother of two and beginning to wonder how I would feel as a real mother.

I fell in love with these little girls, and I desired right then to have my own little girl that I could keep and name Rebecca—all the time knowing I was to proceed with the adoption of the child I was carrying. I was deeply aware of how much I loved this unknown baby. I concluded that my primary responsibility was to love and nurture this wee one, pray for him or her, and take good care of myself right up until the adoption was formalized.

A short time prior to the birth I was transferred to a Christian residential home within the hospital facility and there met a Christian nurse-midwife who became my friend. She prayed with me and stood by me when I went into labor. I delivered a darling little baby girl whom I named Belinda. "Rebecca" was reserved for a baby I could keep in the future. My friend and I committed Belinda to the Lord as we prayed daily for her future.

Over the following two weeks I would go to the nursery and care for her by giving her the bottle and holding her close. All the time I had such a peace because I knew beyond any doubt my decision to make Belinda available to her new parents was God's plan for both of us.

I received a letter from my mother advising me that my father was not well. So after Belinda's adoption was finalized, I returned to my parents' home. I also returned to my airline position and resumed flying duties. Shortly thereafter, I was promoted to in-flight training of other flight attendants. This time I was not only based in my hometown but living in an apartment with Christian girls.

Everywhere we went in uniform we drew attention, and when I entered a Christian gathering on my way home from duty one evening, the young man leading the singing didn't just notice me, he

**A TIP TO REMEMBER**

Allow your adopted child to feel a part of your family history. He may be curious about his birth family, and you'll need to decide when and how much he should know. However, ensure the child knows that your heritage *is* his heritage. Focusing on sharing your legacy with your adopted child is a beautiful way to say that he or she is truly a full part of your family and home.

asked me out. He was a fine Christian leader and within a few months we were married. My family was so relieved!

In the years of our marriage we have produced four children—the first a beautiful daughter whom we named Rebecca. As a special blessing for my husband, she was the first girl in his family for three generations!

This is the husband and family that was God's plan for my life, and I've been amazed at how God has kept my heart free from anguish and regret of the choice I made and committed to him such a long time ago. I know I would not have been able to function as a wife and mother needs to if I had continued to bear guilt and shame. At times as I recalled little Belinda, I'd ask my husband to hold me while we prayed for her.

A number of years ago, when the laws changed, I decided to let the adoption authorities know where she could contact me if she wanted to. I was supplied with copies of her original birth certificate and also an amended one, which provided the details of her adoptive family, including Belinda's new name: Melissa.

Recently, I decided to look at the Internet white pages for her adoptive parents' whereabouts. Incredibly, the only name listed that was an exact match was her adoptive father! He was a delight to speak with and quickly volunteered their family situation and their daughter's family details and whereabouts as well. He assured me he would be seeing her in a couple of days and would give her my information.

Two weeks later the phone rang and a beautiful voice announced, "This is Melissa." As we talked, she told me that a month before she had been praying for me too. How perfectly our God facilitates these vital encounters in our lives! And what a joy it is to know she gave her heart to Jesus when she was eleven years old, is now married to a man of God, and has five children between ten years and ten months. She is home schooling them and leading a women's Bible study group.

Melissa and I have shared many long chats on the phone and even her ten-year-old son asked to talk with me. He even asked me to pray for him.

My father died thirty-four years ago, and in her ninety-third year, my mother has restored our relationship. On Mother's Day, I was able to tell her the wonderful news that she actually has another five great-grandchildren and that someday she will meet them in glory. Mine is a continuing story, but certainly a reminder that we can make difficult choices and trust God's perfect order and provision for our lives, for the Lord has given me an unexpected legacy.

## THE ACCEPTING GRANDMOTHER BY ANGIE GARRETT

When my mother was just twenty-one years old, her husband was tragically killed in a car accident. She was left alone to care for their fifteen-month-old son, David. She had no idea how she would raise him by herself in a time when very few mothers were in the work-force, and it wasn't long before she began searching for another man who would be willing to love both her and her son.

Nine months after her first husband's funeral, Mom met my father. They were soon engaged. My grandmother's first comment on hearing that her oldest child was marrying a woman who already had a son was "Oh, goody! I get to be a grandmother!" She was not resentful that she had not been around for his birth or the first two years of his life. My father's commitment to raise David as his own was enough for her. Grandma simply accepted my brother as fully as if he were really her blood relative. Over the years she proudly introduced him to friends as the oldest of her five grandchildren.

**A KEEPSAKE FROM YOUR HEART**

Create a journal about the adoption for your child to read when she is an adult. Include, among other things:

All the events leading up to and surrounding the adoption.

How you felt when you got the news that your child was available and on the day that things became "official."

Letters to your child. One should express your feelings about her being a part of your family. Others might be written during important life events affirming your love and sharing the positive things you see she brings to your life and home. Include moments when parenting her was a particular joy and a few of the ways your love may have been expressed during the difficult times.

Years passed, and as an adult David began dating a divorced woman who had a young daughter. Her father was rarely around and saw her only occasionally. When David decided to marry this woman, he accepted her daughter and agreed to raise her as his own. He figured that Dad had done it for him, so he could do the same for another child. My grandmother's first comment on hearing of the engagement was "Oh, goody! Now I get to be a great-grandmother!" To Grandma, the news that my brother officially adopted this child as his daughter after her birth father signed away rights was a mere technicality. She proudly accepted this new child as her own kin and tells everyone that she is the oldest of her five great-grandchildren.

Now this great-granddaughter is pregnant and expecting a daughter of her own. Grandma's first words when she heard this news were "Oh, goody! Now I get to be a great-great-grandmother!" I'm sure she'll one day proudly introduce this new little one as the oldest of her great-great-grandchildren. Maybe she'll have five of them.

## AMELIA'S STORY BY CHRISTY LARGENT

Her dark black eyes darted furtively from side to side as she scurried down the deserted alley. She paused to shiver in the frigid early morning mist as she stumbled down the uneven road. The solid metal front of each shop face seemed to stare inscrutably at her as she slipped past. The towering apartment buildings looming over the alley showed few lights at this early hour, so she felt less exposed than she had expected. Yet the fear was still there; the dread and the sorrow pressed in on her when she let her mind linger on the act she was about to perform.

She finally reached the bottom of the alley and looked up. Yes, there were the two red lanterns and the tall welcoming sign indicating this was the Fuling District Social Welfare Institute. This was the place. This was the reckoning spot. It seemed every sound was silenced as she gently placed the plain brown box marked "Fuling Pickles, Hot and Spicy" in front of the gate. The bundle in the box stirred. Gently she reached down and rearranged the green bunting for the hundredth time. Rags really, but it was all she had to keep her precious little bundle warm. In response to the movement, the eyes of the baby girl inside fluttered open, and her rosebud mouth emitted a tiny kittenish mewl.

The young woman shivered again at the enormity of what she was about to do. This was one of the last acts she would perform in this year of 2003, and it was the unthinkable. In just mere seconds she would have to do the hardest thing she had ever done in her life. Tears coursed down her round brown cheeks, and a few fell onto the face of the precious baby looking up at her. She knew it wasn't safe to linger, but the woman felt the fabric of her very soul tearing apart piece by piece as she began to move away. She dropped one last kiss on those sweet baby cheeks, inhaled for the last time the sweet baby smell, and she was gone. The darkness of the moment enveloped her as she slipped away into the shadows.

From her vantage point in the shadows she watched and waited. She contemplated the painful course of Chinese history that had brought her to this moment. She watched the box sitting in front of the gates of the Fuling District Social Welfare Institute and waited for someone to find it. The box held her greatest treasure, her very lifeblood and essence of being—her daughter. She could not keep this precious gift given by whomever it is that creates life, but she could be sure that the little innocent could have a chance at a life. She had heard that many foreigners—"Waiguoren" they were called—adopted babies from this place, and in her heart of hearts she hoped this would happen for her daughter, hoped some family could give her a full and happy life. A life like she saw on the TV. Maybe even an American couple would adopt this girl, and her flesh and blood would reap the riches of the golden country. Who knew? And so she waited to make sure the grizzled old guard who opened the gates promptly at six every morning would see the unassuming box. She waited to make sure he would look inside and find the precious bundle wrapped in green bunting. She hoped that someday, some way, the little baby would know how much she had loved her, and how much she wanted the best life for her.

This is the possible story of the events that transpired in the early morning on December 30, 2003 in the city of Fuling, China. I say possible, because we will never know the true story. You see, my daughter, Amelia AiYan, really was abandoned at the orphanage gates—no note, just wrapped in green bunting. My husband, Tom, and I adopted her from China on December 20, 2004. She became part of our family from that day forward.

The idea of being without family roots is a disconcerting thought. How do you work on a legacy when it all starts with you?

For our daughter, it means we will do everything in our power to recreate the first moments of her life. When we visited the Fuling District Social Welfare Institute (orphanage) we took lots of pictures of her hometown of Fuling and the surrounding countryside. Statistics tell us she is probably from the country and most likely from a family with one older sister, but we'll never know for sure. Establishing a legacy means we'll discuss all these issues and ideas, look at pictures, and create scenarios. We will travel back to the orphanage as she gets older and will explore her Chinese heritage. We are committed to making every effort—from learning the Chinese language to traveling to and maybe even living in China for a year or so—to show our Amelia her biological culture and meld it together with our American culture. Sometimes it even seems as though my Caucasian husband and I have become a bit Chinese during this whole evolvement of our family! Heritage and legacy definitely go both ways!

Although the background of Amelia's biological roots is limited indeed, we do know her spiritual roots. These spiritual roots are what we will stress and strengthen as the years go by. We know God allowed our infertility to bring us to the moment of adding Amelia to our family. We know our family has been designed by God to bring him the most glory, and of course we know God's plan is always perfect! I'm so thankful God chose Amelia for us. We think we are the most blessed parents on earth, and we're looking forward to sharing this legacy of the grace and providence of God with Amelia.

## AN ADOPTED HERITAGE

Is there anything about your legacy that relies on genetics? Not really.

A legacy is so much more than biological. It includes the values you share with others, the character traits you encourage, the talents you pass on, and the way you touched a life. An adopted child becomes part of your family and shares in your family's heritage. When you embrace him in your heart and bring him into your home, your legacy becomes his.

# 13

# CHILDLESS LEGACY
## ℳARITA

*I* feel like a proud mother eagle watching her chicks soar. At least, I guess this is how a mother might feel when her children do well. Never having given birth to children of my own, I can only assume. But I have given birth to the dreams of many.

Hardly a week goes by that I don't receive a book in the mail— a book that was written by someone I trained, nurtured, and encouraged through the CLASSeminar or the other events held by CLASServices Inc., which is designed to help launch speaking and writing ministries. With each book that arrives, usually with a thank you note, I smile and am filled with joy at these outward signs of their successes.

I've heard that the goal of parenting is to raise your children to no longer need you. Much like a mother bird cares for her chicks until they can fly, parents gently nudge their children out of the nest to fly off to their own lives.

These authors are like my children. Their success as they leave the nest makes me that proud mother bird. One of the most recent books to come across my desk is *The Prodigal Brother* by Sue Thompson. On the dedication page she wrote, "I am deeply grateful to CLASServices, Inc. for showing me the door and telling me how to walk through it."

In our offices, we have a bookcase full of books written by the graduates of our programs. Many of these books hold dedications or acknowledgments that are similar to the one Sue Thompson penned. Some do not. But it doesn't matter. Parents don't bear children to get credit for the work they do in raising them. They love them and rejoice in their achievements—even if their role in their children's success is never acknowledged. With each book that arrives in our offices, I am encouraged and know that what I'm doing is touching lives—more lives than I could touch on my own. This bookcase represents the legacy I'm leaving.

Novelist Gayle Roper has been on the teaching team of our ministry for more than ten years. While Gayle has always been a writer who speaks (I'm a speaker who writes), the Lord has been increasingly blessing her writing. She has won many awards and been nominated over and over for the Christys, the Academy Awards of the Christian fiction world. At the time of this writing, Gayle now has contracts for ten books, all of which are due within five years. When she told me this meant she had to resign from our team, I was sad, but I also rejoiced. The bird is flying from the nest. I celebrate her success with her.

I may not be a parent, but I can live my life in such a way that others are touched, that my fingerprints are being left on the lives of others. My students carry on my DNA: Development, Nurturance, and Achievement. I work to develop them, I nurture them, and I help them achieve. Whether you have children or you don't, I hope this book has inspired you to live your life focused on leaving a lasting legacy, even though you may never know the long-term impact of your efforts. Like a parent, we do not touch the lives of others for the accolades we may receive, but because we are called to live up to the legends.

Karen Kilby sent me the following testimony that shows that even those of us who are childless can shape a life, push others to greatness, and leave a lasting legacy.

## AN EVERLASTING LEGACY BY KAREN R. KILBY

"Why don't you write down the stories you've shared with me?" my friend Carol commented while visiting from Milwaukee.

I looked at her not quite believing what I'd heard. *What makes her think I could write something someone else would want to read?* I wondered. Telling someone what God had done in my life was one thing, but writing it down was another.

Carol continued talking as if my skeptical response had not registered. "Now that you're sharing your home with your daughter-in-law, Erin, you have a built-in mentor and editor—your own personal coach! Didn't you tell me Erin is an English and creative writing teacher and has had her own stories published? You really need to take advantage of what God has provided."

Just a few days before, Erin had made a similar comment. "I'll help you, Karen. I know you can do it."

Writing was something I never would have thought of doing. Yet, a verse from the Bible came to mind with Erin's initial encouragement. "Be very careful never to forget what you have seen God doing for you. May his miracles have a deep and permanent effect upon your lives. Tell your children and your grandchildren about the glorious miracles he did" (Deut. 4:9).

*Well,* I thought, *I like the idea of sharing the glorious miracles God has done in my life and passing them down to my children and grandchildren. Maybe I could put a collection of stories together in a notebook for them.*

As I sat at the computer, one story after another seemed to spill out over the keyboard. True to her word, Erin made suggestions and corrections, helping to bring each story to fruition.

"I think we need to send some of these essays out to publishers," Erin commented as we put the final touches on a story one day.

## A SINGULAR IMPACT

Watch a child on occasion for a couple that could use a night out alone.

Play games, such as basketball or Monopoly, with a friend or neighbor's child. Children need many positive adult influences.

Mentor a child, a teen, or even a younger adult in your career field.

Establish or assist in a community service or charity organization.

Pass along your gifts, skills, or talents to others by teaching them—formally or informally—what you do best.

*Who would I send them to?* I wondered. Then I remembered seeing a notice requesting stories for the *God's Way* book series in the weekly update Marita sends out from CLASServices. I had received some training from Florence and Marita and had been receiving the weekly update e-mails ever since. But having no desire whatsoever to become a writer, I only skimmed the "Writing Opportunities" section. With the push from my daughter-in-law, however, the memory of this posting came to the forefront of my mind. I went through my old e-mails and found the one with the request for stories.

Several months went by. Then one day as I checked my e-mail messages, there it was! "Your story, 'A Marriage Made in Heaven,' has been accepted for publication in *God's Way for Women*." I could hardly believe it! My story would be one of thirty-eight stories of women living a life of purpose God's way.

Erin and Carol were even more excited than I was. Giving me a hug, Erin said, "I love the art of writing, but you have a purpose larger than yourself. I'm blessed to be a part of the contribution."

When I called Carol to share the good news, she said, "I can't wait to see your own book for sale on the bookshelves!"

*Wait a minute!* I thought. *Here she goes again with another crazy idea. Who would want to buy my book? It's one thing to have a story included in a collection with other writers, but why would anyone want to buy a book of my stories? I'm not famous; I'm just an ordinary woman trusting an extraordinary God.*

"Maybe, just maybe," God seemed to say, "an ordinary woman just like you would want to read your book, hoping to discover how she, too, could become a woman of purpose trusting an extraordinary God."

As I wait to see the legacy of my book take place, I am continually blessed to see several of its stories published in other books. Wanting to leave an everlasting legacy to my family is important to me, but leaving an everlasting legacy to God's larger family is also important to him. Without the skills and encouragement Marita and Florence have poured into me, I wouldn't have dared develop these stories or even think that I might be able to write. Because of their investment in my life, I can say I'm a published writer—an achievement that's allowing me to write of the glorious miracles God has done in my life so my children and grandchildren can read them. These stories are an ongoing legacy.

## INSPIRING NEW LEGACIES

What a treat it is for me (Marita) to hear stories like Karen's. Even though I do not have children, I am leaving a lasting legacy. A legacy doesn't have to be from parent to child. It doesn't even have to be left to someone you know. Another Karen, Karen R. Power, was inspired to leave a lasting legacy in a different way. Like Karen Kilby, Karen Power attended our Personality Training Workshop. Like me, Karen Power does not have children, but she is not letting that prevent her from having a positive impact on the lives of others.

Here's what she wrote about her legacy.

## THE LEGACY BY KAREN R. POWER

As Florence addressed the class that first day, I couldn't help believing I was a part of something much larger than just a conference. I wasn't sure how big it was, but within the next three days I would begin to find out.

It was the first day of the Personality Trainers Workshop in December 2003. I was there to learn the "Personalities" from some of the best trainers in the industry—Florence and Marita Littauer. I had been teaching their material to the new hires at the company where I work and was looking forward to finally meeting them. I expected to learn some helpful information and see great teaching modeled; little did I know that I was about to embark on a life-changing experience. The milestone of becoming a Certified Personality Trainer would be secondary to a far broader purpose.

Florence said, "I'll share my experience and stories with you. As you grasp the concepts and continue to develop, you become 'my children.'" With that statement, I knew the "something bigger" was beginning to unfold and a deposit was being made into my life and the lives of the forty other participants.

During the next three days, we laughed, loved, cried, and learned with each other. Florence, Marita, and their staff truly invested their expertise into each of us. Still, they gave more—their love, concern, prayers, advice, counsel, encouragement, and support. Marita even offered the notes from her speech "Come As You Are" for us to use as we spoke to groups in the future. In my experience that was unheard of, unprecedented, and downright amazing!

In the months since, I've learned much more about CLASS, Florence, and Marita. I've learned that the organization goes beyond developing skilled communicators. At its heart is *ministry*—helping people find direction for their lives, healing for their wounded souls, encouragement to use their God-given gifts, and a network of believers who will support, pray for, and love each other.

When I learned Florence, Lauren, and Marita were working on this book, I finally grasped what I sensed beginning on that first day of that workshop: Florence's legacy continues into my legacy. As I have listened to their teaching and read their books, I've often thought, *What an awesome heritage Florence and Fred are going to leave behind for their daughters and son.* My challenge with that thought is that I'm single with no children. How can I leave a legacy?

Later when I had a chance to visit personally with Florence, I shared this whole idea with her. That's when the final piece of the "something bigger" came into place. A Christian legacy of giving for kingdom purposes falls into the kingdom's economy. It's about multiplication not addition. I had been thinking that it was me *plus* the lives that heard the message I was given to speak or write. By making a contribution to the CLASS Scholarship Fund, it multiplies exponentially: me plus the lives I touch multiplied by the recipient(s) of a scholarship and the lives they touch. God is now using me to work through multiple channels. Now that's legacy!

I've attended the CLASSeminar and the CLASS Reunion and plan to attend Upper CLASS in the future because God has made the funds available for me to do so. I know, however, that others are willing and ready to attend but need financial assistance. If I can be a part of sending one person to a training conference sponsored by CLASS and it changes only that one life, it's worth it. My legacy continues through every life that one person touches.

Jesus spoke to the multitudes, yet he touched one life at a time. His legacy continues with each story told, each book written, and each life changed. My legacy is to encourage others to be trained by CLASS so they may go out and teach others. As Paul wrote to Timothy, "And the [instructions] which you have heard from me along with many witnesses, transmit *and* entrust [as a deposit] to reliable *and* faithful men who will be competent *and* qualified to teach others also" (2 Tim. 2:2 AB).

## TOUCHING OTHER LIVES

I (Marita) have touched people through the training I offer, people like both Karens, who in turn touch others—Karen Kilby through her writing and Karen Power through her financial giving. But what if you're childless and not blessed financially as Karen Power is, and you don't want to be a speaker or writer as Karen Kilby is? How can you leave a legacy?

Look around you. Nearly every mother of young children I know would like a little break from time to time. Those of us without children of our own—or even those without children at home—can become like an aunt or uncle to the children of our friends.

*Giving Back* (1991) was my third book. It has long since gone out of print, but one of the ministry ideas presented in the book continues to bear fruit in my life. In the book, I highlighted the work of Colleen

Weeks, whom I met at one of our CLASSeminars. A recording she made inspired me to watch for the children of my friends who might need a nonparental, positive adult influence in their lives.

Colleen's message—born of her own experience when she was a teen—was to mothers of young teenage girls. She suggested that their teens needed an adult friend, younger than the teen's mother but older than the teen. Ideally, this friend would be a Christian and a good role model for the teen. Colleen pointed out the value of a responsible adult a child could go to when she had troubles or needed advice on issues about which she was not comfortable talking to her parents.

As I listened to Colleen's suggestion, I remembered a family friend who lived in our home when I was a teenager. She was that positive adult influence for me. I remember the driving lessons she gave me long before I was old enough to drive and the "life tips" she offered still come to mind when I need them.

I agreed that having a third party involved is a great idea, and I believe God told me I was to be that person for someone else's teenagers.

At that time, my friend Connie's two girls were entering their teen years, so I committed to be that friend to them. Emily borrowed some of my fancy dresses when she needed them. Amanda wore my formal jacket to a recital. I was touched to be one of only two adults invited to Emily's beach party for her sixteenth birthday. On one visit to my home, the girls expressed an interest in the *Victoria* magazine I had on the coffee table, so I sent them a gift subscription. In return, they sent me a thank-you note that read, "Marita, thank you so much for your thoughtful gift. We will enjoy *Victoria*. I appreciate the way you let us know how much you care. You are one of our favorite grown-ups! Keep up the good work." Later in a note to me, Connie wrote, "I appreciate the love and attention you give my children.... Nothing can ever repay the thoughtful time and affection you have shown them. Thanks!"

Looking back, I wish I had done more. I wish I had kept in touch better after we each moved away, but even a little is better than nothing. After all, when you touch a life with love, you touch a life forever.

Around that same time in my life, a young family moved into a condo near the one we were renting. They had a little girl who took an instant liking to me—and I to her. I was sad when they moved away. One day Chuck saw her father walking down the road. Of course, Chuck stopped to see if he was okay. His car had broken down, so Chuck took him home. By then, they were living in a brand-new starter home neighborhood. The house next door was vacant and the builder was having trouble selling it. This former neighbor suggested to Chuck that we should buy it. We did.

We lived next door for years. Once again, this little girl loved coming to our house to visit. Even though my house is not geared toward kids, I created places and things that were within her "welcome zone." I kept a special makeup collection for her to play with—real adult makeup, not play toys. It made her feel very grown up. Sometimes she would knock on the door and ask if I could play just as I was getting ready to go somewhere. I'd invite her in for a few minutes while I was getting ready, and we'd put on our makeup together.

Occasionally, I'd be in the kitchen cooking dinner and she'd come downstairs with makeup all over her face and the jewelry I allowed her to use—several necklaces at one time. She'd say, "I can't find your 'pincher earrings.'" Though I have pierced ears, she knew I had two pairs of clip-ons she could wear.

I have pictures of her standing on a chair at the stove while she helped me cook dinner. In one of my favorites, she has chocolate all over her face while she stirred brownies. I praised her for her efforts and she basked in my affection. One day I commented that she probably heard similar things at home, because she really was a good girl. She grew thoughtful for a moment and then said. "Sometimes, not very often. Mom and Dad are very busy."

Around the time we moved from that neighborhood, they moved away as well, and though we stayed in touch through Christmas cards, our lives went different directions. Years later I had a speaking engagement in their area. I contacted the family to see about visiting. They were warm and welcoming. As I drove up to their house, I berated myself. *This is crazy! What was I thinking? It's been years since I've seen my little friend. She's a teenager now. She won't have any interest in me.* I parked near the front door. It flew open, and my little friend—now a preteen—ran out to greet me. She jumped up and hugged me hard. I stayed there for the weekend, sleeping in her bed while she slept beside me on the floor. I was clearly there to visit with her, not her mom.

## AN ETERNAL IMPACT

Teach a Sunday school class or children's club.

Mentor a younger Christian. Start by simply spending some time with him or her.

Find a church ministry that fits you and get involved. It could be through music, hospitality, leadership, or anywhere else God calls you.

Share your faith with younger family members such as nieces and nephews.

Give your time and/or money to a trusted evangelistic organization. Better yet, find ways to get involved in evangelizing your own hometown.

One evening of my visit when I helped her mom make dinner, she said, "Those times with you were very special. She still remembers them with great fondness." We stayed in touch, sending letters back and forth for a few years until, once again, our lives went different directions. Although I'll always wish we'd stayed in better touch, I know that for that time, I had a positive influence on a young life.

You don't have to go out to the highways and byways to find a child in need of a friend—just look at the children of your friends and neighbors. Where I live now, I again have little friends. One of my best friends has two children, and she has no family nearby who have the time, space, or interest in having them stay overnight. As this friend was sharing a concern with me about her marriage, I realized part of the problem was that she and her husband never had a night alone. I came home and talked to Chuck, asking him if we could take her kids, Weston and Waverly, once a month. He agreed.

So I committed to have Weston and Waverly over to our house frequently—not once a month, but often enough that they leave things at our house for next time. Chuck has a slot car track, and he's given Weston a car that is only his. When he visits, Chuck and Weston play with the slot cars. Waverly helps me cook, and we do girly things like a paraffin wax manicure and pedicure.

I remember the first time Waverly spent the night. I was in bed when I heard whimpering. I slipped out of bed and tiptoed into the guestroom. Waverly was scared. She had not been away from home much, and had never slept in our house. I asked if she wanted me to sleep with her and she did. I crawled under the covers with her and stayed there until she fell asleep. She's had no fear ever since.

She is older now. Since her mom is the emcee for the Glorieta Christian Writers Conference that I run, Waverly always wants to come. She hangs out with me and is my little helper. She has participated in a writing class for children, has been paid to critique a children's book manuscript, and has acquired a sizeable collection of autographed books. One day she declared she would not read any book that was not autographed. When I go to places where there are authors of children's books, I get her autographed copies of age-appropriate books.

Though I love my nephews and nieces too, they don't live near me. Chuck and I have done special things with them—even though we can't have the same daily input in their lives as I have with my friend's children. In this way, we can influence young lives, even though our influence within our immediate family is sometimes more limited than we would like.

Like us, Cheri Liefeld is childless. But she is blessed to live near her niece and nephews. Here is her story.

## LIKE A CHILD BY CHERI LIEFELD

Not having my own children, the time I spend each week with my one-year-old niece and three- and five-year-old nephews is precious to me. I look forward to handing family traditions down to them. I look forward to tea parties with my niece and I hope to pass on my love of cooking to all three children. I have family heirlooms such as Dad's cameras and Grandmother's china that I will give to them one day, but the thing I pray about the most is passing on the love of Jesus and my story of how I accepted him as my Savior.

I grew up a preacher's kid. I practically lived at the church because I was very involved in everything from Sunday school to Awana to being the angel in the Christmas pageant.

Now, as an adult, I enjoy talking with kids about God and watching them discover Jesus and the old familiar Bible stories.

One week right before Easter, my nephew Luke—who was four at the time—was learning about Communion at the Christian preschool he attends. That weekend he went to his grandfather's for an afternoon and asked Paw for crackers and grape juice. When his grandfather asked why, Luke replied, "We can break bread and have Communion."

Recently I asked Luke what he had learned at Sunday school that day and at first got the classic "I don't remember." Then a minute later, he said, "There was this boy and he kept hearing someone call to him. He would run out and they would say, 'It's not me. Go back to bed.'" I laughed and said, "Oh, you learned about Samuel." For quite some time, we talked about how God spoke to Samuel. We have also had a few more difficult conversations, like the day Luke offered to "die for us" if he could just have his favorite toy or stay up a bit longer. I smile when I remember the times I have spent with Luke.

Through my speaking and the various groups with which I'm involved, I am frequently reminded that many people grew up with no knowledge of God. As children, they were not taught about Jesus and how he loves them. As adults, they struggle to understand. They didn't learn "Jesus Loves Me," have "sword drills" (contests to see who could find a Bible verse the fastest), or have the opportunity to perform in Christmas pageants. They missed out on the various ways to use a hymnal to amuse yourself during a particularly long and dry sermon or to learn all the verses to "Just As I Am."

I see what a gift it was to know Christ as a child, asking him into my heart at five years old with my mom by my side.

As children, we had pure hearts that could easily accept God's love and embrace it before we grew disillusioned or cynical, before our hearts were broken. I believe that knowing about Jesus when I was a child stuck with me when I was too broken to believe God cared. The verses I memorized in my fifth grade Sunday school class to win that fancy camera played in my mind and were a lifeline when I struggled to find my way back to God later in life. Matthew 18 talks about becoming like a child to enter the kingdom of heaven. It is harder to find that childlike faith as an adult, which is why I pray that my niece and nephews come to know Jesus while they are still children.

With the memory of my childlike faith in mind, I've started praying at bedtime with my niece, Livi, whenever I have the opportunity to baby-sit. The night I started this practice, I put my hands together and began praying as she lay in her crib looking up at me. When I said, "Amen" and opened my eyes, she sat up, put her hands together, and said, "Pray, Mommy." So I kept my hands folded, and we prayed for each person in the family—including her Mommy. Now each time I pray with her, my eyes open to the precious sight of her holding her little hands together, joining me in the prayer.

I pray that as she grows, that childlike faith will stay with her and that she will always remember Aunt Cheri's influence on her life.

## AN ACTIVE IMPACT

Pick one child or adult you hope to influence. (Alternatively, it could be a group through which you can have an impact.) Prayerfully, seek ways to share your heart, your gifts, and your faith. Commit to investing in these lives for at least one year, and find at least two specific actions you will take to positively influence each person's life. For example, "I will impact my niece's life by playing soccer with her once a month and buying a children's devotional we can work through together after our soccer games."

## FOLLOWING THEIR LEGACY

Karen Power's nieces and nephews do not live near her. But remembering something special her grandmother and great-grandmother did for her, she is now doing the same thing for her niece. Following the legacy they left in her life, here is the legacy Karen is leaving for her.

## THE POSTCARDS BY KAREN R. POWER

Most of my dad's family lived in Southern California, while I grew up in northern Florida. Back in the 1960s when I was a child, cross-country travel was not as convenient and fast as it is today. Visits with my grandmother and great-grandmother were few and far between. Fortunately, these two wise women knew how to reach out through letters and postcards and give a little southern girl a thrill. It was always so much fun to go to the mailbox and find a postcard from some far-off place with my name on it. In the beginning, my mother read these to me, but as the years passed and my postcard collection grew, these captured memories became my special treasure.

Now many years later, I'm a single adult with no children of my own. My job requires me to travel more than I'd like, and lately I've been struggling with traveling alone and wanting someone to share the sights and experiences. On a recent business trip to Southern California, just a few miles from my dad's hometown, I realized that what my grandmothers did for me, I could do for the next generation: my nieces. My youngest niece, Samantha, is six years old. She is at a perfect age to continue a family tradition. She loves learning, and her reading skills are improving every day.

On this particular trip, I was having dinner in Redondo Beach, looking at sea lions in the harbor with a couple of friends and fellow CLASS grads, when one of them said, "Our dolphins are black instead of gray like the ones you've seen on the east coast." That statement sparked a new purpose in my travels.

Now with each trip I take, I am "alert to life" while visiting new locations. I pick up a postcard from that area and make sure to share one tidbit of information I've learned while visiting there. I try to make it appropriate for Samantha's reading level so she can understand and learn. I also mail it before leaving so it's postmarked and dated from that city to add an extra measure of authenticity. My sister recently told me that Samantha really enjoys going to the mailbox and finding something there with her name on it. I can hardly wait to see her again at Christmas to share some of my experiences with her firsthand. Which reminds me, maybe I should look for a unique album for her to store her special treasures in....

If you don't have children of your own, think of your nieces, nephews, or the children of your friends who would enjoy learning a little more about who you are, what you do, or places you've visited.

## EXTENDED FAMILY

Karen has found a great way to stay in touch with her young niece who lives across the country. When my (Marita's) nephews were old enough to travel on their own, before school activities—and later jobs—occupied all their vacation time, they came to visit us one at a time. They have especially appreciated their time with Chuck. I am very much like my sister, and they don't need more maternal influence! They have a great dad, but he's more of the studious type. Chuck is a guy's guy. He has lots of toys that they don't have at their house. Much to my sister's chagrin, he takes them shooting, motorcycle riding, and bicycling.

My middle nephew, Jonathan, has connected with Chuck in a special way. Because of Chuck's influence in his life, Jonathan now owns his second motorcycle. His first was a used Yamaha Chuck picked out for him here in New Mexico. It was his Christmas present the year he turned sixteen—paid for jointly by his parents, grandparents, and Uncle Chuck and Aunt 'Rita. Jonathan drove that motorcycle all through high school and into college.

Jonathan wanted to spend his twenty-first birthday celebration with Uncle Chuck—on a Harley. So for Jonathan's spring break, Chuck flew to California, and they each rented a Harley and drove up and down the coast on Highway 101. This multiday motorcycle trip has been a highlight in Jonathan's life.

Also, because of Chuck's influence in his life, Jonathan is an avid bicyclist. He has been on the bike patrol, a part of UCLA's security force, and during his last year of college, he worked at a bike store, greatly enhancing his bike paraphernalia inventory.

Jonathan has now graduated from college, and time is limited for both he and Chuck. Rather than a gold Cross pen or a savings bond, Jonathan opted for quality time with his uncle as his graduation present. When Chuck discussed a gift with Jonathan, they decided that Chuck was to meet him in Las Vegas, where Jonathan is now working, and they would share a two-wheeled weekend.

Yes, those of us without children can still make a difference in the world. There are many ways to leave your legacy! Look around. Whether or not you have children, there are people—adults and children—whose lives you can impact.

# 14

# TRACING THE LEGACY
## *Lauren*

Tracing your family tree can be a bit like a treasure hunt. There are sometimes dead ends. Other times, you make an amazing discovery, such as that you share a career path with a great-great grandparent or that you are related to someone famous. You may also discover some ugly realities. These "skeletons" can help you understand your own past and that of your relatives. No matter what you learn about your family, it can help you understand who you are. And as you pass this information on to others, you are creating a valuable heirloom— one that tells future generations who they are and where they are from.

We always knew my father's grandparents were from Germany, but one day Dad's employee said, "You name my country." Because of his broken English, Dad didn't immediately grasp what the man was saying. The employee said it again. "You name my country— Littauen!" Research revealed that in Germany, Littauen is the name used for the country we call Lithuania. In Germany, a person from Lithuania is a Littauer. We now suspect that hundreds of years ago, Dad's ancestors lived in Lithuania, moved to Germany, and were given the label "Littauer."

I had the opportunity to visit some business colleagues who lived in Germany and I shared my Littauen story. They immediately concurred, as if it were third grade knowledge, and whipped out a pre-World War II map. Sure enough, there it was in print: Littauen.

Last year, Randy came home from work with a surprise for me. While going through a recent stamp purchase at our store, he discovered a large envelope addressed to a baroness living in Glendale, California. It was covered in Lithuanian stamps and dated 1922. When he flipped the envelope over, he noticed that the return address was from Littauen! Now I can hold in my hand the proof that a Littauer is a person from Lithuania.

## WHO ARE MY ANCESTORS? DID THEY LEAVE A LEGACY? by RANDY BRIGGS, SR.

At one time or another in your life, you've probably asked yourself the questions, *Where did my ancestors come from? Who were they? Where did they live? And what did they do?* These fairly simple questions aren't always easily answered unless your family has kept really great records or some genealogist has done all the work for you. Unfortunately, my family had neither, so I had to start from the beginning.

Our family has always been pretty close knit. When I was a child, we spent quite a bit of time together for celebrations, holidays, or just because we liked to get together. During all those times we always seemed to get along and have a great time.

My dad's parents lived the closest—just twenty-five miles away—so we planned to spend every other Sunday together. I remember the women cooking while the men swapped stories or talked about sports. Dinner was usually followed by card games, when there was always more talking. I was a great listener.

Occasionally, I was invited to my grandparents' house to stay for a few days, and that was when Grandma and I got to talk. She shared a lot about her childhood in the Cass family. She told stories about her life on the farm and the wonderful times she spent with her parents in Iowa. The Casses had come to Jackson County, Iowa, in the 1840s and had farmed all that time. I remember a big Cass family Bible that belonged to my great-great-grandfather, John. It had ornately carved wood-like covers and was elaborately illustrated. In the front of the Bible was a list of family members with dates of birth and death. The Bible was interesting to look at, but I knew none of the people it named except my grandmother's parents. Grandma also had large photos on the wall of her parents and grandparents. I remember the picture of John Cass especially well because he had a long, thin white beard and looked really old to me. He lived to be ninety.

I was in my early thirties when I embarked on creating my formal genealogy. By then, most of my older relatives were gone, so I missed the opportunity

## WHERE TO START

You'll want to collect as much preliminary information as you can obtain from relatives before you begin.

Begin on your home computer. Search major genealogical Web sites. In particular, search for references to older family members' names, and research the history of the towns where your family lived.

The local government where your family lived can provide guidance in finding birth and death certificates, marriage licenses, and property deeds. Contact city hall or county government offices. The location of important documents can vary from state to state, so do some checking ahead of time.

If you have a date of death, your first stop should be the obituaries in the local paper, where you may find a wealth of information.

Make copies of what you find for anyone else in your family who is doing genealogical research. It might spark a helpful insight.

to ask questions. I remembered my grandmother's huge family Bible and photo albums, but they had been given away when she died. I needed other sources for determining my roots, so I started by listing all the family members still living and their vital statistics, births, marriages, and so forth. Then I checked with each one, confirmed my facts, and asked them questions about what they remembered about their ancestors. That technique worked well for a while, but I eventually had to turn to more formal sources.

Fortunately, my grandmother had left me a large book containing the history of Dubuque County, Iowa, where my Briggs ancestors had settled. Looking in the index I found my great-great-grandfather's name listed. The autobiographical entry mentioned that he had been born in Maine in 1816, but no town was listed. That helped, but not a lot. So I went to Dubuque, the county seat, to see what I could find. The library held many books about the early county history, but I hit pay dirt in the obituary files. There I found many Briggses, but one was of particular interest. He was a son of my great-great-grandfather's brother, and the file listed his birthplace as Hampden, Maine. Knowing my ancestor had traveled to Iowa with his older brother, it stood to reason that they were probably from the same town. It was only a potential clue, but it seemed like too great a coincidence to ignore.

On my next trip east, while attending a family gathering in Maine, I took a day off and drove up the coast to Hampden. I had discovered Hampden had a historical society when I checked directory assistance.

Upon my arrival, the docent brought out a huge folder filled with Briggs records. I found out that my great-great-great-grandfather, Otis Briggs, had been the local Baptist minister and justice of the peace. The names and birthdates of his children, including my great-great-grandfather were listed in the records, as well as Otis's date of death, but I saw no information about where he had come from. I did, however, learn that his wife, Ann Williams Briggs, had died in Hampden and was buried nearby, so I drove to the cemetery to search for other clues there.

Once again I got lucky. Her very large headstone contained much of her life history. She had been born in Wrentham, Massachusetts, to the Reverend and Mrs. William Williams (another minister!).

Needless to say, my next trip took me to Wrentham, where I found a wealth of information about the Briggs and Williams families at the local library. My research revealed that I had descended from a relatively long line of Baptist ministers who had graduated from Brown University in Rhode Island. In fact, the Reverend Williams had been in the first graduating class at Brown in 1769 and was instrumental in preserving the Brown library during the Revolutionary War. He had gathered up the many volumes, transported them back to Wrentham, and hidden them. Once the war ended, the Reverend Williams returned the books to the university, and that collection bears his name today. I have visited the library and have seen the books he so carefully protected and the large cabinet in which he hid them. The Brown Library also has Williams's graduation diploma from 1769, which I was privileged to hold. It's the only surviving diploma from that first graduating class.

Research in the Brown University Library also turned up information on the Reverend Joel Briggs, Otis's father. He had been the first pastor of a Baptist church in East Stoughton (known today as Avon), Massachusetts, for nearly fifty years. We drove to that church, were welcomed by the current pastor, and were shown all their records pertaining to Joel Briggs. To my surprise, Joel was from Norton, Massachusetts and had been a Minuteman in the first call to arms in

April 1775 when volunteer troops were called to Lexington and Concord. What a thrill to find out that my ancestor had participated actively in our nation's fight for independence! It was equally thrilling to find Joel's headstone in the cemetery inscribed "Defender of Religious Freedom."

Subsequent travels to Massachusetts have yielded tremendous finds, including the entire Briggs genealogy back to the year 1549 in England. All this work had been done by professional genealogists who printed their findings in the quarterly publication of the New England Historical and Genealogy Society (NEHGS), a great organization located in Boston. Fortunately, my research in Hampden and Wrentham paved the way for the ultimate connection to this wonderful body of work done by other researchers. You don't have to do all the work yourself.

It is so important not only to learn your ancestor's names, but to try to find out who they were and what they stood for. As a child, I thought all the Briggses had been farmers. In fact, my background is varied with educators, farmers, pastors, soldiers, and patriots—all the kinds of people that made America great.

I have taken you through my search for ancestry just to show how I connected my family back to England in the 1550s with very little

**WHEN YOU'RE THERE**

When traveling to a specific city to research, check out:

- Libraries
- Cemeteries
- Churches
- Professional organizations a family member may have been involved in
- The local newspaper
- Government offices
- The actual neighborhood where your family lived, when possible, to find long-term residents
- The phone book (If your name isn't overly common, you may find others who share your name. Meet with them, if you think they may have some helpful information.)

I have an ancestor who attended a Lutheran church with his wife, though his background was Baptist. He had a disagreement with the church, rebelled, and so on. He wanted to please his wife but would not consent to their being buried in the church cemetery. So he approached the next-door neighbor, a farmer, and bought a piece of land just over the property line next to the church. Well, may he rest in peace, but in time the church expanded and, needing more land, bought the adjoining property. Now my headstrong ancestor and his wife are in the church cemetery after all! We only have so much control, dear fellow!

*—Stuart Osland*

original information. Yes, it really can be done. Reconstructing your genealogy is a matter of connecting a series of stepping-stones to the past. Lauren and I have often combined genealogical research with vacations, and our kids haven't even minded. Many times, when I suspected someone important to our family had been buried in a particular cemetery, we'd pull in, and we all would fan out to see who would be the first to find "grandpa." More often than not, one of the kids would find the headstone before I would. These turned out to be great family times and, more importantly, opportunities to build a family legacy.

## PRINCE EDWARD ISLAND BY RANDY BRIGGS, SR.

A couple of years ago, following the death of my father-in-law, Fred, several Littauer family members took a Memorial Day trip to Massachusetts to visit his grave and plant the requisite six pots of geraniums, a family tradition. Since we were all gathering on the east coast at the same time, I jokingly suggested we fly up to Prince Edward Island, the ancestral home of the MacDougalls, Florence's mother's family. To my knowledge, no one in the family had been there since

S ometimes there aren't sufficient family records to do an adequate genealogical search. National organizations, such as the NEHGS already mentioned, have fantastic libraries just waiting to be explored. The Internet contains hundreds of sites, many of which are free, that can help you find the clues you need to proceed. The genealogical library of the Mormon Church is the greatest repository of information of family lineage in the world. Available through Ancestry.com (for a fee), you can access all the census records, Social Security records, many military records, and work that any other genealogist has registered there. A truly remarkable amount of information is available.

*—RANDY BRIGGS, SR.*

1898, and there were many blanks in the family tree. I was pleasantly surprised that so many wanted to go—so go we did.

We flew to Halifax, Nova Scotia, rented a car, and drove across the bridge to PEI. What a charming, laid-back kind of place. It was full of farms and open space, and even the towns had a different feeling; no one was in a hurry. After all, where could they go? The whole island is only about a hundred miles long and a few miles wide.

In Charlottetown, the provincial capital, we found the record office and library, where Lauren and I spent the next couple of days doing research. Fortunately, local genealogists had done a great job indexing most of the island's inhabitants, with references to the specific local records and their locations within the library. We found so much information—including relatives we never knew existed— that I'm still trying to absorb it all. The MacDougalls had lived in Tyne Valley located in the western part of the island, so the next day we drove there, not knowing what we would find.

As we crested a little knoll—there are no mountains or big hills on PEI—we saw below us a small vale with a stream running through it. A few businesses and homes were clustered around. Of the dozen or so stores that comprised the town, two were cafés, right next door to each other. We picked the cuter of the two and went in to have lunch. To my surprise, I discovered what I found to be the world's greatest oysters: Malpeques. They are named for the bay in which they are harvested—right next to Tyne Valley.

The walls of the café and also the back of the menu were covered with historical facts about the town. We scoured the pictures and writings for a hint of the MacDougall existence, but to no avail. The waitress was pretty talkative, so we told her of our quest. She asked the name we were researching and when we said, "MacDougall" she replied, "The postmistress across the street is named MacDougall... maybe she could be of help."

After a delicious lunch, we wandered over to the post office about fifty feet away. Judy MacDougall was helpful and even indicated that her husband outside was actually Florence's distant cousin. Their grandfathers were brothers. James Ellis MacDougall, Florence's grandfather, had left home at a young age, moved to Halifax, and then went on to Merrimac, Massachusetts. The PEI MacDougalls knew

## GETTING IT TOGETHER

Get a binder and divide it into the following sections:

- Your complete family tree
- Files on each individual family member—This will include a photograph (when possible), copies of all documentation you've gathered, a summary about what you've learned about the person, and a list of questions about him or her you'd like to have answered.
- A section for summaries or transcripts of interviews with family members
- A list of research resources with contact information
- Information needed for future research trips

he went to Massachusetts, but the families lost touch once James died in 1930.

Judy put us in touch with other MacDougall relatives on the island, including Gary MacDougall, the editor of the primary newspaper on PEI. We called him when we returned to our B&B in Charlottetown, and the next morning he dropped by for breakfast and a morning chat.

We spent the better part of a week in Prince Edward Island and were fortunate to meet wonderful relatives. What a thrill to reunite a family that had been separated for more than one hundred years. We can hardly wait for a return trip. Researching one's family need not be boring; it can be an exciting adventure of discovery!

# 15

# RECORDING THE MEMORIES
## FLORENCE

*E*ven with e-mail and faxes, a personal letter is still something to be treasured. You can't get attached to a slick white sheet of copy paper with black print. They're all the same. When writing a letter, a person can choose different stationery, types of pens, and colors of ink. I have so many of each that it often seems to take me longer than it should to decide what I feel like using, to determine what the recipient would like the best, and then to make my selection.

What are some of the appropriate times to write a note or send a card with a note on it? New babies, birthdays, holidays, graduations, weddings, or just a day that the Lord put someone on your heart. These latter ones often make the best impression because you feel no obligation.

One very special type of letter I've written is to each of my grandchildren on the day each one was born. I described where I was when I heard their birth was imminent and how I managed to get to the hospital on time.

When my second grandson, Jonathan, was being born, I was speaking at a luncheon, and the chairman let me start early so I could get to the hospital on time. The girl who had written down the message had heard "drive 210" as if it were "drive to 10." So I headed off on Interstate 10 looking for an exit that never appeared. When I found myself west of Los Angeles near the ocean, when I was supposed to be in Glendale—east of Los Angeles—I could have cried. We didn't have cell phones in those days, so I had to locate a pay phone to call the hospital and find out what to do. "Turn around and go back to where you came from." Gratefully, I did arrive on time—just before Jonathan was born. But I was so exhausted by the time I got to Lauren's room that I wanted to hoist myself up onto the hospital bed and take a nap!

In each child's birth letter—to be put in their baby books for future reference—I told how I felt emotionally about seeing them for the first time and how thrilled I was to be their grandmother. It was important to me to write the letter that day since I knew I wouldn't feel the same the next.

## BLESSING LETTERS BY LOU WORKMAN SOUDERS

Once my Christmas decorations are up and most of the gifts wrapped, I begin to think of my blessing letters to my family.

Years ago, when my daughter and two sons were young, I learned how important it is to give verbal as well as written blessings. I began by writing Christmas blessing letters and sticking them into the hand knit stockings hanging on the mantle. I sit and pray for each person, now including three grandchildren, and ask God to help me encourage and praise each one with my words. I make each one personal and end with what I will be praying for them in the coming year.

I hope that one day they will take the time to reread their letters, remember milestones in their lives, and feel my love even after I am gone. I take joy in watching all of them read their letters and look to me with love and gratitude. That is my blessing.

What a constant joy it has been for me (Florence) to have Linda Jewell in our office. She is consistently cheerful and an uplift to my spirits. Through her work as Executive Director for CLASServices, she has developed several resources for speakers including a "Booklet on Booklets," a "Tip Sheet on Tip Sheets," and a "Tape on Tapes." In her personal ministry, she shows people how to write special letters. She also speaks to women's groups on the value of personal correspondence. She has written several booklets that encourage and equip people to pick up their pens and express themselves through note-writing and journaling.

The following is one of my favorite of her "letter" stories. I hope you enjoy "Sister Mary Gabriella" as much as I have and that it inspires you to write a "legacy letter."

## SISTER MARY GABRIELLA BY LINDA LAMAR JEWELL

My sister, Jannet, is almost two years older than I am, but when she started school, I pitched such a fit that my mother sent me the next year, even though I was only five.

My father was Catholic, and we attended St. Columbus in Durango, Colorado. The school was small, so first and second graders were together. Sister Mary Gabriella seated me next to Jannet.

One day she called on me to read from our Dick and Jane books, "Oh, Oh, Oh. See Spot run. Run, Spot, Run!"

Sister Mary Gabriella said five words that had a profound impact on my life: "Class, Linda reads very well."

This was my first public affirmation, and I felt proud when I sat down next to my older sister, whom I adore.

Sister Mary Gabriella's five words were like a life preserver I held on to tightly in the years to come.

Within eight weeks of my starting first grade, my parents divorced, and my sisters and I went to live with my non-Catholic grandparents in the country. There I attended a three-room school—where again first and second graders were together.

The next summer we moved to a larger community. Not only were the first and second grades not together, but there were two second grades!

I was placed in the "dumb" class along with some older boys who had failed first grade, Native Americans who spoke English as a second language, a young boy with a speech impediment, and other younger second graders like me.

Because of Sister Mary Gabriella's five words, however, I *knew* they had me in the wrong class! I refused to believe I was dumb.

That year I became a target of the bully from the other second grade. He was a big kid and I was a skinny runt. After recess one day we lined up at the water fountains. He smarted off to me—I replied in kind. He slapped me—I kicked him in the shins. That year I earned a reputation as a "shin kicker" because if anyone gave me any baloney I'd kick them in the shins and run like the wind. Nothing the class bully said or did to me could shake my conviction that Sister Mary Gabriella clearly saw my abilities.

Two years later, my fourth grade teacher saw in me what Sister Mary Gabriella had seen and moved me into the smart class.

Forty years later, while writing letters of appreciation to people who made a major impact in my life, I wrote a letter to Sister Mary Gabriella, thanking her for her five words of grace that kept me from believing lies about myself. In a way that only God could have directed me, I located her. She was in her eighties by then and didn't remember me; she'd taught a lot of first graders since 1955! But I had the honor of talking with her on the phone and mailing her my letter of appreciation.

Now I teach others how to write notes and letters of appreciation. I use this story as an example to encourage others to express *their* appreciation in writing. I'll tell my students, "This is not about my stories or my letters of appreciation; it's about *yours*." Then I'll challenge them with, "Who in your life has made a positive, profound impact on your life? Live a life of no regrets. Today, before it's too late, express your appreciation in writing to that person."

(Authors' Note: In hopes that Linda's story—and all the others in this chapter—has encouraged you to "pick up your pen," we have included an abridged version of Linda's booklet as an appendix to equip you with the techniques to write a letter that others will cherish—one worthy of saving through the years.)

## SCRAPBOOKS

Scrapbooks can become family heirlooms as we keep records of pictures, awards, and family information. I (Florence) started pasting newspaper articles about plays I was in and honors I received long before scrapbooking classes became popular. As a teenager in a family that took few

## INSPIRING LETTERS

If you need a little inspiration to begin letter writing, here are a few tips to make the task more appealing:

- Splurge on some decorative stationery that reflects your personality.
- Buy pens you love. Consider the feel of the pen as well as the color and flow of the ink. Try a fountain pen, which adds distinction to your handwriting.
- For a truly personal touch, buy a wax letter seal at a candle shop. They seem indulgent but can be fairly inexpensive.
- If regular letter writing is difficult or too time-consuming for you, start with pre-stamped postcards. Interesting, quirky, and beautiful ones are available at stationery stores and art museum gift shops.

pictures, I got copies of school photos, pageant casts, and Sunday school class rolls. These were treasures in a family without such collections.

My first scrapbook was filled with high school activities, showing me on the stage winning the poetry reading contest and an action picture of me in the cast of the senior play, *The Fighting Littles*. I have my graduation picture and an assortment of pictures of young men who graduated the same year. Looking at the book, you might think I had a large assortment of boyfriends, though I actually had none. But I was on the yearbook committee, and when we threw away the picture proofs of each individual, I retrieved from the trash some of the shots of the best-looking young men and pasted them in the book. If you don't have a romantic past, you can always create one. This action was, perhaps, the beginning of my career as a creative writer.

My college scrapbook has my quarterly report cards, my invitation to become a member of Kappa Alpha Theta (the first Greek letter fraternity known among women), and a picture of me and my date, with me wearing a borrowed gown of blue chiffon and receiving the award as third runner-up to the queen of the Gardenia Ball.

During my time as the drama teacher of Haverhill High School, I made pictorial records of every play I directed, every award I won, and every time I was elected president of another organization. I was, at that time, a professional president and once became the president of the Connecticut Speech and Drama Association on the first day I attended—before I had even joined.

When *LIFE Magazine* chose me as bride-of-the-year (May 18, 1953), you can imagine the surge of interest Haverhill had in my life. I have two scrapbooks of this zenith experience, and my favorite picture is one of the *Haverhill Gazette* photographer taking a picture of the *LIFE Magazine* photographer taking a picture of me!

When my socially correct mother-in-law arrived at the church for my wedding and saw the high school band tuning up, twenty girls fluffing around in net dress as my court, and numerous photographers at work recording it all—she threw her hands in the air and exclaimed, "Oh my, what is this? Some kind of a circus?"

After Lauren was born, I went back to high school teaching and directing the senior class plays. Our production of *The Boyfriend* won the Connecticut state top award and went on to become Best High School Production in New England. I created a step-by-step scrapbook of this show—including cast pictures, newspaper reviews, and plaudits.

Later as our family became real Christians instead of faithful churchgoers, I began giving my testimony at Christian Women's Clubs. I was excited to see the large percentage of women who prayed with me to receive Christ. Naturally, I wanted to keep records of this new phase of my life, so I came up with a plan. I bought a simple camera and had someone take my picture with each club chairman. After I spoke, I instructed the ladies that if they prayed with me to receive the Lord today, they should hand me their nametag on the way out so I could pray for them. Not only did I pray for these new believers by name, but I put all the nametags from each group in scrapbooks. On each page I would put the picture of me and the chairman, the name of the club, the date, the number of people attending, and the number of people who prayed and asked Jesus into their hearts. For ten years I made these scrapbooks of Christian Women's Club successes as I spoke around the country. I have a whole shelf of these books, and when I take one down to review, I am thrilled to see the proof of God's harvest, and I laugh as I observe my various and assorted hairstyles and outfits throughout those years.

What records have you kept of your life? Have you ever asked

**M**y grandmother was the youngest of nine children—only seven of whom survived childhood. Her family came to Lubbock, Texas, in a covered wagon in 1906. During my last semester at Texas Tech, I sat down with my grandmother and her oldest sister, Hattie—who was ninety-six, twenty years Grandma's senior—and tape recorded hours of conversations about their life on the high plains of Texas. I heard many tales about living in a dugout, getting lost in their own thousand-acre pasture, and other amazing adventures.

Then I transcribed and edited the entire recording into a book, preserving the West Texas dialect and, with my grandmother's input, adding illustrations such as old photos, current photos of the farm as it is today, and a family tree lined up with a world events timeline.

Only one year after the book was complete, my great-aunt Hattie died, and the following year, my grandmother began showing symptoms of Alzheimer's. Although my children were born before she died, they were never able to know each other. But I have her story, in her own words, in the book she and I put together.

*—KATHERINE BELL*

---

your parents or other relatives for pictures or scrapbooks they have of the family? It's amazing how willing people are to share memories with those who care enough to ask. My daughter-in-law, Kristy, asked her grandmother if there were any records or pictures of the family's past. She not only produced a scrapbook with a family tree back into the 1800s and the birth and marriage certificates from her great-grandparents down—but most exciting, her grandmother gave her the scrapbook because Kristy was the only one who asked.

If you wish to have a legacy to share with your children, ask around the family and see what you can find. You might be the only one who asked.

My friend Bonnie Skinner is a great encourager of other people, yet she decided she should do something special to lift up her own spirits.

She devised a "Victory Log" that she writes in every night. Others might call it a journal; Bonnie calls it her Victory Log. "I record five blessings for each day. I remember late one afternoon when I realized I had not had a blessing all day, so I went out to Wal-Mart and observed the sadness of some of the customers. I greeted the people as if I had been hired as a hostess. As I cheered up the lonely ones, I received five blessings worthy of recording."

It's important to continually fill our hearts and minds with positive thoughts, fill our body with proper food and drink, and fill our spiritual tank with the love of our Lord Jesus through prayer and Bible study.

As Bonnie records her victories, often in times of sadness, she hopes her grandchildren will read these later and be encouraged by how she handled difficult situations. "As I get each day into perspective and live the abundant life, I write it all down to pass on to my loved ones. My Victory Log is my legacy."

When I first went to visit my friend Peg Butts in Ohio, I was amazed and impressed with her basement family room. She had a classroom and worktables set up with all kinds of paper, glue, and ribbons—a haven for people who like to make things. I could hardly wait to sit down and get to work. She explained to me her ministry of scrapbooking and how she encourages women to make creative memories for their families. I asked if she would share some ideas with my readers, and she sent me the following.

## SCRAPBOOKING BY PEG BUTTS

For many years, my husband and I took lots of slides and pictures of our family, friends, vacation trips, and special occasions. Unknowingly, we placed them in albums that were unsafe for photos and that even hastened their destruction. Sometimes information about the event or photo was written on a sheet of paper and included in the back of the album, but most of the time nothing was written at all. While photographs give a pictorial document of the occasion, it is the descriptions—the who, what, when, where, and why information—that explain to the viewer and future generations the story behind the picture.

I can remember taking time with my mother to find out who our ancestors were in the various family photos. My great-grandfather was a photographer, so we had several old family albums, unnamed, of course. We documented their names with their pictures, and I learned more about my heritage. Mother was the last of her generation that would have known who these people were. So many people's pictures end up in the trash because they lose the connection with the family as well as the story behind the picture.

When we returned from living in New Zealand, a friend of mine asked if I would like to attend a Creative Memories™ workshop. Since I had pictures of a recent trip to put in an album, I thought this would be a good idea and that scrapbooking with other women would be more fun than doing it alone.

After I finished the album of our trip to London and Scotland, I realized that I had a larger and more important album to do. Every other year my father's side of the family held a reunion for one week. In other words, we took our vacations together. The twentieth such reunion was coming up, and my photos were scattered in various places. Wouldn't it be great if I could have one album telling about these fun times? The album was a big hit at the reunion and triggered other stories of our great times together.

Another album I made was for my dad who was in an assisted

**H**as reading this chapter inspired you to want to begin scrapbooking? Are you unsure where to start and feeling a little overwhelmed? You're not alone.

Over the many years I've been scrapbooking and speaking to mothers' groups about creating lasting memories for their children, the most often asked question is, "Where do I start?" I tell them, "Start with bite-sized projects."

When I first began scrapbooking, I started working with my oldest photos. I felt I couldn't start with my most recent pictures until the album was caught up chronologically. My enthusiasm waned quickly. I wanted to work with the photos I'd taken on our recent trip to Disneyland. After much thought, I came up with a simple solution, which I believe you'll find helpful. I decided to make theme albums rather than a single—with several volumes—chronological album.

Theme albums are easier to catch up and keep up while you work with events such as birthdays. My favorite theme album is my family album. It includes a yearly family picture (we take one every October for our Christmas cards), the milestone baby pictures, and my kids' yearly school pictures. Each of my children has a smaller version of this album with wallet-sized photos they will take with them when they leave home.

*—RAELENE SEARLE*

living apartment. The album has pictures of his children and their children, Dad's brothers and sisters with their families, and several recent events honoring Dad and the people he has blessed. This brought his family close to him every day and gave him a wonderful way to share his photos with those who came to visit. Also, the journaling reinforced Dad's memory of these important events.

On Father's Day my brother, Jon, received an album with his granddaughter's photos and messages from his son, Brian, on the importance of his father's love. What Brian wrote touched our hearts.

My granddaughter, Allyson, a fourth grader, and I are working on a school album that records her activities in each of her grades. Working together is a fun way for me to be involved with her and learn about her friends and what's happening at school.

Can you imagine how impressive an album would be that covered the growing-up years of an individual? What a wonderful gift for a graduate. Just a few pictures each year with stories about that year recorded in an album doesn't take much time or money.

Does an album page have to be creative? Certainly not! In fact, adding a lot of extra stickers and paper can detract from the photos. I often tell my customers that their write-up about the picture is the best decoration a photo can have. Children and adults are interested in what their parents have to say, not how cute the stickers are.

Recently, one of my customers made an album for each of her children and gave it to them for Christmas. Her only son died a few months afterward, but his album was made at a happy time and continues to bring joy to her son's family. Another customer made an album about the life of her husband who had died two years before. Because of her husband's death, it was a difficult album to make, but it did a lot to help heal her aching heart. She wanted generations to come to know about him and the blessing his life was to those who knew him. As one customer shared pictures of each relative in her heritage album, she included a family recipe that was special to that person and brought back good memories of them.

## SAFEKEEPING MEMORIES

Save some small mementos to keep in a scrapbook with your pictures:

- Airline tickets stubs
- Theater ticket stubs
- Postcards from places you visit
- One or two special projects your child completed during the school year
- The envelope that came with a particularly important letter
- Newspaper clippings or headlines from a special date in your family history
- Programs from weddings you attend

What a terrific way to preserve those yummy meals.

One gift I like to give a bride and groom is the collection of pictures I've taken of their wedding and friends. I take photos that the professional photographer normally doesn't take. For example, I try to include the sign of the building or church, an outdoor scene that shows the weather, and pictures of their guests. My hope is that these photos help the couple tell more of the story of their special day.

Do you want to make a difference right where you are? How about preserving your family traditions and stories? Pass on the events of your family's life to the next generations. What a gift that would be for the future. Preserve the past, enrich the present, and inspire hope for the future. Pass on your family story.

## JOURNEYS WITH JOHN BY LINDA LAMAR JEWELL

Along with fifty other authors, I listened to what Dan Benson, director of book development at Cook Communications Ministries, had to say. The other authors focused on the kinds of books the publishing house wanted. But I zeroed in on Dan's comment that after the Bible, the book that most influenced his life had only seventeen copies in existence. This book continues to influence his business and personal decisions. Excited, I thought, *Now, that's a story!*

Seventeen copies! Who would write a limited-edition book that had such impact and influence?

Intrigued, I leaned forward to hear that the author of this treasured book was Dan's father, John Benson. Dan's speech to the authors shifted to other topics, but my attention wandered as I wondered about the book Dan's father wrote.

Several years later I had the opportunity to talk with Dan about his father's book. In a large, sunlit hotel atrium, Dan sat on a couch sipping Starbucks coffee, and I sat in a nearby armchair drinking spiced tea as we discussed the treasure he'd received from his dad. That morning, I learned *Journeys with John* came from Dan's father's research on the family tree and his reflections on life. John began the work after he retired and continued off and on for three or four years.

Wanting to be able to picture the book, I asked Dan to describe it. I learned that *Journeys with John* is roughly 150 pages of family facts and stories, printed front and back on letter-size paper and bound in a brown leatherette three-ring binder. On the inside front page John included a copy of a hand-painted insignia thought to be the family crest or coat of arms. After that, John arranged his material in time sequence of his ancestors and then added stories from his own life.

John, an amateur photographer, included copies of photos he took over the years. He then used his software to wrap the story around the photos and include captions for each one. In the book appendices, John also included additional photos with one-page write-ups of interesting facts and findings that didn't fit in smoothly with the main text.

I also wanted to know how the book was given. Was it at Christmas, a fiftieth wedding anniversary, a family reunion? I learned that John Benson, an unassuming man, didn't give this gift of gifts with fanfare. Dan received *Journeys with John* in a box along with other presents. In fact, when Dan opened the pages, his first reaction was one of mild interest. However, after a few times of reading just a couple of pages, Dan was hooked on the book.

I was also curious on how the book impacted Dan. I learned that Dan already knew his father was the "best dad he knew how to be." Yet, reading *Journeys with John* gave Dan insight into his father's life—including stories about how he met and married Dan's mother, reflections on the addition to their family of each of their four sons, and how John came to trust the Lord in the circumstances of raising a family.

From his growing-up years, Dan remembered his dad showing love for his family more with actions than words. *Journeys with John* gave Dan a chance to better understand in retrospect his father's emotions, decisions to be strong for his wife and four sons, and to trust in the Lord through some tough situations.

Every few years, Dan pulls *Journeys with John* from its shelf and rereads his father's story. It's a chance to get to know his dad a little bit better through stories that clarify and offer insight into John's decisions and actions. Although John died a few years after he completed it, the book is a tangible reminder of Dan's dad's reputation that continues to influence Dan's choices today. When Dan is faced with tough business decisions and pressure from himself and others, Dan remembers his father's sterling reputation. Dan's heritage—John's legacy of a good reputation—continues to influence Dan.

Because John made copies for all the immediate family, including all the grandchildren, I asked Dan what would happen to his copy in the future. Dan replied that he would probably want to give it to someone who knew John well.

While talking to Dan, I couldn't help but think how I—and many other people—would love to have a book of our ancestors' life journeys.

When we finished with our caffeine and conversation, I thanked Dan for his time and willingness to share the story of his dad's book. As I walked away through the large hotel lobby, I thought how we each make a choice about whether or not we record our family history or our own story. I can't make a choice for my ancestors or other family members. Yet the longing for my own heritage in writing strengthened my resolve to continue to choose to write family heritage and my legacy letters for my son, my extended family, and future generations.

After meeting with Dan, I also reflected that too often family heritages and personal legacies are lost in unrecorded time. Not so for Dan Benson. In *Journeys from John* he can see the generous gift his father gave his immediate family and future generations. In catching a glimpse of his father's ancestors and of his father, Dan and his family can reflect on the results of their own choices and who they might become.

Each of our lives serves as the fulcrum point between the heritage we've received and the legacy we leave.

Both heritage and legacy are the summation of choices. One of the most important choices we make is to invest our time and efforts in recording them for our posterity. Dan's life—and his family's life—is richer for the choices his father made.

Dan's story highlights that heritage letters are worth our time and effort. Invest in this priceless gift. Take time. Start now.

In a society where we extol youth and beauty, we often neglect older relatives who have a wealth of stories about times we did not know. How much more interesting these recollections are from the mouths of those who lived it than from pages of the history books.

## LETTERS FROM MOM BY LORI J. SEABORG

When I was ten years old, my missionary parents decided to move from Missouri to Papua New Guinea with my three brothers and me. We children were excited about what would surely become a grand adventure. The only catch was that we would have to spend thirty-four weeks of each year at a mission boarding school, while our parents remained far away in the jungle where they lived among the natives.

The jungle was a primitive place. There were no phones, no

Internet, no faxes, and no telegrams. The local post office was a two-and-a-half-hour hike away over mountain passes plus a half-hour trip over dirt roads in an overcrowded pickup truck. All my parents had for regular communication with us was a one-way radio.

Once a week, on our assigned radio day, we kids would walk up the steep hill at our school base and speak into a radio to our parents. Everyone on the mission field who owned a radio could hear us talking, so it was certainly not a private conversation. It actually wasn't a conversation at all, since our parents couldn't talk back to us. They could only listen.

The one-way radio may have helped my parents feel better, but it didn't fill the void in my heart. I was facing many more weeks at school without any communication from my parents whom I adored!

Just when I was getting discouraged, however, the letters started coming. Most often, they were from Mom. The letters were always at least a week old because of the country's slow mail system, but we didn't care. We were just delighted to hear from our parents!

Mom had a gift for writing, giving silly details of what was happening in their tribal location. She'd tell me what my native friends were doing, and she'd write

## START SMALL

Recording your memories can be an intimidating project to start. Begin small and the results will eventually add up.

Keep the stack of photos from your recent trip in a convenient place. Choose one each day and, using photo-safe ink, write the date the picture was taken along with the names of the people and places in the picture.

Pick one person you feel could use a caring letter and write a short note to him or her on the first day of each month.

Decide you won't leave a family event or holiday celebration without taking at least one picture.

Begin a tradition of writing legacy or appreciation letters. Choose an event to prompt the writing of these letters such as a birthday or holiday.

down the antics of our dog Snuggles and Rascal, our aptly-named cat. She'd write of the price they paid for bananas that morning and about what kind of bread she'd baked from scratch that day. She'd let me know which mountain Dad had hiked to visit a new tribal group and how many times it had rained during the week.

Even though it was difficult for my parents to send mail, we received letters several times a week. They often came four at a time, with one letter per child. Mom had become creative with the mail delivery. On the days Dad couldn't make the time-consuming trip into town, Mom would hire a native who was always happy to hike to town with a little change in his pocket.

Through the details in her letters, Mom kept us children in the midst of our parents' daily lives. Although we still wished we could be with them, we felt a part of the memories our parents were making in the jungle.

Later, I flew away to attend college in the United States. Mom's frequent letters followed me, even though it took more than two weeks for the letters to make the trip from Papua New Guinea to Florida.

Each letter my mother wrote to me, and any letter I have received from her since, has been saved in shoe boxes. The letters mean more to me than any material thing I could have received from my mother.

Now, twenty-four years from the day I began attending that boarding school, I am also a mother of four. Although I homeschool my children and am with them daily, I still write letters to them in journals. When they're older, I'll give each of them their journal of letters and they, too, will know the treasure that is in a letter from Mom.

## UNUSED GIFTS BY LINDA LAMAR JEWELL

When Grandma died, my parents and sisters, aunts, uncles, and cousins faced the sad task of dismantling my grandparents' home. Normally a noisy bunch, we worked quietly, each with his or her own memories of Grandma and Grandpa.

During those June days, I worked in the hot garage and the attic overhead. There I found a few treasures, such as my uncle's baby dress Grandma had saved for more than sixty years. I also found many unused gifts in their original packaging that well-meaning friends and family members had given my grandparents over the years. Knowing Grandma and Grandpa, they had probably smiled, thanked the givers of the gifts, and then put the gifts in the attic until they could figure out what in the world to do with them.

The following winter I remembered the experience of cleaning out my grandparents' garage of unused gifts. I grew cranky about Christmas because I thought it too commercial. However, God has a sense humor and showed me in Esther 9:19 that the Jews celebrated their deliverance from their enemy "with gladness and feasting, as a holiday, and for sending presents to one another." This verse inspired me to take a fresh look at my Christmas gift giving—a way to celebrate with others our deliverance from the Enemy of our souls.

I believe that heritage is the gift we've been given by previous generations, and legacy is the gift we give to future generations. I now write at least one heritage letter and one legacy letter to send to my family each Christmas. A sample of the stories I wrote the first year follows.

*Dear Ones,*

*The autumn Great-Aunt Nell was eighty-five and I was forty-nine, she reminisced about how much her grandmother, my great-great-grandmother Parsons, loved flowers. While gathering the round, flat*

**271**

seed pods from the lower skirts of pink hollyhocks, Aunt Nell and I chatted. Pausing at an old-fashioned, single-bloom variety, she shared seeds and stories about how Grandmother Parsons taught her to make hollyhock dolls.

I, on the other hand, meandered through more recent memories—splashes of dahlias and hanging baskets of bougainvillaea near my own mother's porch. I smiled remembering Mom's delight when my sisters, Jannet and Sharon, sent her a hundred daffodil bulbs one fall to bring sunshine to her soul the next spring. I recalled gathering handfuls of wildflowers from the crazy-quilt patch of color Mom still grows in the mountain meadow outside her office window.

While wondering if green thumbs are hereditary, I suddenly comprehended my rich heritage—a love for flower gardens—handed down from mothers to daughters. Surely my mother also learned her appreciation for flowers from her mother. Everyone who knew Grandma knew that she loved flowers.

I recalled a day of blue skies forty years earlier when I joined my grandmother in her cutting garden planted south of the house. Like colorful jewels in jumbled rows, flowers separated the vegetable garden and the expanse of emerald green lawn edged with bridal wreath. Entering the cutting garden was like stepping into a Monet painting. With the sun kissing my face, I waded through waist-high bachelor buttons to look bleeding hearts in the eye.

That long-ago day, Grandma's crown of white hair touched my sunbleached bangs. We both leaned down, and she showed me how to deadhead a spent iris without disturbing the remaining blooms and buds. She pointed out petals easily bruised by carelessness and disregard.

Grandma's flower garden doubled as life's classroom. Without words, Grandma's tender care for her iris impressed on me that, like flowers, some people bruise easily and that I must handle them with gentleness. With the dignity of new maturity, I felt grown up because Grandma shared with me one of many secrets of womanhood. Today, I still remember Grandma's lesson. When removing spent iris blooms, I have gentle hands.

I trust that my grandmother's mother, whom we called Grandma Lou, shared her love for flowers with Grandma. Ten years ago, while driving through a residential area, tears welled up when I spotted an unexpected bunch of lavender iris—the color I associate with Grandma Lou. Although she passed away two decades earlier, I still missed her spunk, her common sense, her frank, loving questions. Prompted by the unexpected emotional response on my drive down the side street, I later planted Pacific Mist, a lavender-colored iris, in memory of Grandma Lou.

Surely, Grandma Lou learned to love flowers from her mother, Great-Great-Grandmother Parsons. Aunt Nell later took me to explore the long-deserted Parsons' home place. Rogue trees and overgrown weeds filled the yard. No budding beauties nodded hello. However, knowing Grandmother Parsons' love for flowers, I closed my eyes and imagined her yard in full bloom. I wished I could open the iron gate and meet Grandmother Parsons in her cherished flower garden. I'd chat with her about her favorites, and then arm-in-arm we'd contemplate a backdrop of hollyhocks dolled up in red-ruffled flounces. Woman-to-woman, I would say thank you for passing along a heritage of love for beautiful flowers.

Aunt Nell brought me out of my reverie with an offer of heirloom hollyhock seeds. Surrounded by flowers, I felt a bond with my *great-great-grandmother, whom I never met. Curious, I asked Aunt Nell if Grandmother Parsons' mother or grandmother loved flowers. She didn't know. I may never find out. But deep in my soul, I believe that like the hollyhock seeds Aunt Nell gave to me, Grandmother Parsons also handed down a priceless inheritance.*

*Perhaps I, too, can share the love for flower gardens with a daughter-in-law, a granddaughter, or a great-granddaughter. Or, separated by time, even a great-great-granddaughter. This is why I'm writing to you—the future yet-unknown-to-me generations. My prayer is that you, too, will appreciate your heritage. It includes a love for flower gardens—an everlasting bouquet preserved by generations of women.*

*Forever yours,*

*Linda Heinz LaMar Jewell (1949–)*

*Betty (B. J.) Frame Heinz Harris (1930–)*

*Mom Goldie Harris Frame (1905–1992)*

*Grandma Lula Parsons Harris (1885–1969)*

*Great-Grandma Lou Alcena Ripley Parsons (1851–1938)*

*Great-Great-Grandmother Parsons*

After the letter about growing flowers, I added photos of six generations of women in my family, starting with Great-Great-Grandmother and ending with my niece. A great-aunt helped me find old photos, which I scanned. Two aunts helped me identify names and birth and death dates of the different generations.

Years from now, will someone find my gifts unwrapped in a garage? No, I don't think so. The special gift of knowing more about our heritage and our legacy is something that money can't buy—and is as precious in the giving as in the receiving.

# 16

# PRESERVING THE MEMORIES

## *Lauren*

*H*ave you ever wondered, *What year did we vacation in Yosemite?*
or *When was the Jansen family reunion?* Randy and I often discuss our past trips and family events when we're traveling.

Last fall, we went on a weekend getaway to celebrate my birthday.
As we ate breakfast at the Apple Farm in San Luis Obisbo, our typical
topic of conversation came up. Each date and event grew foggier as
the discussion proceeded. We decided, right there in that restaurant,
to document what we could remember. On the placemat, Randy
chronicled family trips, important events that came to mind, and any
major parties we'd hosted. After our meal, we went straight to Office
Depot and purchased two spiral notebooks. One is for the first twenty-
five years of our marriage and the other is for the next.

That night in the hotel room, I headed every three pages with the
years since our marriage. Throughout the remainder of the weekend,
I entered any key dates and events we remembered. Once I returned
home, I began looking through calendars and photo albums for information to store in our journals. I'm a long way from finishing the first
twenty-five years, but at least I have a place to record the information.

I've made entries for the funny names my husband has made up for each of our sons, the plays we've been in, the years our boys changed schools or graduated, our twenty-fifth wedding anniversary party, and other milestones. I want this to be a simple record of what has happened in our lives.

Someday, these notebooks, written in my handwriting, will serve as a valuable document for family memories. Consider creating something similar for your family.

## THE CAMERA IS ROLLING by RANDY BRIGGS, SR.

Older relatives are precious and valuable resources. Value them and make yourself available to the decades of knowledge they possess and are often willing to share.

For years I threatened to videotape my uncles Donald and Daryl, my mother's brothers, but I never had an opportunity I thought was "just right" until recently.

My wife and I, along with our son Jonathan, just spent a few days in Iowa visiting my mother's side of the family. Our visits are usually punctuated by a family get-together and this trip was no exception. We met at my cousin Jerilyn's home, and twenty or so of us celebrated family by having a barbeque in the driveway. We spent several hours visiting in the balmy evening air and had a tremendous time swapping stories. As the stories got started, eighty-seven-year-old Uncle Donald, who is virtually blind, began adding his "two cents' worth." Jonathan, quick on the uptake, revealed his digital movie camera. We set it up on a nearby card table and managed to capture almost an hour of "pure Uncle Don." Everyone except my uncle knew he was being taped, so we all egged him on, prodding him for more information. The tape is a gem and will thrill generations to come. He is a wonderful and colorful man whose stories will live for decades.

The next day we ventured to the family farm where my uncle Daryl has farmed for more than fifty years. My family has owned the farm since my immigrant great-grandfather bought it in 1905. My mother and her brothers were all born on the farm, so the property obviously has tremendous meaning to us all.

The first year Daryl bought the farm from my grandfather, in the forties, he had a pretty good harvest. Feeling flush, he bought himself a new tractor: a bright-red B model Farmall. He knew the tractor would allow him to till the fields better, as well as complete other chores necessary to the overall productivity and profitability of the property. When his father saw his new purchase he asked, "Where'd you get the tractor?" My uncle told him he'd bought it with his profits. Grandpa responded that if my uncle had so much extra money, he could pay off his loan right then and there.

Obviously, my uncle didn't have enough to pay off the loan from his father, so he was forced to swallow his pride and sell the tractor. Today, it seems like a very hard line to take with a son, but in those days immediately following the Depression, it was a reasonable and not totally unexpected demand, which my uncle honored.

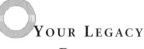

## YOUR LEGACY PRESERVED

Tips for preserving your memories:

Use acid-free paper and pens, when possible, for any writing you intend to last into the future.

If you need encouragement to set aside time for working on your family history. Invite several friends to come over to work on their own family histories too. Have food, music, and fun.

Save family e-mails on CD-ROM.

Preserve letters and cards in a binder or box. Organize by date or by the family member who sent it.

Have slides placed on DVD for easier viewing. Consider narrating the show to tell the stories behind the pictures. Share copies with other family members.

Many years later, my uncle heard of a farm auction nearby and attended in hopes of finding something he could use. There, right in the middle of the sale items, was a well-used Model B! He placed the winning bid, transported it back to the farm, and painstakingly and lovingly took it completely apart and rebuilt the machine. Today, it is his pride and joy, and every time he gets the chance, he displays it and drives it in parades.

Imagine my joy when Jonathan captured Uncle Daryl telling the story of the Model B on videotape. He seemed oblivious to our taping and just rambled on and on. Once again, we have preserved his memories for future generations. How I wish video cameras had been around when my mother and my grandparents had been alive.

## THE LOST ART OF WRITING LETTERS BY SANDRA SCHOGER FOSTER

Letters found in an old trunk in the attic, in a box in the garage, or in a desk drawer connect us to our heritage. Reading them over and over floods us with memories and puts us back in touch with old friends and relatives. Legacies can be uncovered and embraced in letters. The electronic age has pretty much taken over, and letter writing may someday become a lost art.

My maternal grandfather, Harry O. Paschal, was a great letter-writer. Many miles separated us, but we felt close because we bridged the distance by writing letters. When I see his or Grandma's handwriting, I see their faces. When I read their words, I hear their voices.

Grandpa ended most of his letters with "Nuf-Ced." His creativity made them interesting. Once he opened a small flowered sack and wrote on the inside. He drew ducks or birds along the margins. He made capital letters in the salutation fancy for emphasis. Even when he didn't feel well, he kept writing to us. When he lost his hearing, letters became the only way to stay in touch. The box of letters and birthday cards I've saved from him and my grandmother are treasures. Reading them, I'm back in time to the date postmarked on the envelope. I'm so glad he took the time to write, because generations that follow him will have a peek into his life.

One letter said, "You were a bundle of curiosity when you were a little girl, Sandra. Very anxious to see everything and find out why, who, where, what, and how come. Now what else should I write to a granddaughter who's so loving and kind? Do you know we have never seen your children?"

That was all I needed to hear. I started planning for us to fly to Florida the next year. The pictures I took of my children in 1974 with their great-grandparents are invaluable.

In a letter dated 1976, Grandpa recalls that visit. "Dear Sandra, I'll never forget our last look at you at the airport as you left for California. Ray and the two children had gone onto the plane and you stayed as long as you could with us. Someone hollowed [sic] out 'time to leave,' and you very hurriedly kissed and hugged us again and ran to get on board. You were out of sight and then in a second you stuck your head back out of the door to see us once more. A big smile was on your face. I see it yet." It was special to have the details of that long-gone moment captured in his letter.

A cherished letter from him in the late 1970s went like this:

*Well, as you know, G'ma is nearing the time to leave this life and go to heaven, and it will leave me with a broken heart. My Ole Pal, Effie and your grandpa have been together constantly for over 70 years. Effie was my first and only true love. We went together steady three years and ten months before we married. The dear Lord has been so good to us.*

*Effie was a Christian before I was. She is the one that got me going to church. I went so I could be with her. My first day with Effie was July 23, 1905. I'm just as sure she was meant for me as 2 + 2 = 4. She is so sweet, and to think I have to give her up grieves me. Oh, Sandra, it's been so heart breaking to see her look so bad. I go to see her every day in the hospital. I want her to get well and stay on with me like it used to be. One night I patted her sweet face and told her visiting hours were over and it was time for me to go. She held up both arms and put them around my neck and pulled me down and we began to cry. We both cried together.*

Grandpa reached out to me and let me see his heart. My children and grandchildren will read these letters someday and remember the legacy he left.

Grandpa wasn't the only person who wrote to me. My grandmother also wrote often. In one of her letters she said, "You always say, 'Write to me, Grandma' in your letters, so I am writing to you, my dear same-birthday granddaughter."

I've also kept letters from my children—notes written from summer camp, when they went on choir tour, and after they left home. Kristin wrote from choir tour, "Mom, we are having a great time. I met someone in one of the churches that knows you. I think he was your old boyfriend." Another letter from her: "Mom and Dad, force Bradley to write me. He promises, yet he never does. I've written him twice already and have heard nothing. Thanx for sending me to college at Point Loma. I wouldn't trade this experience for anything. I'd better go. I have homework. I may not be home this weekend. I'm dating a cute guy named Mike. Love always, Kristin."

Our son, Bradley, sent letters about his adventures in various countries overseas while he was in the U.S. Air Force. One letter said, "It rained and rained here in Guam. I don't know if we will ever dry out." From Turkey he wrote, "Some buddies and I flew from Ankara to Istanbul. We went to a supper club and they asked us what country we were from. We posed as Canadians in case of trouble. At one point in the program they asked each table to stand and sing their national anthem. My buddies and I didn't know the words after 'O Canada, O Canada' and stumbled around trying to fake-sing it. We couldn't stop laughing. Can't wait to get home and see you guys. Love, Brad."

Reading and rereading a letter from a loved one is a walk back in history and gives hope to the next generation.

As my dear grandfather used to write, "Nuf-Ced."

## LIFE IN THE STORE BY THE REV. JAMES W. CHAPMAN

Imagine growing up in a home where the front room had an ice cream chest, a cooler for soft drinks, a twenty-foot long candy case, Hostess cream-filled cupcakes, and many other childhood delicacies! That is precisely what my sister Florence, brother Ron, and I had. In 1936 when we were nine, five, and one years old, our parents moved us into three rooms behind a small variety store in Haverhill, Massachusetts. In a video of my mother reminiscing about that move, she paints a picture of quiet desperation. It was

### FAITH OF OUR FATHERS

Use a family Bible to record births, deaths, marriages, and spiritual milestones.

When obtaining information on general life history, search for or ask for information on a family member's spiritual life.

Consider purchasing a special gown or outfit for your baby's dedication or baptism. If you can, find one that has been used in your family before.

Create a spiritual journal in which you can share your own spiritual journey. Include special sections for God's blessings and answered prayers.

1936 and the Depression had not relaxed its grinding grip. My father was fifty-eight and my mother thirty-eight. When my brother was born that year, they saw no way to keep the family together. They planned to have my mother move back with us to Merrimac, Massachusetts, where we would live with our grandmother until my father could find work.

Then came the sermon!

One of the great preachers of that day was Harry Emerson Fosdick, one of the first to use the radio for religious programming. On a Sunday when my folks were seeing no resolution to their problems, Fosdick preached a sermon titled, "Hang on a Little Longer." It was precisely the message my folks needed to hear, and they decided to wait a bit. Not long after that inspiring sermon, they were notified that a former employer of my father's had died and left him and others $2,000! Their astonishment and joy could not be measured. That was a significant amount of money in 1936.

Shortly thereafter, my mother took us kids up to Merrimac for a visit, where she saw an ad in the *Haverhill Gazette* offering a small store for sale in Haverhill, the next town. She called "Chappie"—her name for my father—and told him about it. He took the train up. They went over, looked at it, and decided to buy it.

Thus the Riverside Variety Store was born. And that is how our front room had all those wonderful objects for our daily indulgence. We lived in the three rooms behind the store with just a door separating our living quarters from the store. For a couple of years we had two bedrooms upstairs before the landlord took them away. During that period, to get from our kitchen to the upstairs bedrooms we had to walk through the store, greeting customers as we paraded through in our pajamas, receiving good wishes from all assembled.

Then we went into the "tank room," which I presume none of you reading this will have had. It contained a one-hundred-gallon tank of kerosene, which we sold to the customers for fuel. As I look back on that fire hazard, I realize we lived literally one misdirected match away from oblivion! From the tank room, we wended our way up a flight of stairs, lifted a trap door in the floor above, and entered the multi-window sunroom. I thought this room with windows on three sides was beautiful. However, as I mentioned, the landlord soon felt those quarters were much too spacious for a family of five, so we retreated back to the three rooms

This all sounds pretty Paleolithic, I'm sure. And in many ways it was. We had no hot water, so there was always a kettle of water simmering on the kerosene-fueled stove in the kitchen; the only heat in the three rooms was from that stove. There was no bath tub, so we washed as best we could—which was probably not very well—in the large, black kitchen sink about six feet from the door to the store. As I perched up there on the counter by the sink, bathing, it could not help but pass through my anxious mind that a few feet away in one direction was a store with people coming and going, and from the other direction could suddenly appear my brother or worse—my sister! Baths tended to be short.

All these details set the stage for the observation that we virtually lived in the store. We all waited on customers. We all visited with them. We knew almost all of them and even had special names for many of them. They were our extended family. The ice cream and candy were dandy, but the people were the real charm of the store. We kids did everything there was to be done. We stocked shelves. We cleaned the "tonic chest" (soft drinks for you who have never lived in New England). The only phone we had was the pay phone in the store, so we contrived elaborate signals with our friends who knew if their signal ring sounded they were to call us back. In that way we saved a nickel!

My father died in 1948, three days after Christmas. It was a stunning blow. My sister was home from her senior year at the University of Massachusetts, I was a senior in high school, and my brother was in the eighth grade. I had never thought about my father dying. For thirteen years he had gotten up before six to catch people on their way to work on the 6:10 bus. With an hour's nap in the afternoon, he was able to stay open until eleven—a sixteen-hour day—seven days a week. (He closed the store for Thanksgiving and Christmas afternoons and an hour each Sunday for church.) Why should a kid worry about such a man dying?

My mother and he had gone to Boston for the day and then were to meet friends for an evening at the theater. This was the first time in thirteen years that they had gone away together for so much as a day! My mother said in retrospect that it was as though he wanted to see everything there was to see in the city he loved so well. He did, until he collapsed of a heart attack and died coming up out of the Boylston Street subway station. My mother returned home alone to tell of the tragedy. She tried to hold the store together for a couple of years as I went off to college and my sister came back to teach at our old high school where my brother was still a student. It was too much for my mother to handle, however, and she soon sold the store and went back to care for her aging mother in Merrimac, where she had grown up.

The store ceased to exist, but its memories took on a life of their own. Whenever any of the three of us gets back to Haverhill, we go straight to Tilton's Corners, where the building still stands. Even today as I look at it, it is illuminated by the memories of people, candy, risky bathing, and big jugs of kerosene for the kitchen stove. I could draw a diagram that would be accurate to within a foot or two, showing where everything was fifty years ago.

Now take a great leap forward with me to the 1980s. The store is long gone. My mother has followed my father to what must have been their great reward. When my wife and I would visit antique stores, I would say, "We used to sell that in the store!" One day she said, "Why don't you start collecting things that you remember from the store?" So I did. I bought boxes of soap powder ("Rinso White! Happy little washday song!"), milk bottles from the Clover Leaf Dairy, and all kinds of tobacco cans we had sold. After a few years, I had more than 150 items that we had stocked in the store. My sister had some old items that had really been in the store, and she contributed them to my collection. We had a bright orange gasoline pump outside the store

## JUST GETTING STARTED

Pick one or two of the following ways to record family memories:

Videotape family memories as they are shared, or film important places you visit.

Write letters and keep the ones you receive in return. Do the same with e-mail.

Create a "life-event" journal. For every important moment or holiday, jot down one or two special memories. Make a separate one that will bring things up to the present day by writing as many memories as you can, a few at a time.

Have your digital pictures placed on DVD.

Write notes to keep with your mementos and family heirlooms that tell their stories.

that dispensed Gulf Gas into thirsty cars if their owners had the proper ration coupon! My brother found one exactly like it and shipped it to Michigan, where we had built a cottage on the shore of Lake Michigan. It now stands proudly in the living room of the cottage, marking the entrance to the "store." When the light in the globe on top is on, the store is open to the grandchildren.

What store, you ask? In 1973, my first wife and I had built our cottage, a large A-frame to house our six kids each summer. The corner room on the main floor was my workshop, out of which some remarkable achievements emerged over the years. In 1998, after my wife died after a long battle with breast cancer and I was on my own, I built a small barn behind the house for the workshop. Thus I had an empty room where the shop had been. I remarried in 2000, proudly showed off the cottage to my new wife, and told her about the store and the stuff I had bought. She noticed the orange gas pump in the living room on her own, and suggested that I turn that room into a museum of the store.

We went to work mounting shelves, building stands for two glass showcases we bought at an antique sale, and erecting a counter for the cash register and other nostalgic items from the store. Carolyn made red, white, and blue skirts for the stands the cases were on, and I found a straw hat like the one my father wore from Memorial Day to Labor Day every year. Florence had saved the actual white apron our father always wore. We bought fifteen clear glass bowls and filled them with penny candy typical of the thirties and forties. We had root beer barrels, Necco wafers, malted milk balls, the strips of paper with little dots of candy on them, the wax bottles with sweet liquid inside, Bit-o-Honey, and a host more. We had planned a Chapman family reunion for July of 2001 and decided to make it the dedication of the "store." And so all were invited!

The great day came, and about sixty people descended on little Saugatuck, Michigan, for the big event. On Friday evening, we gathered the clan and told the story of the "robbery" and the "fire," two hallowed events in the original store's history that my children and grandchildren have heard probably too often over the years. Then my brother, Ron, presented us with an antique pay phone just like the one we'd had in the store. Finally, we cut the ribbon and turned on the gas pump light, and the store was opened!

I don't know when I have enjoyed a scene as much as watching all those little grandchildren crowd into the store to buy their penny candy. My nephew Randy is a coin dealer and generously provided a hoard of coins, a few bills, and even silver dollars from that era. So the kids were actually spending money from the thirties and forties!

We opened the store that weekend about three times each day and had a crowd every time. On Saturday evening, we catered a dinner comprised of food we ate in the kitchen behind the store, including Spam (not the Internet variety!) with cloves stuck in and a mustard-and-brown-sugar crust, canned B&M Baked Beans, and Spanish cream made from tapioca pudding. The young grandchildren were not sure that this was an era in which they would have liked to live!

Before everyone left on Sunday, we had had a worship service on the bluff above the lake, a maypole dance like we used to do at the church across the street from the store, and in many other ways relived those ancient days of living in a store.

Every family has a history, a heritage, a story to tell, and a place to be revisited. Ours is the store in Haverhill. I hope to go back there next year and show my new wife and her daughter the site of so much memory and illumination. The store is now an apartment, but the shape of the building is still the same. The three crescent steps that led to the store still mark the entry to the apartment. It is not hard to translate it back into what it was for us so long ago.

Some years ago we were back there and as we stood outside trying not to look too threatening, a car pulled up and a young woman got out. I stepped forward and told her I had grown up there when it was a store. She recalled having heard about the store and invited us in. My heart almost stopped! To enter again into that hallowed spot! And so we did! Everything was changed, but everything was the same. The bay window, the door to the kitchen from what was the store, and the three tiny rooms—shrunk by the ages—were still there. I think that, through my visits to Haverhill with my children and now their children, much of my history is alive to them.

Now with the store in Michigan, they share each summer in what went on there and hear again the stories that comprise so much of my biography. After one of the family times at the cottage, one of my daughters asked the children what they had enjoyed most about their stay at the lake. Three little voices piped out in unison, "Grandpa's store!" Hearing that made it all worthwhile to me. I felt the legends of the Riverside Variety Store would live on for at least another generation. I suspect that when my sister, brother, and I lie dying one of these days, many of our thoughts will be, to steal a line from General MacArthur, "... of the store,... and the store,... and the store."

## OLD STONE HOUSE by RANDY BRIGGS, SR.

When my Cass ancestors moved from New York to Iowa in the 1840s, they ultimately settled just north of the town of Monmouth. My great-great-grandfather, David, built out of locally quarried stone a two-story house that, for several generations, the Casses called home.

A number of years ago my uncle took me to see the old house. It stood empty, and I was granted permission to go inside and look around. I walked all around the property and then went inside, video taping and narrating as I went. What a thrill to step back into my family's history and see the place where many of them had been born and lived.

A year later I returned to do some more documenting and much to my horror, the house had been torn down! I was crushed as I had considered offering to buy the place just to keep it in the family. Obviously, I hadn't moved fast enough, but how grateful I was to have taken the time to do that videotaping. Don't wait to document your family history.

## BLESSING THOSE WHO HAVE GIVEN US WONDERFUL LEGACIES BY KARLA LOVELESS-DILLON

A few years ago, my husband and I asked friends and family to share how my parents had blessed them through the years. I didn't want these comments kept hidden and shared only at their funerals. How nice it would be (though somewhat embarrassing for such a humble couple) to show them the impact they had made on others. Months later at our Christmas Eve gathering, I presented Mom and Dad with a book full of blessings.

As important as it is to pass on the blessing of a legacy, it's just as important to bless backward, if at all possible. Following is the letter I wrote to my parents:

*Dear Mom and Dad,*

*As I was preparing for Christmas this year, I thought back to all the Christmas traditions in our home. We were blessed that all our holidays were filled with brightly wrapped packages that held our heart's desires. The house was always decorated, the Christmas story acted out by the cousins, and Christmas dinner topped off with pumpkin and butterscotch pies.*

*I also began to think about all the wonderful gifts I have received in my lifetime. I want to share with you those which have come to mean the most. The most precious gifts have been the lessons I have learned from you.*

*When Karen and I were very young, we would race from the '57 Chevy, across the street, and up the steps to our house. I loved it when I got to be with Dad. If it looked like we were going to lose, you'd just sweep me up in your arms and off we'd go. You were the strongest man alive! And I always knew I was safe in your arms. This gift of feeling safe and protected while running at full speed was a wonderful foundation on which to grow. I could step out, take a chance, and still feel the comfort and support from Mom and Dad.*

*One of the very best gifts I received was your time. We spent a lot of time together as a family. Whether it was Sunday drives, Friday league bowling, driving across the country, darts in the garage, or simply dinner around the table, I always felt that you wanted us to be with you, that you enjoyed us. You always took the extra effort to be active in our lives—PTA, costumes, plays, parent-teacher nights, all the while being chauffeur, cook, and counselor. By your example, I have learned that giving time to those we care about shows how much we value them. You have made me feel valued all my life.*

*Dad, you have been a man of integrity, loyalty, and honesty. You have stood firm when others have made compromises. Your strength of character and your steadfastness have been like a light guiding others to a higher, more moral pathway.*

*Mom, you have been a woman of gentleness, compassion, and wisdom. You have listened to the woes of many and yet continue to treat everyone with dignity and respect. You have a great way of putting others at ease and drawing out their best qualities.*

*Both of you have taught me how to have a serving heart. You continue to use the gifts you've been given to help others in any way you can. You have taught me how to love simply by being who you are and by the way you raised me. And the most important thing you taught me was about Jesus. What you taught me about him will have an eternal impact on the generations to come.*

*I am so very blessed and proud to have you as my parents. You have done a wonderful job in raising your children and have touched the lives of countless people. I love you.*

The letters I wrote are more precious to my parents than any expensive gift.

## Capturing the Moment

CLASS Speakers had just purchased a video camera and some studio lights to film our speakers during advanced training. Because I (Lauren) was going to be the videographer, I set everything up in my living room. Grammy Chapman was living with us at the time, and I explained I needed to learn how to use the equipment. I asked her if she would read three-year-old Jonathan a bedtime story there in the living room so I could learn how to do everything. Grammy was never interested in new technology and was afraid if she touched anything wrong it would "blow up"!

Having no idea what all this equipment meant, she willingly sat in an overstuffed chair. Jonathan, in his fuzzy yellow sleeper, climbed up in her lap and sat quietly while Grammy read him a story. When she finished, with the camera still rolling, I took Jonathan to bed, and Randy slipped onto the couch to visit with Grammy. We hadn't planned what came next, but it became a precious moment in history.

Knowing the camera was still recording, Randy started asking

Grammy about her family, her childhood, memories of her father, and what her life was like raising children during the Depression. Because he was an in-law and hadn't been raised on these stories, she happily conversed for more than an hour.

Set the stage for some of these once-in-a-lifetime moments, and you'll be amazed at what you might capture.

## YEARBOOKS FOR MY CHILDREN BY SUZY RYAN

Each year during school, I purchase a three-ring binder and page protectors and create a book for that school year for each of my children. I store report cards, pictures, and projects they have completed in there. By the end of the year, these volumes are rather thick. My husband teases me that the kids won't be happy to have to cart twelve enormous notebooks to their new homes after college. I am not deterred, however, because I see them look through their binders throughout the year.

Since I've done this for more than ten years, I've found it actually reduces clutter because I only pick the cream of the crop to include in their books, and now that they're older, they choose for themselves. The rest is trashed without guilt.

I also keep a journal for my three children, which I started when they were babies. I write twice a month about what they're doing and how they're maturing. I love recording their history for them and hope they'll continue this tradition with their own children someday.

## IT'S REALLY WORTH IT

An old stone house, a store, and a tractor. They all held special meaning to those sharing their stories in this chapter. And, they were all legends worth preserving. Each of these stories was captured differently, but each will be kept safe for the coming generations. Family members will enjoy seeing on film the remains of the home that sheltered their ancestors, children will have a first-hand experience of grandpa's childhood in the store, and everyone will appreciate the first-hand account of the tractor and the life lesson it taught. It doesn't matter if the things you want to keep are as everyday as your children's schoolwork. You and future generations of your family will appreciate the things you preserve. And it often only takes a little creative effort to ensure your family history becomes a legacy for years to come.

# 17

# WHAT WILL YOU DO?

## *FLORENCE*

*D*ear Friends,

Thank you, thank you!

Thank you for being my friend over the many years of my Christian ministry. Thank you for coming to the seminars, some of you so many times you could recite my life growing up in three rooms behind my father's store by heart—and be convincing! Thank you for coming to CLASS and answering God's call on your life to share your faith with others. Thank you for coming to Bible studies in our home, looking at the artifacts we've written about in this book, and observing our family's dedication to the Lord Jesus in our everyday life. Thank you for loving my two daughters through their years of ministry—first beside me and now also on their own. Thank you for noticing how my husband, Fred, honored me, cared for me, parted the Red Sea for me. Thank you for supporting me at the time of his sudden death, and for writing of his life-changing effect on you. Thank you for keeping in touch with me and praying daily for our family, for my health and ability to keep going year after year.

Now, to those of you who didn't know me and bought this book because you liked the bright blue plate on the cover, has it been a blessing? Have you received new ideas for your home and your heart?

My hope for all of you is that the words in this book will translate into motivation to create new family traditions, to remember and communicate the good things in your past, and to prepare a legacy for the future. That what you've read will not add to your daily burdens, but make them lighter and give you a renewed sense of purpose.

We've titled the book after a simple household item with little monetary value that represents an emotional memory for me. I still have it and will pass it on. Remember, it's not the cost of the item—it's the story behind it that brings value.

What treasure do you have in your attic, basement, garage, or storage shed? Does your mother have memories of your childhood that she would give you if she knew you'd display them? Are there cradles, quilts, or wedding gowns hidden away in cardboard boxes? Find them, bring them out, and tell their story. Pull your children away from the TV, sit down with them, and tell them about your life and your possessions.

Once you've gathered up some treasures and told their stories, what can you do with them? Using a little creativity, and some of the ideas presented in this book, you can decorate walls with all kinds of memorable items. Set groupings of similar items on a table, shelf, or mantel. I have a collection of little cream pitchers Fred bought for me all over the world. He chose a different one each day for my morning coffee. He loved making the selection from more than fifty choices, and I loved that he cared enough to give me variety. Marita has on display an old bicycle with a basket full of goodies heading for a picnic. Guests stop in their tracks when they see a bicycle in the living room. "I never would have thought of that" is the response she hears most often.

Does your family sit down together for at least one meal each day? Do you discuss topics of interest to them? Do they look forward to their time at the table? Can they bring a friend home for dinner? Our policy was, I would feed anyone, but my child had to ask my permission *before* inviting friends. My children enjoyed helping to prepare meals. Some parents want the children out of the kitchen, but this produces adults who get married and can't cook a simple meal. "McDonald's again?" Both my daughters are gourmet cooks and love to entertain. Do you have company for dinner at least once a month? Are your children learning hospitality? Remember, it is not the expense of the food that brings value, but the feel and the fellowship that brings value.

"Tradition! Tradition!" sang Tevye in *Fiddler on the Roof*. Tradition is what binds a family together even when they grow up and move away. It's heartwarming to hear children—even adult children—say, "I always look forward to..." Are you creating any traditions that will last? Over the years I gathered up holiday table decorations and place-mats. I had two shelves in the linen closet devoted to storing these centerpieces. I would bring them out one or two weeks before the holiday. I decorated for everything, even Groundhog Day! The children looked forward to these changes, and my daughters have followed these traditions in their own ways.

Are there talents that have come down through the years? Show your children how their ability was passed down from Aunt Ruth. Emphasize talents and help your children to get involved in something they are good at; bring out their best. My mother's family was all musical. My father was a talker. My brothers and I are all professional speakers, and Jim is also musical. All three of my grandsons are professional musicians. What thread runs through your family? Are you doing anything to encourage this talent?

How about collections? Building a collection can be both fun and educational. Help children choose something they can look for when on vacations—something historical or biographical or theme oriented. My son-in-law Randy has the world's only complete collection of "siege notes" issued by General Charles Gordon in Khartoum. He has collections of Gordon's books, journals, artifacts, statues, bronzes, and autographs. I have been collecting memorabilia of Winston Churchill for years. My father, born in England, loved Churchill and insisted I listen to him speak on the radio during my teenage years. I have his books, tapes of his speeches, figurines, Wedgwood pieces, souvenirs, and even a teapot of him. On my coffee table is a grouping of his books topped with an antique bust of Churchill. It is unique as a decoration and educational as well. When people know you collect a specific type of artifact, they will find you presents all over the world.

How about Christmas? What, besides presents, gets your child excited over the impending holiday? What do you do every year? Do you have special dishes? Do you go to church on Christmas Eve? Do you make getting out the decorations an event? Do the children help polish the silver, select the tree, or help wrap the presents? In our family we each choose a certain wrapping paper for our gifts. I have silver boxes, Lauren uses blue with silver snowflakes, Marita wraps in Christmas rabbits. (Yes, there are such things.) When we get together on Christmas, we all know one family's gifts from another. Develop some holiday traditions and pass them on as part of your family legacy.

Do you make your family trips something the children look forward to, or are they long, boring drives without any meaningful conversation? We've given you some fascinating ideas to make the trip—not just the event—exciting. How about historical trips with a family study of the area before going? How about making your next trip one that will make history come alive?

As you think over your childhood, are there any missing branches on the family tree? Have you often wondered why Uncle Harry disappeared and why no one has mentioned him in years? Are any pieces of the puzzle missing? Ask about any untold stories. The knowledge, followed by understanding, may fill in gaps in your family's history. Why did my mother never tell me about my brother Arthur? She was so ashamed that she didn't have the money for a cemetery plot and a proper burial. Now I understand.

Are there adoptions in the family that may be untold stories? My adopted son is grateful for my choosing him, and he is so caring, kind, and considerate of me. What a blessing he is as my son. Are you childless by choice like Marita? Do some people try to make you feel guilty? Can you have a legacy when you don't have children? Can you be a very special aunt as Marita is? She has passed her knowledge of speaking and writing on to thousands through our CLASSeminars. I'm sure God is pleased with her living legacy.

Are you curious about your family tree? Where did you come from? What kind of roots did you have? My son-in-law Randy, who is a history-loving numismatist, has spent years researching both sides of the family. On our trip to Prince Edward Island we found direct descendants of my grandfather MacDougall's eleven siblings. We went to some of their homes, visited, and looked at photo albums of my relatives. What a blessing it is to find records and pictures of those who came before you. How eager we should be to start scrapbooks for our children so they can see ancestors they've never met. We all have a heritage. We must record it, preserve it, and picture it. As the Bible says, write it down for future generations.

Last but not least is our spiritual heritage. We can't pass down what we don't have. Do our children know our Christian testimony? Have we made being a believer a vital step to a full life? Have we taught our children verses, taken them to Sunday school, enrolled them in church activities, and shown them the joy of the Lord? It's hard to get our children excited for the Lord if we are negative and complaining ourselves. It's almost impossible to have children desiring to go to Sunday school if we don't go to church.

We've shown you some of the ideas that we have used in our family life to pass on a joyful legacy. We don't expect you to do all of these things, but each of you can adapt some of them into your life. Our hope is that you will consciously pass on your talents, possessions, and passions to your family members and teach others to collect artifacts and share their ideas and significance. With families scattered around the world, it is more important than ever to unite our families in faith, words, and deeds. You can establish a living legacy that will last through many future generations. Show your family why each blue plate is special.

# WRITING HERITAGE AND LEGACY LETTERS

Writing heritage and legacy letters isn't a linear process; it's weaving memories together. It's recording remembrances and research after reflecting about what's interesting and important from your life and family history.

You may start at any point. Perhaps a recently discovered photo or a conversation with a grandparent triggers a memory. Maybe curiosity about the migration of your family prompts you to interview relatives or search regional history books or census figures. You may come up with more questions to ask as you write up your notes after interviewing a grandparent.

What works for one family won't necessarily work for another. You can choose to write these letters alone, particularly if circumstances make input from other family members awkward. However, if at all possible, involve other family members. Pray that your family relationships will be strengthened in the process. Communicate with all others involved to ensure your relationships aren't harmed. Tap into collective remembrances. Various loved ones can contribute—a story, a fact, a document, a photo, an interpretation or an insight.

Look at ways to maximize various family members' strengths. For instance, if you are a good researcher and your sibling is a good writer, work as a team.

A special note to orphans: Heritage doesn't only come through our biological family, but also through adopted and foster families. Even if we are not legally adopted, we may still receive some of our heritage from those who adopted us into their hearts—aunts and uncles, grandparents, spiritual mothers and fathers, teachers, coaches, family friends, and neighbors. If you don't know who your biological family is, you can still write heritage and legacy letters by interviewing those who passed their heritage to you.

If you are in a situation where gathering family history is difficult, you can begin now and write for your children, grandchildren, nieces, and nephews, or for yourself.

When I teach letter-writing workshops, I only have one rule—do what works for you. However, I hope you will try the different things suggested here to see what will work for you as you write your own heritage and legacy letters.

## REMEMBER

Our memories are a good starting place when writing heritage and legacy letters. Remember the big things—as well as the little things that speak volumes.

We can remember:

Character traits of family members.

Possessions we hold dearly.

Family sayings, proverbs, quotes, Scriptures and mottos.

Guiding principles in our life or our ancestors' lives.

Significant national/international people and events.

Significant personal relationships and events.

Illnesses/diseases that run in the family.

Why we love what we love well.

What makes an ancestor special to you.

How ancestors spend their time/skills they taught others.

## REFRAME

I once heard that children are the best observers—and the worst interpreters. With time and experience we sometimes have the incredible opportunity to reframe a hurtful memory—and see how blessed we were. For instance, when I was five and my parents divorced, my sisters and I lived with my grandparents. Like many children of divorce, I wondered why my parents didn't love me enough to keep me, or if I caused the divorce in some way. As an adult, when I divorced my son's father, I realized the incredible love my parents showed when they divorced and, faced with unsolvable circumstances, allowed my sisters and me to live with my grandparents.

## REFRAIN

Sometimes we remember something painful, or a family history of which we are ashamed. We often wonder if it should be included.

On one hand, the Bible tells us we are to speak—and by inference write—the truth in love. Would practicing this teaching help future generations understand their ancestors and their own humanness? Would it help them see that they can learn from their mistakes, ask for and give forgiveness, and know freedom?

On the other hand, the Bible also says that love covers a multitude of sins (1 Peter 4:8), and you may not want to include some painful memories.

Regardless, we must be proud of what is good and right, not of what is bad and wrong. Shameful deeds should not be glorified. When shameful situations occur, you can report on them factually. Handled with care, we may be able to use these circumstances as gentle warnings to warn and deter thieves, alcoholics, or bullies in future generations, for example.

When I find shameful information, I usually let it rest for a while. We may need to journal about our memories or feelings to put them in perspective and ask God's understanding of the situation and wisdom as to whether or not to include certain information or stories.

In years to come, we may be able to reframe a shameful family heritage with information, insight, or forgiveness.

## Research and Request

### People and Places

Consider who may be willing and able to help in your research:

Family members

Family historians

Librarians

In addition to the people who might be involved, consider places where you can find more information:

Your own home

Family members' homes

Local museums

Local, genealogical, university, public, or private libraries

Internet

Family get-togethers

Newspaper offices

Local bookstores

Schools and churches

County courthouses

Cultural fairs and festivals

### Plans and Preparation

As you begin, have a goal and consider steps you'll take before you begin writing your heritage and legacy letters. Adjust your plans based on what you've been able to find and not find.

Brainstorm topics and format.

Prepare interview questions.

Plan the format. Your content shapes your format as much as your format shapes your content. Give yourself flexibility to change your format, especially in the beginning. There are a variety of formatting options, layouts, and bindings. For instance, you might prepare:

Individual letters written over the years, sealed and addressed to individuals.

A collection of letters slipped into sheet protectors placed into a three-ring binder.

A scrapbook with stories written around the pictures or pictures placed on one page and a related story placed on the facing page.

A family cookbook or genealogy with family stories or world events interspersed as separate sections.

A memory book or a tribute to parents or grandparents.

A yearly update for or about each of your children.

Copies of letters, lines of poetry, pictures, documents, artwork, mementos, or words from songs in a memory book.

A private printing of a bound book.

A commercially printed bound book with guided questions.

## Pull It Off

*Deadline*

Regardless of your format, consider a deadline for the final product and intermediate deadlines for finishing a draft or completing the finished letter or book of letters.

Whether the deadline is driven by Christmas, a birthday, a special anniversary, a family get-together, a school project, or a community project, work backward from that date. Consider breaking the project down into smaller goals to meet on a weekly or monthly basis.

Allow time for others' input, interviews, and times when you can't work on your legacy and heritage letters. If you're running out of time, consider if it's better to have a one-page letter completed than two longer letters half done.

*Accountability Partner*

If you work better with an accountability partner, agree to reasonable goals each week and report back on your progress.

*Alertness*

Be alert to information and insights in casual conversations. For instance, my mother was fond of Aunt Ora, but I didn't know why until the afternoon I told Mom I usually used Aunt Ora's recipe for holiday dinner rolls. Mom told of Aunt Ora's visits during a time when other family members ostracized her. From my casual comment, I gained an insight into Aunt Ora's character and my mother's affection for Aunt Ora.

*Family Involvement*

Others in your family have interests and talents that might lend themselves to a heritage and legacy letters project. Make choices that work well for you. However, if you're working with others, discuss choices that impact all those involved in piecing together and recording your family heritage.

*Time Management*

Like a Boy Scout, "Be Prepared." Think about what you would like to know and how you can achieve it. Pre-plan interview questions, but be prepared to be flexible. Think ahead to the supplies you'll need, the visits you'll need to schedule.

Plan to make those calls or visits and write those letters before it's too late.

## REFLECT

Set yourself up for success from the beginning.

### Function

From time to time, reflect on why you are writing heritage letters and their importance to you and to others. You may find that the importance of these reasons varies based on the information and artifacts you are finding, the changing circumstances of your own life, and the wisdom that comes with age.

### Focus

In addition to focusing the project, we need to examine our motives in what we include and exclude. Heritage and legacy letters aren't the place for gossip, bitterness, anger, or vengeance. They are a place to highlight family love, history, and values.

Also, focused letters are more powerful. (See "Record" section for more details on how to focus your heritage letters.) As you craft each letter, ask yourself, "What is my heritage—and what should be the focus of this letter?" For instance, in a heritage scrapbooking class, one woman identified her family's faith in God and a strong work ethic. She could write one letter focused on her family's faith in God and a second letter focused on their strong work ethic.

If you're writing more than one letter, ponder your choices of the focus of the collection of letters: Do you want to focus on previous generations; your generation (self, siblings); or future generations (your children, nieces and nephews)? Or a combination of all three?

Note what you have, need, and want in order to go forward.

*What You Have*

Sometimes when we obtain information, we may ask ourselves, So what? Now what? What does it mean? or What do I do with this?

*What You Need*

Do you need to do more research?

Do you need to reassess your interviewing methods? If you've prepared interview questions or have already interviewed family members, reflect on what worked and what didn't work. Step back and see the process with new eyes.

Do you need to reassess your time line? Do you have reasonable expectations to finish a project by a holiday, birthday, anniversary, wedding, or birth?

Do you need encouragement? Whether it's Scripture, a quote, a picture of your grandparent or your grandchild, reflect on what will keep you motivated when you can't remember important people, places, and dates, when your research efforts fizzle, or when you're struggling to articulate your thoughts and feelings.

*What You Want*

Consider your dreams and goals for writing heritage and legacy letters. If you could interview anyone, what would you want to know? Where would you go? While your wants may not get satisfied, asking these questions may trigger interview questions or additional research.

## Form

The clearer your focus, the easier it is to determine your form. Because it sometimes takes time to focus your letter(s), however, be flexible when considering the form. After the first or second draft, you may land on the form that best suits you and your project.

Following are some questions to ask yourself as you reflect on choosing the final form of your heritage letter(s):

Now that you know what you want to say, how do you want to say it? What writing techniques might work best for you and your story? e.g., (a) newspaper article (organized in most important to least important information); (b) classic feature story (lead sentence, summary paragraph and story); (c) screenplay (scene-by-scene); (d) profile (anecdotes and quotes); (e) chronological (date order); (e) pros and cons; or (f) comparison and contrast. Can you tie the story up like a ribbon by quoting someone or making a reference in the ending paragraph to someone or something first introduced in the opening paragraph?[1]

Can your form change over time? For instance, can you write one letter and mail it in an envelope now and use that letter later as the starting point for a series of letters in a bound book?

Reconsider the style and creative touches you want. Does printed material in a family quilt or a preprinted border on a piece of stationery give you any ideas?

Do you want your letter to be on paper or a particular electronic format?

How long do you want the final product to last?

# RECORD

## Write

Like every good writer, focus each topic. You don't have to cram everything you know into one letter. Sometimes we'll get some interesting tidbit that doesn't tie into the story we are relating. Ask yourself if this information is the seed for another heritage or legacy letter. Or add sidebars or quotes of interesting facts that aren't the focus of the story but are too good to throw away. Or you can save all the extraneous information in a file folder or a separate computer document until you need it for something else.

If you get stuck determining the main theme of a story in a heritage letter, skim the following questions to see if they help you clarify your focus[2]:

What am I trying to say?

What is the meaning of this?

Is there a recurring message?

What is the point of this story?

What are the results of the words or actions in the story?

How did this incident change my life, the life of a family member, or someone else's life?

How has someone changed or grown as a result of the experience or event being recounted?

How has someone grown through an experience, loss, or joy?

Why tell this story?

What is timeless about this story?

What does it teach or show?

What difference did this person's life, words, or actions make?

What was the problem and solution?

What were the goals and results?

What are the central statement(s) of the story?

If you've jotted down topics for an outline, try rearranging the items to come up with something catchy or memorable. Sometimes simple outlines are the easiest to follow, such as arranging the material by generation.

Once you've written a rough draft, label each paragraph with one word, then print the document and cut the paragraphs apart and regroup or rearrange them manually. Then rewrite or retype the letter or cut and paste the paragraphs in a word-processing program to see if each idea more naturally flows into the next.

Depending on the organization of your material, you may want to write out funny incidents, interesting facts, or tantalizing tidbits. These may be a simple listing or in story form. If this is what you're doing, give the listing a brief title or introductory sentences to shape the reader's expectations.

## Write, Rewrite

*Six Easy Pieces*

To make any letter come alive, you can include six easy pieces. (1) Identify a value, standard or principle held by you or an ancestor; (2) include a related attribute, quality, trait or talent; (3) tell a story, example, event, or experience; (4) find the who, what, where, when, why, and how; (5) fill in the word picture you're creating with sights, sounds, smell, taste, touch; and (6) most importantly, express your—or their—feelings.

*Rapid Write*

Next, set a timer and write rapidly for five to ten minutes. Don't edit at this point. Ignore spelling, grammar, and penmanship (it only has to be legible enough for you to read). You may be surprised where this exercise takes you. Keep writing for the entire time. If you get stuck, write about having nothing to say or start on the next subject.

*Write a Draft*

Now is the time to begin rough editing. Using your rapid writing as a "taking-off" point, write a draft of your letter. If it works for you, make a rough outline of your letter.

*Revise*

Now is the time to begin to polish your letter. Check spelling, including names and locations. If you're writing on one side of the paper in longhand or typing your draft, cut the paragraphs apart and arrange in different order to see if the ideas flow more logically from one to the next. If you're using word processing, do a spell and grammar check, realizing that they are not all-knowing. Save your document under another file name and cut and paste different paragraphs to see if this improves the flow of ideas.

*Read*

Read your draft out loud to see where you stumble, for duplicate words, and for changes you'll want to make.

*Review*

Later, have someone review the draft and final letter for accuracy and readability. Many of us cringe from being critiqued, but it can be a blessing to have another pair of eyes look at our work and speak the truth in love. Ask other people to read your heritage letter and note where they stumble, grammar and spelling changes, factual corrections, or fair interpretations.

Not everyone is a gifted critiquer. If someone is harsh or not helpful, thank them for their time and find another person or group to critique your letter.

## Wrap Up

It has been said, "Write all the words you need and not one more." Know when to stop. Stretch yourself—if you're a slob, put more effort into your letter than you would normally. If you're a perfectionist, give it up before you lose your sanity.

Now that your heritage or legacy letter is completed, wrap it up with love and give it for a gift. Other helpful hints are:

Make copies for each child or member of your family.

Make a copy for yourself to enjoy.

Make extra copies for future children, grandchildren.

Make another copy for the safety deposit box to pass along with
your will.

Keep a log of names and addresses of people to whom you've given
copies.

Keep a copy or computer backup and store it in a safe place.

Keep another copy to mark corrections.

Date the original and each major revision.

Between drafts in the writing process, you may also be taking the other
steps, remembering, researching, and reflecting.

## REPEAT

The previous activities—remember, research, reflect, and record—are related.

Each of these processes may prompt you to take a next step. For instance,
sometimes a photo will bring to mind a memory, and sometimes a remem-
brance will trigger a search for a photo.

Writing heritage letters is not always a straight ascent up a mountain, but
rather a hike with others over a trail that spirals around the mountain to get
to the top. Sometimes our steps do not lead us in what we think is the right
direction; some even seem to take us farther away from where we want to go.
Sometimes we must detour around rocks in the trail—and at other times we
have to wait at rest stops and wait for others to catch up with us. However, by
repeating these processes, we make the previously unattainable a reality. For in
the end, the circular trail will lead you to the top of the mountain, where you
can look down and see where you've come from, and look up to catch a
glimpse of heaven.

## QUESTIONS TO KICK START INTERVIEWS

When interviewing, keep it simple and ask for what you would like to know.
When possible, ask for the opportunity to ask additional questions that you
will think of later.

Use the following questions with previous generations when researching and recording your heritage. Focus a heritage letter by narrowing it to
the answers to one or two of these questions. (For simplicity's sake, the
ancestor in question is female. Of course, the same questions apply to a male
forebear as well.)

What are the ancestor's vital records? (This includes full name, birth
date and place, spouse's name, marriage date and place, date and
place of death, and place of burial.)

What is her nationality?

What is the meaning or translation of the family name?

Where did she move from and to, and why?

What was her job or source of income?

What community, military, or governmental positions did she hold?

What was her education?

What language(s) did she speak?

How is she best remembered by others?

What is she most noted for?

What are your favorite memories or stories about that person?

Why is this ancestor special to you?

What are or were her character traits and strengths?

What was a typical day like for her?

What inventions and discoveries were made during her lifetime?

What historical events happened during her lifetime?

Who may have access to her journals, diaries, other documents,
Bible, photos, mementos, or artifacts?

How did her faith impact her life?

What have you found about this ancestor that interests you?

What kinds of entertainment did she enjoy?

What decisions did she make that affect you today?

What was her home like and where was it located?

Use the following questions as a starting place when you want to share

**313**

your memories and values with future generations through a legacy letter:

What are your vital records? (This includes full name, birth date and place, spouse's name, marriage date and place.)

What kinds of creative talents do you have and enjoy?

Who were the influential people in your life and what was their influence?

What people and circumstances most influenced your generation?

What family memories are precious to you and why?

Who was your favorite teacher, and what was your favorite school topic, and why?

Who is your favorite non-school teacher, and what have you learned from him or her?

What are some of your earliest memories?

Do you have a Bible verse that means a lot to you?

What is your greatest personal victory?

What is your greatest regret?

What people, events, books, poems, songs, paintings or other artwork, or creative endeavors have influenced you most in the choices you've made?

Are there family or other mottos or proverbs you live by?

How do you describe the setting of your youth (home, neighborhood, school, town, and/or country)?

What were your interests as a child?

What are your skills, interests, hobbies, passions?

What lessons have you learned in the good times and the hard times?

How has world history influenced your personal choices and history?

What have you learned from your ancestors that you want future generations to know?

What is important to you in your faith and beliefs?

What of your medical history and that of your ancestors may be important to future generations?

What traditions are important to pass on to future generations?

What kinds of entertainment do you enjoy?

What is your favorite place or scene of natural beauty (such as mountains, oceans, forests)?

Who are your heroes and why?

Use the following questions as a starting place when you want to share with your children your memories about them in a legacy letter:

What funny things have they done?

What are their triumphs?

What sad things have happened?

What character traits have they exhibited that you wish to reinforce?

What are their highlights of the previous year?

What family vacations, gatherings, or traditions have they been involved in?

What new things have they learned?

What are their accomplishments (school, sports, music, art, activities, church)?

What are their character strengths and traits?

What do you want to challenge them to do?

What memories or stories do you have about them that they might want to hear?

What are the lessons they've learned in hard times?

What Bible verses best describe your hope for your children?

What advice do you want to give your children?

What affirmations do they need to hear?

What are your favorite stories about what your children said or did?

Why did you name your children what you did, and what do those names mean?

What special-to-them (not hurtful) nicknames do they have, and how did they get them?

What blessing do you want to give your children?

How have your children been a blessing to you?

What is your promise of unchanging love?

What wisdom have your children shown that is beyond their years?

What attributes, qualities, or traits are you proud of in your children?

How are your children like a family member they wish to emulate?

What are the clues God may have given you as to his purpose for their lives?

## INTERVIEW QUESTIONS & TIPS

Every reporter has his or her own style of interviewing. Jan Jonas, editor and reporter of the *Albuquerque Tribune*, specializes in interviewing and profiling local people. The following are tips from Jan to help you interview others for your heritage and legacy letters:

Verify correct spelling of names and dates for as many generations as possible. Be as specific as possible.

Prepare a list of what you want to know. Jot down stories you've heard or read about what you want to know more about and to jog your memory.

Do not feel compelled to keep the interviewees on track. To find wonderful stuff, let them chase hares.

Don't be afraid for the conversation to go somewhere you aren't prepared to go. It's fun to let them go down a path you didn't anticipate. These are jewels—feel privileged.

If an item is compelling, roll with it. Have a handle on where you think you want to go, but do not feel that's exactly where it has to be.

If a comment sparks a question in your mind, ask it. For instance, you may want to ask questions such as:

Was it cold that day?

What were you wearing?

Do you associate food or music with that memory?

How does that person connect with other people in the family?

What were your feelings toward that other person?

Who else knows where I can learn other family stories?

You may learn that you have some favorite questions that trigger memories.

What was it like growing up?

What was school like and how important was it to you?

If you could have been or done anything, what would that be?

What one thing would you go back and change if you could?

Is there any experience so important to you that you wouldn't trade it for anything?

What was it like the first time you rode in a car? What did it feel like?

What was the first TV program you watched? Did you have a favorite show?

What did you listen to on the radio?

What was it like to raise children when you did?

How do you think things have changed?

What is the best advice you can give?

What was the best advice you ever received?

Don't ask questions and walk away, but interact with the person. Care about people in general. The best part about interacting with another person is getting a peek at some point in the past.

You may also have a few standard questions that mean the most to you and get the most answer for the least question.

Why was this person special to you?

What diseases/medical conditions were hereditary?

What were some personal experiences, tastes, beliefs?

Were you afraid? Happy? Resentful?

Did you have other friends?

Were you lonely?

Did you like to dance? Did you get to dance?

Were your parents strict with you?

Did your parents differentiate between you and your siblings?

What were your early marriage years like?

What are your greatest joys/regrets about raising children?

What do you regret most?

What do you consider your biggest achievement?

What is your favorite book, pastime, movie, song? Why?

What are some family mottos and proverbs?

What are the biggest turning points in your life?

Why did you move?

What were some family nicknames?

What were your nicknames?

What were the family priorities? Did you approve?

Sometimes people don't want to remember certain events—such as soldiers after a war—or may need to shelter their loved ones and themselves from certain memories. Some parts may have been so horrible that they don't want to remember but can't forget, and can never tell anyone. If the person thinks that it is better left unsaid, respect her decision and don't press that issue. Give her the dignity of making that choice. Each person's life is so rich with memories, we don't need to probe a sensitive memory. Don't go where you're not invited. If you get there accidentally, don't hang around.

Some older people delight in being naughty and will say what their mother would have a fit in knowing. What you learn and how you learn it depends upon the other person's personality as much as your own.

In addition to Jan's helpful tips, here are additional interviewing tips for gathering information for heritage and legacy letters:

Ask permission to record or take photos.

Take a picture of or with the person providing stories and information.

If possible, ask the person to go with you to show you the old homestead, the school that figures in the story, the childhood neighborhoods. Take pictures if possible.

Ask the people you're interviewing if they have or know of local books with relevant information. Visit local bookstores and ask if they have books with local history.

Give yourself plenty of time to listen. Make several visits if possible. Sometimes the best stories or nuggets come after a period of time and an increased level of trust.

Listen, listen, listen. Listen with your ears, listen with your eyes, listen with your body. This is not about you.

Explain the purpose of the interview.

Offer to send a copy of your write-up and solicit corrections.

Write a thank-you note for sharing their time and memories.

Keep a contact list of people you've interviewed and where you've gotten information. Write up your interview notes. Keep your notes in one place.

Special thanks to Linda Jewell for being willing to share this information from her booklet *Writing Heritage and Legacy Letters*. For more information on the letter- and note-writing resources Linda has available, please visit www.thepowerofyourpen.com. To inquire about Linda teaching a note-writing or journaling workshop, contact CLASServices at 505.899.4283 or speakers@classervices.com.

---

1. MANY OF THESE QUESTIONS WERE GENERATED BY THE ARTICLE "FIRST COMES FOCUS THEN COMES STRUCTURE" BY MARK H. MASSÉ, PUBLISHED IN *WRITER'S DIGEST*, AUGUST 2001, 32–33, 61.
2. IBID.

# CONTRIBUTORS

When we sent out a message to our readers that we were going to write a book on the joy of family legacies, they sent us stories from their personal experiences. We couldn't use them all, but we have selected some of the best for your enjoyment. Although my two daughters have written about half the book, I wanted you to know that what we've shared with you is not singularly unique to our family, but contains similar ideas that were sent in by others for you to adapt for your family.

Different sections of this book are written and edited by me, Lauren, or Marita. When the stories are authored by others, we have included their names. The majority of the contributors are graduates of our CLASS (Christian Leaders, Authors and Speakers Seminars). We know that you've enjoyed the multitude of ideas presented here and are inspired to make your family heirlooms both visible and special.

## CONTRIBUTORS

DIANE BAIER SPRIGGS
KATHERINE BELL
JANET TAYLOR BIRKEY
JONATHAN BRIGGS
RANDY BRIGGS, JR.
RANDY BRIGGS, SR.
PEG BUTTS
JAMES W. CHAPMAN
RUTH E. CROW
MICHELLE DIERCKS
JUNE DURR
KATHLEEN M. EDELMAN
SANDRA SCHOGER FOSTER
ANGIE GARRETT

LINDA J. GILDEN
JOY HUSTON
LINDA LAMAR JEWELL
KAREN R. KILBY
CHRISTY LARGENT
WENDY LAWTON
CHERI LIEFELD
KARLA LOVELESS-DILLON
NALLEY T. OSLAND
STUART OSLAND
GOLDEN KEYES PARSONS
KAREN R. POWER
MARY ANN REMNET
SUZY RYAN

LORI J. SEABORG
RAELENE SEARLE
BONNIE SKINNER
PAMELA SONNENMOSER
BETTY WINSLOW
ROSE SWEET
LARISEE LYNN STEVENS
WENDY STEWART-HAMILTON
PAT THOMAS
LOU WORKMAN SOUDERS
RICCI VERQARA
BARBARA VOGELGESANG